The Lioness of Judah
A Jewish Lion Tamer's Memoir of Resistance and Survival

by Sara Hauptman

As told to
Sue A. Oliver

Dancing Queens Press
Colorado Springs, Colorado

Dancing Queens Press

965 Carlson Drive
Colorado Springs, CO 8091
First Printing April 2006

Dedication

This book is dedicated to Nathan Hauptman, my loving husband, and to Guy Hauptman, my son, for whom I survived.

Table of Contents

Acknowledgements

I would like to thank Sara's family who readily recalled information for the writing of this book. Guy Hauptman, Mariette Rozen Doduck, and Esther Rozen Brandt resurrected painful memories to help me understand background information and details about Sara's life.

Thanks goes to Amy Hughes, the granddaughter of Maurice Gilbert, who gave me a plethora of information about the Belgian Resistance in which her grandfather and other family members participated with Sara.

A special thank you goes to the members of my critique group, Margaret, Cindi, Marcella, Joan, Heather, and Irmgard, who encouraged me, helped me with editing and were always there to give me their input.

To Kay Esmiol, I appreciate your creativity and help when I needed you.

I would like to recognize JT and Clara Oliver who read the early drafts and reminded me to show Sara's sense of humor.

In addition, I would like to thank my husband, Alan R. Oliver, for his love, patience and understanding as Sara and I worked on this project. Go fishing any time you want, Alan.

Finally, thank you, Mom, for nurturing my love of writing.

Sue Oliver

PREFACE

"You can't go yet," I told her. "God and I aren't finished with you. I've already lost one mom, and I don't want to lose another. Don't die!"

Sitting beside Sara Hauptman's hospital bed, I prayed for her recovery. I felt guilty for being gone when she needed me the most. While visiting my sister in Utah, I was engulfed with an inexplicable depression on Christmas Eve. I couldn't identify its source until I returned to Colorado and found out Sara was in the hospital and had nearly died.

When I entered her room, she said, "You'll have to finish the book on your own." She was ready to die, but I wasn't ready to let her go.

Whenever someone would leave the hospital room, she would have me open the door to the hallway. Ever since the concentration camps, Sara can't bear to be in a room with the door closed. I asked her about it once and she told me, "When the door is closed, I feel like I'm being put into a gas chamber."

Over the next few days she improved. Always a fighter, she managed to pull through and escape death as she had so many times in her past.

I first met her when she spoke to the students at the school where I teach. She told them about her experiences during the Holocaust. When Sara entered the gymnasium that afternoon in

1996, I couldn't see her over the students. She was tiny with short, curly, dark hair that was graying gracefully, and she had a smooth complexion—not at all what I had imagined a Holocaust survivor to be. She didn't look hardened from her years in the camps. Glowing with appreciation when a student handed her a bouquet of flowers, Sara personified what every grandmother should be.

She asked that General Gritz, an American liberator of Buchenwald, speak first. Somewhat shy and humble, she thought his story would hold the students' attention, and hers could be second. After General Gritz was finished, Sara walked to the podium. She asked for a cup of water and that the microphone be removed from the podium. At four feet eleven inches, she was too short to be seen behind it. Unafraid to face an audience of over three hundred middle school students, she told them her story of living in Belgium during World War II. Her French accent was difficult to understand at first, but we listened closely to her incredible story.

She began with her arrest and being sent to a camp in Belgium, Malines. From there we heard about Auschwitz and Dachau—the selections, the punishments, the food, the daily fights for survival, the tortuous work, the news of her family members' deaths, and finally liberation.

A thunder of applause followed her story. Spontaneously, the students gave her a standing ovation. They crowded around her afterward, asking to see her tattoo and hug her for sharing her life with them. After all, she's living history.

Before she left the auditorium, I asked her if anyone were writing her story. Veiled comments such as, "Thank God I had my children before the war because I couldn't have any after it," led me to believe there were many incidents she omitted for the sake of the young students.

"Yes," she told me, "someone is working with me." Then protectively, General Gritz ushered her from the gymnasium.

When I delivered the students' thank-you notes to her, she told me the woman who was working on her book wasn't carrying through, and she asked me if I knew someone who could write her story. I nearly jumped out of her kitchen chair to say, "Yes, I'll do it!"

Over the next few years of taping interviews, researching, eating her wonderful cooking, sharing our lives every Friday afternoon until sundown when she'd light her candles for the coming Sabbath, this remarkable woman became a part of me. We adopted each other; I now had another mother for mine who had died, and she had a daughter again. Somehow God knew we needed each other.

Every Friday became a new revelation as she told me about her life during the war. She fought back on many occasions and was involved in the resistance. As a cover for her underground activities, she became a lion tamer with the circus. In the camps she survived severe punishments. Awed at this petite woman's remarkable life, I can still remember telling my husband Alan, "You'll never believe what Sara did."

I also gained ten pounds from eating at her home. No one can enter Sara's house without a plate of goodies or a full dinner being thrust upon her guest. Mountains of sandwiches, boxes of pastries, and homemade soups were always on hand. As a true Jewish grandmother, she'd admonish me, "Eat more. You're too skinny."

Taking her to see the Ringling Brothers and Barnum and Bailey circus turned out to be one of the highlights of our research. While we watched the lion trainer, she critiqued his performance as far less dangerous than when she had performed. Suddenly she remembered the name of the lioness she had assisted when it gave birth, Mitzi. Her remarkable memory continues to amaze me with recollections of conversations and events that happened over sixty years ago.

It took longer to write her memoirs than I expected. Wanting to have all the details fully researched, I contacted the museums at Malines, Auschwitz and Dachau to collect dates and information. However, she wasn't listed at Dachau and Auschwitz. It took a while for her to remember she was using a false name when she was arrested, Sura Miodownik. Once that was pieced together, the dates fit perfectly.

During this time I also suffered a ruptured disc in my spine which made it impossible for me to sit down for five months.

When the pain was too much, Sara would send me home and reassure me we could work on her book later. Full of compassion, Sara was there to hold my hand when I underwent back surgery. Since she had been in the same hospital with her own medical problems, which are myriad, all the nurses and doctors knew her and loved her. I felt like I was with a celebrity.

After Sara's illness, she moved to El Paso in 1997 to be closer to her son, Guy. Her leaving created a chasm of heartbreak in the entire Colorado Springs community, but it was most deeply felt in Temple Shalom, in her friends, and in me. No one can fill Sara's shoes.

Whenever Sara told me about events in her life, she told them as conversations and scenes. Her memory of what people said in situations is remarkable and accurate, as verified by relatives and the granddaughter of Maurice Gilbert, a Belgian resistance worker. I had to be true to her story-telling techniques and used her words in the memoir. Being an actress is what saved Sara's life numerous times, and it is only natural she would remember the "lines of her life."

When we tried to think of a title for her story, I first thought of using her number from Auschwitz, A23140; however, her memoir contains far more than just her time in this one camp. Then thinking of all the times she had to fight for her life, her fierce pride of being Jewish, her time in the circus and the resistance, I created the title that truly epitomizes Sara Hauptman. She is, indeed, the Lioness of Judah.

Sue and Sara in El Paso, Tx.

CHAPTER 1 – PARIS
JUNE 14, 1940

As the German soldiers paraded past me on the *Champs Elysées*, I shook my fist and jeered at them from the unusually quiet Parisian sidewalk. Even if others were afraid to voice an opinion, I wanted the Nazis to know I wasn't waiting with open arms for their arrival. The swastikas on their flags, their emblems of hatred, repulsed me.

Other citizens of the conquered capital stood in silence that Friday around noon as the tanks, armored cars, and motorized infantry invaded through the western end. Many stores were boarded up, but one baker's shop still sold his goods to customers. I needed bread, and since I couldn't hear gunfire or bombs, I risked taking my baby with me to the bakery. Some machine guns were posted along the way, but no one gave them cause for alarm. Small groups of people sat along the boulevard or in cafes.

As I stood among a small crowd of women outside the bakery, I heard one woman cheering for them as she fanatically waved her perfumed handkerchief. In her frenzy to show them her support, she pushed against my baby and nearly made me drop him. He let out a wail, and I shifted Guy to my other hip. I smoothed his baby-fine, blond hair and wiped the tears from his eyes. After I was sure that he was not harmed, I glared at the woman. Not only was she stupid to support the German soldiers and the Nazi cause, but she didn't apologize for hitting my child.

"Go back with them to Germany if you love the Nazis so much," I yelled. "Get out of France."

She turned to face me with her hands on her hips. I doubled my right hand into a fist, ready if she were to touch my child again. She mumbled some expletive and gave me a "go to hell" look. Only the fact I was holding Guy kept me from punching her. She stepped closer to the sidewalk to show the green-uniformed soldiers her support.

Guy began to cry again, and I comforted him. "Don't worry, *cherie*. I'll protect you." However after seeing the triumphant German army pass under the great *Arc de Triomphe* that afternoon, I wondered how much longer I could protect him. The Nazis hated Jews, and the German army had us trapped.

Dispirited, I bought the bread and made my way back to my apartment building. The few French people I passed on the way also mourned the fall of Paris as the realization of occupation sank in, and a sense of despair descended upon all of us.

The combined French and Polish armies had not withstood the German *Blitzkrieg*. My husband, Nathan, had been part of the Polish army that had tried to regroup in France. We had been living in Belgium before the war, but Nathan still held Polish citizenship. After the fall of Poland in September 1939, more than 100,000 Polish soldiers fled to Paris, and the Polish government in exile drafted its citizens living in other European countries. Nathan was one of them. Even though we were living in Brussels, he received orders to report to a camp outside Paris.

My mother begged me not to follow him to France and to stay in Brussels. When I told her I had to be with the father of my son, she asked me to leave Guy with her and not take the baby. I wouldn't hear of it. Carrying four-and-a- half-month-old Guy and two bottles of milk, I arrived at the train station in Brussels and showed Nathan's letter to the conductor. He allowed me to board the train going to Paris, and I joined Nathan in France.

Nine months earlier when I first arrived in Paris, Nathan's friends, Herman and Frank, had helped me find an apartment. The landlady, Jeanette, was a kind, older woman who treated us like her own family.

When I reached my apartment building, I began the long walk up the stairs, wondering if Nathan were back. He had been looking for contacts to get us back to Belgium, but nothing looked promising, especially after King Leopold of Belgium had capitulated. For more than a month we had received no word about my family or what happened to them when the Germans invaded Belgium back in May.

I opened the apartment door and took Guy to the bedroom to

change his diaper. After I got him settled on a blanket on the floor, I prepared our meal.

I was glad Nathan had deserted the Polish army. Why should he fight for a country that despised him? The Poles regularly conducted pogroms on the Jews, persecuting and killing people. They burned Jewish homes, stole belongings, beat up the men, and terrorized the women and children. That's why Nathan's father insisted on his leaving Poland and learning to be a tailor with his cousin in Belgium.

By the time Nathan returned to the apartment, I had our meal ready. Guy was awake and ready to play with his Papa. Nathan picked him up and sat at the kitchen table as I put the food in serving dishes.

I told Nathan about seeing the Germans entering Paris along the *Champs Elysees* and how one French woman was actually happy to see them.

Nathan had seen people's reactions too and informed me that the Germans had sealed off every exit to Paris. I had never seen this look of consternation on Nathan. In the past he could handle anything with ease and didn't worry, not even when we had to tell my mother that we had eloped against her wishes. The uncharacteristic creased lines on his brow made it clear that Nathan had never faced such a situation before.

"What should we do?" I asked him.

"We wait," he said. "But we need to be ready." Nathan rose and went to the bedroom. He returned with his Polish army uniform. "After we eat, we burn this."

I nodded in agreement.

"Talk to Jeanette tomorrow about someone outside Paris who could take care of Guy. He'd be safer if he were with someone who's not Jewish." Nathan picked up the scissors and put them on top of his uniform before he returned to the table.

I had lost my appetite and pushed my plate away. Just thinking about giving Guy to someone else made me nauseous, but Nathan was right. We had to make plans. As I did the dishes, Nathan cut up his uniform and burned all the pieces in the stove.

A few days later, Jeanette found a farmer's wife whom she trusted to take care of Guy. I took him there for visits and made sure she understood that we would come back for him. If we could not, she agreed to return him to my mother, Chana Rozen, in Brussels.

I tried to convince myself it was no worse than leaving Guy with a babysitter. After all, my own mother had hired a nanny for my brothers, sisters, and me. With eleven children, dear *Maman* needed extra help taking care of all of us. This lady might turn out to be like my own nanny, Catherine. However, each time I left him with her, I wondered if it might be the last time I would see my child.

As the weeks progressed, life under the German occupation became worse. Daily the Germans posted signs on kiosks, informing the people of Paris about new regulations. We saw arrests on the streets and knew about people who suddenly disappeared without a trace. The Germans made raids any time and any place.

Swastikas appeared everywhere. Worst of all was seeing the Nazi flag flying from the highest point of the *Tour Eiffel*. Soldiers patrolled the streets, and gunfire occasionally broke the silence of the night. Any time I went out in public and passed a German soldier on the street, my stomach would tighten, and I held my breath until he passed. I tried to act normal and hoped he didn't notice me. Each trip to the market became an exercise in terror. I searched for familiar faces, but didn't maintain eye contact too long. A sense of foreboding made me hurry home after any outing. I tried to act confident while praying for invisibility.

CHAPTER 2--A PARIS PRISON
1941

*M*onths after the Germans invaded France, our lives hung in a balance of secrecy. We prayed that anyone who knew Nathan had been in the Polish army would not to betray us. Nathan could only hope his Polish military papers would not be traced. The Germans still looked for French or Polish soldiers who had escaped. Whenever Nathan left the apartment, I trembled, wondering if I would ever see him again. Then one day my worse fears were realized.

Heavy boots thudded up the wooden stairs. The familiar sounds of a German raid filled my heart with fear. I moved closer to the front door and listened in silence, hoping they would pass by as they had on other occasions. Then fists pounded my door. I jumped back from the loud sound like an animal hearing the hunter's rifle. The dreaded command *"Auf machen!"* sliced through me.

The Nazis had come for me. *Had they discovered I was Jewish or were they here to arrest Nathan as a prisoner of war?*

Dropping a dust cloth, I tried to calm myself. My heart thumped so loudly it drummed in my ears. I wiped my hands on my apron, and my mind raced as I concocted a lie to tell them about Nathan. My knees nearly buckled as I stood by the door. Taking a deep breath and blowing it out, I grasped the cold knob and turned it.

An SS officer's black uniform filled the doorframe. He advanced through the doorway, and I retreated.

Avoiding his eyes, I focused on the silver skull on his collar. "What do you want?"

"Out of the way." With one forceful sweep of his arm, the tall SS officer brushed me aside. Two other men barged past me, crushing me against the door. A second SS officer with darker blond hair took charge of the search as the tall officer watched me. The third man in his early twenties—close to my age—wore the green uniform of the *Wehrmacht*, the regular army. My mind couldn't concentrate on anything but the colors of their uniforms. I kept my eyes averted from their faces because a direct look might seem a challenge to attack.

The younger enlisted man overturned chairs, pulled up the brown sofa cushions, and searched every inch of the living room.

My heart pounded even faster. To conceal my terror, I shoved my shaking hands in my apron pockets. The officer had not asked about Nathan. Moreover, he had not called me a Jew. I hoped this was just some door-to-door search the Germans conducted so often.

From my position in the living room, I could see one of the SS officers saunter into the bedroom and jerk open the wardrobe door. He grabbed Nathan's black jacket, searching the pockets. As he finished with one garment, he yanked another of Nathan's hand-made suits from the hanger. Then he called to the others, "Here are the suits."

I didn't understand their interest in Nathan's clothes, but I was glad he had burned his Polish uniform.

The young soldier joined the officer in the bedroom while the tall SS commander detained me in the living room. The two Germans yanked the rest of Nathan's jackets from the hangers, searched the pockets and threw them on the floor. Sweating, the young one picked up a gray, pin-striped jacket Nathan had sewn. He tried to push his pulpy arm through the sleeve, but that green toad could never fit into Nathan's clothes. When the officer in the room signaled him, the young one threw the jacket on the floor, grinding his black boot into its fine fabric.

Tightening my hands into fists, I glared at my tormentors.

The tall officer enjoyed my discomfort as the others ransacked the bedroom. He stood in the doorway between the rooms and glanced casually around the bedroom and then back at me in the living room. In German he ordered the enlisted man to go through the dresser drawers.

The toad jerked the drawers open, emptying their contents on the floor. Guy's baby clothes fell like tiny snowflakes amid my sweaters and undergarments. They had all noticed Guy's tiny shirts, shoes and socks, but they didn't care that I had a child. I thanked God that Guy was with the farmer's wife outside the city.

Then the soldier found Nathan's underwear.

The tall officer whirled on me and raged, "Where is the man? These clothes belong to a man. Where is he?"

I steeled myself against his sudden attack and said the first thing that came to mind. "I don't know where he is. The clothes were here when I moved in."

The officer didn't believe my poorly constructed lie and continued the barrage, getting louder and closer to my face each time. He towered over my five-foot frame and shouted, "Where is the man? Where is he hiding?"

"I don't know. I tell you the clothes were here." Even though I told an unconvincing lie, I had to stick with it.

He grabbed me by my arm and slung me into the bedroom. With a final smugness, he said, "You have ten minutes to pack a bag. You're under arrest."

I could tell he had done this many times. He knew the routine well enough. Tell the person being arrested nothing. Out of fear the victim might give away information. I refused to play that game. I would not betray Nathan.

Rubbing my sore arm, I looked about the defiled room. I didn't know where to start. Clothes were everywhere. I got my little yellow suitcase from the closet and packed several blouses and skirts, along with some low-heeled shoes. Careful not to pick up anything touched by the Germans, I put in some panties, bras, and slips. After I put in a sweater, I closed the suitcase.

Taking off my apron, I tossed it on the bed. I had been cleaning house when they arrived, and I would have to wear my dusty skirt and blouse out in public. *When Nathan returns to see this mess, he'll realize the Nazis have me. I would never leave the house like this. He'll know to get out.*

Like jackals waiting to attack, the three German soldiers watched my every move. With his hand on the back of my neck, the young one pushed me out the door and hurried me down the stairs ahead of the officers. They didn't bother to close the door behind them.

Jeanette, my landlady, was not home, but she would realize something was wrong when she saw the door to my apartment wide open. Hopefully she could warn Nathan in time, and he could escape to Belgium. He could do nothing to help me now. My only hope was that my captors wouldn't discover I was Jewish.

The young soldier pushed me toward a black car and shoved me into the back seat. Circling around the car, he opened the adjacent door and sat next to me. The officers sat in the front. I felt like a common criminal and avoided the sympathetic looks from occasional passersby.

The car roared away as if we were on some urgent business. Every time an officer glanced back at me, my skin crawled, but I was determined not to cry. I wouldn't let them break me. They continued to look back and forth at each other with smug expressions.

As we drove through the streets of Paris, I couldn't see out the darkened windows very well. Noticeably, the sounds of the city had changed. An emptiness engulfed everything compared to the Paris I had known before the German invasion months earlier. People were afraid to be on the streets. Sirens occasionally pierced the silence, but the Nazi terror had muted the laughter of carefree people sitting at the sidewalk cafes. Heavy diesel exhaust suffocated the aroma of coffee and pastries. Even the leafy, green trees were overshadowed by the wintry blackness of the German uniforms and weaponry.

When we arrived at the prison, located on the outskirts of Paris, the young soldier grabbed my arm, but I pulled away. I got out of the car without his touching me any more. Flanked by the toad and an officer, I walked up to the gray stone building. They left me with a middle-aged *Wehrmacht* soldier at the desk after the officer said, "She had the suits."

I couldn't figure out why Nathan's suits were of such interest, unless they had already arrested Nathan. *Had my greatest fear become reality?*

The Germans processed me like some common thief. I had no trial, and they never told me why they arrested me. The soldier at the desk took my suitcase and purse to a room behind him. On returning, he threw a bluish-gray prison dress at me and pointed to a room across the hall. "Leave the clothes you have in the room."

After I changed clothes, a middle-aged French guard escorted me to a cell crowded with many women. Some had been allowed to keep their own clothes. Many looked like prostitutes with their garish makeup and bosom-exposing blouses, yet others looked as bewildered as I felt. I had heard that the Nazis often planted spies in cells, hoping someone would betray a secret. I had to be careful not to reveal anything about my past, no matter how long my stay would be.

The crowded prison cell with its rusted iron bars banished all thoughts of freedom. Gray and black shadows hung on the walls. The musty air of bad breath and perspiration encircled me like an oppressive fog. No one talked to me. I found an empty cot and sat down.

I spent the rest of the night in silence worrying about Nathan and Guy. Turning on my cot to face the wall, I cried. All night long I had nightmares of an SS officer beating Nathan while Guy screamed in terror. *Where were they?   What was happening to my child and husband?* Somehow I managed to cry myself to sleep.

The next morning I awoke with swollen, red eyes when I heard the other women moving. We were given some bread and coffee for breakfast while others were led out of the cell ahead of me.

Then a middle-aged French guard led me to a laundry room where I was to wash clothes. At least the facility had washing machines, and I didn't have to wash the clothes by hand. Other women were in the laundry area with me, but I was cautious enough to share only my first name.

As I folded clothes, I kept wishing I could go back—back in time when the world was not at war and I was safe in Brussels. All I wanted in life was to take care of my child, to see my husband again, and to be left alone. The laundry I folded should have been Guy's clothes. I passed that day and many others in the same fashion—worrying, keeping everything inside, and telling no one about myself.

I had never been in such surroundings before. Learning to get dressed in front of other women wasn't so bad, but using the toilet with no walls for privacy was crude and embarrassing. Sleeping in a cell with others became easier as time went by. Sometimes women moaned as they slept or called out a name. Others snored. Most of us lay awake in the darkness, thinking of our families. At least we each had our own cot with a blanket and pillow. To break the boredom, we sang familiar songs or told jokes, but with the Nazis in control, no one felt comfortable enough to confide in others.

Each day the moist, hot atmosphere of the laundry room trapped me in its jungle-like humidity. Sweat poured off me, and my sticky dress clung to my chest. At least having a job kept me busy, but I worried about my family. *Did Nathan and Guy get out of Paris safely? What kind of damage did the Germans inflict when they invaded my beloved Belgium?* Only a few months before I had been so self-assured, but seeing what the Germans did when they took over a country completely wiped out all confidence.

Questions haunted me, but seeking answers wasn't safe. All I could do was pray for Nathan's safety. I doubted Nathan and Guy ever made it back home. Nathan was probably in some cell like this or in even worse circumstances. I wouldn't allow myself to dwell on what the

Germans might be doing to Nathan. Guy was probably with the farmer's wife still. I only hoped she would return him to my mother as she promised. He was too young to remember Nathan or me if we were gone a long time.

All of my past life seemed like a dream. At times I wondered if I had only imagined a life outside those walls. I worked, but my mind wandered to Nathan, Guy, *Maman*, and my eight younger brothers and sisters. After Papa died of prostate cancer when I was seventeen, *Maman* had made ends meet by sewing uniforms for the Belgian army, but with the German take-over, she would have little income—just the widow's pension from the Belgian government if she were allowed that small amount now. My younger brothers and sisters depended entirely on her.

Perhaps my older brothers, Charles or Jules, could help her, but they had families of their own. Besides, Nathan helped *Maman* more than Charles did, and Jules wasn't as close to the family after Papa sat *shiva* for him and said the prayer for the dead when Jules married a Gentile woman. Papa even told me he didn't want Jules at his funeral and never reconciled with him.

Maman depended on Nathan more than her two oldest sons. Nathan had been a friend of my older brothers and was always at our house even before I eloped with him to Antwerp when I was nineteen. *Maman* would never have given us her blessing because she didn't want me to marry a tailor who was twelve years older than I was, so we didn't ask her. I went by the cemetery to ask Papa's approval before we drove to Antwerp, and when no voice from heaven forbade me to marry Nathan, I did marry him. On September 23, 1937, a Jewish rabbi married us. That was a little over three years ago from the time I was arrested, but it seemed like an eternity had passed.

The weeks in prison played tricks on my mind, and I couldn't keep up with the passage of time very well. Everything before my arrest seemed like many years ago. However, I couldn't let myself give up hope of getting out. The falling brown and orange leaves signaled the change of seasons and the passage of time. Also I had concealed a tiny piece of paper and a pencil in a pocket and crossed off continuous days, but I had no idea how many days passed before I found this paper and pencil. I had eighty-one marks on the paper and knew I had been in prison over three months. Newspapers and calendars were forbidden. Our menstrual cycles would also indicate the passage of another month. Some women scratched their initials in a hole by the toilet and kept track of the days that way, but I was afraid I'd be caught.

Days merged into an endless cycle. Some women talked about boyfriends, but only in vague terms. Occasionally we sang when the chores were over. A few coarse women told dirty jokes, but I avoided those women. The highlight of the day was when we could walk in the fenced-in, outdoor courtyard. Talking was forbidden, and high brick walls concealed the view of the countryside, keeping us hidden from the people outside. However, breathing fresh air was our one pleasure of the day.

While I was working in the laundry, a woman wearing the same prison garb as mine approached me. I hadn't noticed her in our cell before. Instinctive warning signals went off in my mind when she asked me if I had a husband. As I mopped my forehead with my forearm, I told her I couldn't stand around talking. I stopped cranking the handle of the dryer and opened the door, taking out the clothes to fold. Purposely I moved away from her and continued my work. She got the message and left to pump someone else for information.

Sometimes a woman would be released, but we never knew why she had been in prison in the first place. Suspicion reigned especially when we were questioned at random intervals.

"Frau Hauptman, do you wish to write a letter today?" That question came from the Nazi overseers on a regular basis. "Don't you miss your family? Don't you want to let them know how you're doing?"

"No, I have no one."

My soul ached to know if Nathan and Guy were all right, but I would not place them in jeopardy by writing a letter.

Time continued to crawl along. Then one day while we ate our soup, another prisoner whose name I have forgotten told me a rumor she had heard. She said that close to the time I came, some German soldiers had deserted. An accomplice here in Paris had supplied them with civilian suits, so they could blend in and get out of the fighting. Then the deserters were caught.

At last I had a clue about my arrest, which explained my captors' interest in Nathan's suits. The Germans must have thought I was the accomplice furnishing the deserters with civilian clothing.

About a week after I heard this news, the French guard summoned me. He took me to the entrance of the prison to a changing room, gave me my purse and suitcase, and told me to go.

Throwing down that horrid prison dress, I put on my own things. My skirt and blouse hung on me as though two sizes too large. I took up three notches in my belt to keep my skirt on my thin frame. Right then I didn't care how I looked. After spending eight months behind bars, I was free.

When I emerged from the changing room, I asked the French guard, "Why are they letting me go?"

"*Madame*, I do not know." Then he ushered me to the door that led to my freedom. On the outside he whispered, "Get away from Paris as quickly as you can. It is not safe for Jews to stay here. Even for my wife. Go with God."

He had known all along that I was Jewish and hadn't told anyone. He could have revealed this fact and received a reward, but judging by his comment, his wife was Jewish too. I owed this man my life.

After he gave me twenty-five francs, I rode a bus back into town. I never saw him again, but I will always remember his kindness.

He didn't need to urge me to leave. I wanted to get as far away from that prison as I could. I took a bus back to the main part of town since the prison was on the outskirts. Using a circuitous route through back alleys, I made my way to my apartment and knocked on my landlady's door.

Jeanette was surprised to see me, and she pulled me inside.

When I asked about Nathan and Guy, she told me Nathan came home shortly after my arrest. He had picked up Guy from the farmer's wife, and they left Paris.

I was truly thankful to God for His deliverance. Nathan must have finally found a way back to Belgium. I explained to her about the suits and why the Nazis suspected me of helping the deserters. No ordinary person would have as many suits as Nathan did, but being a tailor meant he had many suits. From that piece of evidence, the Nazis were convinced I was the accomplice.

I asked about my belongings, but I anticipated the answer.

"The Germans took everything, even Guy's clothes," she said. "Nathan said you should go to Herman or Frank when you got out."

After she gave me the message, an awkward silence ensued. I wasn't sure what else to say or do. It felt like home here, but nothing of mine was left. I couldn't even look at our apartment one last time. A visit would resurrect bad memories of the day I was arrested, and other people had rented the apartment. Jeanette could not hold it for us indefinitely.

"Someone might have followed me," I said. "I'd better not stay here too long."

I checked from the window to see if anyone was looking up at her apartment. We hugged goodbye, and I left the building. Before I crossed each street, I looked behind me.

It didn't take long to get to Herman and Freidal's apartment. Herman might be home since his manager, Leo, often ran the restaurant on his own. As I rang the bell, I hoped Herman would help me.

A pretty, dark-haired girl with curls answered the door. The eight-year-old called her Papa.

Herman and his wife, Freidal, entered the room. He wore a long-sleeved shirt and trousers and was folding a newspaper. Though in his early thirties, he had a receding hairline. Herman and his wife, Freidal, were closer to Nathan's age, about ten years older than I. His wife wiped her hands on an apron, apparently just finishing with the dishes. She pushed a dark strand of hair from her face, trying to see who was at the door.

"I was released from prison a few hours ago," I said. "I don't want to put you or your family in any danger, but I have to get to Belgium."

Both of them stood speechless. I realized they weren't sure who I was.

"Sara Hauptman, is that you?" Herman asked.

"Yes." I must have looked like some waif off the street. I weighed about ninety pounds, and my hair must have been a mess. It was no wonder that they couldn't recognize me.

Herman pulled me into the living room, took my suitcase, and shut the door behind him. Freidal put her arm around me and guided me to a chair.

"We asked around, but no one would tell us why you had been arrested," Freidal said. "It's dangerous to ask too much these days."

"I know. I'm not blaming anyone. Everyone is helpless where the Nazis are concerned." I told them about my arrest, the suits and the accomplice. Then I asked about Nathan and Guy.

Herman explained that Nathan had called him before he left Paris. They had arranged that Herman would take me to the border, and Nathan would meet me there. Another friend, Frank, had agreed to help.

I begged Herman to let me go alone to the border, but he wouldn't hear of it. After calling Nathan, both Frank and Herman drove me to the border between France and Belgium. During the more than three-hour drive, I was scared we would be stopped, and the Nazis would arrest me again. However, the thought of being reunited with my family outweighed any risk. Every set of headlights that approached us made my stomach tighten.

When we stopped, I waited in the car as Herman went inside the border guard's booth. He came out smiling.

"It's all set. We bribed him to allow you through. Nathan's waiting on the other side."

"Thank you. I don't know how to repay your kindness," I stammered as I hugged them goodbye.

"We're friends," Frank said. "It's the least we could do."

I waved to them as the guard let me cross with nothing more in hand than my one suitcase and purse. I had nothing else since the Germans had stolen our belongings. For a few scary seconds I stood in the lit booth, nervously toying with the purse's strap. Then the guard motioned to me to follow him. I had no idea if I would find myself in Nathan's arms or a Nazi trap.

CHAPTER 3—A NIGHT'S PASSAGE

My eyes couldn't adjust to the glare of the guard's booth. I blinked several times, trying to regain focus. The guard counted his money, pocketed it, and motioned me to the other door.

As I walked through, I saw Nathan. No one had ever looked so good as he did at that moment. His outstretched arms welcomed me. I ran to him and threw my arms around him, squeezing him as though I could never let him go. His smooth cheek caressed mine, and our lips met in a firm, yet quick kiss. Pressing against his strong shoulders and warm chest, I realized both of us were crying.

"Darling, I missed you so much," Nathan said, stroking my hair. Probably aware of the guard's stare, he continued, "We have to get out of here quickly. Jean is waiting by the car."

"Where's Guy? Is he all right?"

"Yes, he's with your mother in Brussels." Nathan picked up my yellow suitcase and pointed in the direction of the car. "Let's go home."

For the last eight months I had longed to hear those words. I walked next to Nathan and held onto his arm with both hands.

Smoking a cigarette, my younger brother Jean, stood next to the car. He crushed out his cigarette with his shoe and met me with open arms. I had to tiptoe to hug his neck.

"Surala, I'm glad you're home. I thought we had lost you."

"Thank goodness I have good *mazel*. My luck has held out so far."

Nathan put my suitcase in the trunk and tossed the keys to Jean. Jean got in front and started the engine. Nathan seemed to hurry me into the back seat. He hugged me close and told me that being near the border so late could raise suspicions. Others, besides the guard we bribed, could be nearby.

Once we were safely on the road to Brussels, I relaxed somewhat, but I would not let go of Nathan's finely manicured hand. I etched every detail of Nathan's face into my memory. So often in prison I had longed to see the outline of his nose, his thin lips, the way his green eyes lit up when he saw me, and that wonderful smile that won my heart when we were dating.

Even though I felt safer with Nathan, each passing car's headlights made me uneasy. I asked Jean for one of his cigarettes, and he handed me the pack. After I removed one, Nathan lit it for me. Trying to calm myself with the cigarette, I took only a few puffs before crushing it out. I told myself the worst was over, and I was heading home.

"How's Guy?" I asked. "What does he look like now?"

"He's grown a lot. Your brothers and sisters keep him entertained. Mariette treats him like her doll. It's hard to think she's his aunt when she's only three and a half years older."

"That Mariette! She's a doll herself. How are the others? Are they all right?"

"They're fine. You'll see them soon."

All I could think about for eight months was getting home, holding my baby, and seeing Nathan again. I missed them so much.

He kissed me, and we stayed wrapped in one another's arms. I rested my head against his chest, enjoying the first sense of peace I had known in months. Nestled against Nathan, I closed my eyes. I was glad to be back with him, and I felt safe as long as he was with me. Momentarily, I must have dozed off.

A horn blared, and I jerked up, thinking it was the Germans. I shuddered.

Nathan hugged me and told me it was just a passing car, not a Nazi patrol.

I took a deep breath and leaned my head against Nathan's shoulder again and stared into the dark countryside. I didn't want to speak and ruin this illusion of serenity. I feared that if I fell asleep again, I'd wake up and find myself back in prison. After a long silence I saw the larger buildings of Brussels. Home wasn't far now.

Brussels had not been badly damaged when the Germans invaded. Being in Paris when they took over Belgium, I didn't know the extent of the damage. When we entered the city, I saw some buildings were bombed, but most of the city was spared.

After being away so many months, I was home at last. All I wanted to do was hold my baby, but would he recognize me after so long? *Would I be a stranger to my own son?*

Jean parked the borrowed car in front of *Maman*'s apartment building. Nathan would return it to his cousin Mocha the next day. I bounded up the steps, outdistancing Nathan to reach *Maman*'s apartment. When I rang the bell, *Maman* opened the door.

"Sara! Oh, thank God you're here." She kissed and hugged me. "I missed you so much."

I cried and buried my head in her shoulder a few seconds. "*Maman*, I didn't know if I would ever see you again. Oh God, I'm home!"

I stared at *Maman* and saw how she had aged over the time I had been gone. In her mid-forties, *Maman* was still pretty, but she looked tired from worry or keeping up with all the children. *Maman* no longer had the luxury of giving attention to such matters as curling her hair or putting on rouge. Her short, dark hair was tied up in a kerchief.

I pulled away and looked for Guy. *Maman* understood and told me Guy was asleep in the bedroom.

I tried not to wake my younger sisters, Esther and Mariette, who slept in the living room. I tiptoed to the bedroom and opened the door.

Guy slept in his crib next to *Maman*'s bed. He had grown so much, and I realized he wasn't a tiny baby any more. Picking up my precious son, I held him close and smelled the fresh scent of baby powder. He moaned a little and shifted his legs, but he didn't wake up. Afraid that I would wake him with the tears streaming down my face, I returned him to his crib.

Maman watched me from the doorway and told me to sleep in her bedroom. I protested, but I was too tired to be stubborn. *Maman* picked up some bedding and smiled at Nathan and me as she shut the door.

Nathan put my suitcase next to the bed and checked on Guy. He kissed our son goodnight and crossed the room to me. We had to be careful where we stepped to avoid the creaking boards. We didn't want to wake the others since the walls were thin.

Glancing up at the wall above *Maman*'s bed, I noticed the pictures of my grandparents and felt a little self-conscious. It seemed like my grandfather with his red beard and white hair and *Bubbe*, my grandmother with her scarf on her head, watched us, but my heart was filled with so much love for Nathan I forgot everything else.

Pressing myself close to him, I kissed him. It had been so long since we had been together. He undressed me quickly, and I undid the buttons on his shirt. Like first-time lovers we fell into bed, touching each other and renewing senses put on hold for so long.

Nathan in Brussels

Maman and Papa before the war

Sara's siblings before the war
Top Row—Sara's cousin Esther and brother Albert
Henri, Esther, Jacques and Bernard

CHAPTER 4—THE SURROUNDING DARKNESS

I awoke to the sound of a door opening. Thinking I was back in prison, I sat up. In the darkness, I didn't know where I was. I held my breath and shivered. For a few seconds, I listened and waited in a sweat. No echo of the guards' boots sounded as they patrolled outside the prison cell. Then feeling Nathan next to me, I calmed down. I remembered where I was. With a deep sigh, I lay back down and pulled the sheets up around my neck.

I heard my brothers' voices and realized the noise that woke me had been the boys' bedroom door. They slept in one large bed in the sewing room where *Maman* used to make uniforms for the Belgian army. Through the walls I heard Albert asking Simon all sorts of questions about girls. Smiling, I dozed back off and didn't wake up until I smelled *Maman*'s cooking the next morning.

I stretched and reached for Nathan, but he was already up. I checked on Guy, still asleep in his crib. Touching his arm and talking gently to him, I said, "I love you, Guy. *Maman*'s home." I picked him up and held him a few moments. Rubbing my cheek against his hair reassured me I was really home and not dreaming. Then I laid him back down and put on one of *Maman*'s robes. Easing the door shut behind me, I walked into the large area that served as both living room and kitchen. I saw noodles hanging on the back of the chair to dry. *Maman* must be making soup.

Seated at the kitchen table, *Maman* held six-year-old Mariette on her lap. In front of them lay the family Bible. *Maman* was reading to Mariette from the scriptures. Busy as she was, *Maman* always found time to read to the children. All the family names were inscribed in this

Bible, and *Maman* would tell stories about our family as she saw each name in this sacred work.

When Mariette saw me, she jumped off *Maman*'s lap and scurried over. I picked her up and gave her a big hug and kiss.

"You're home! Where have you been? I missed you," Mariette said.

Dancing around the room with her, I said, "I missed you too. I came home last night. Nathan and Jean drove me from the border. You were asleep when I got in."

"Why didn't you wake me up? I wanted to see you."

"You see me now. It was too late to wake you up." I brushed her blond curls from her face. Mariette was sixteen years younger than I was and looked like Shirley Temple.

She scampered toward the boys' room to wake them up.

I reunited with my family. Nathan had not gone to work, and the older children had not gone to school yet. My only younger brother missing was Simon. He was probably off visiting one of his many girlfriends.

Laughing and hugging each other, we interrupted each other talking so fast.

Henri hugged me and then took the darts from the dartboard hung next to the glass door leading to the toilet. He practiced throwing some darts. Mariette watched his every move. For a ten-year-old, Henri had a creative imagination, but I wished he wouldn't be in such a hurry to grow up. He always wanted to be on his own and never listened to anyone.

Jacques was next in line for a hug. At age eight he was two years younger than Henri. Games of any kind held his interest. Jacques headed for a corner of the room to put together a puzzle.

Bernard, eleven years old, was a true scholar. Had Papa lived, Bernard might have attended a *yeshiva* to become a rabbi. However, all hope of his becoming a rabbi had disappeared.

Hearing so many voices all at once was strange. The eight months in Paris seemed an eternity ago, another lifetime I had dreamed in a nightmare.

Nathan entered from the glass door next to the china hutch. Ready for work, he came over and kissed me good morning. *Maman* offered Nathan a cup of coffee.

"Refka, do you want one?" Nathan was the only one who could call me by my middle name and get away with it.

As Nathan drank his coffee, Jean came in with his jacket over his arm. "I have to go. Someone has to work in this family," he joked. Jean had a place of his own, but he must've spent the night here at *Maman's* rather than return to his own apartment so late at night.

I asked if he could stay longer, but he had to get to work.

As Jean closed the door, I noticed my nine-year-old, quiet sister who was fourteen years younger than I. When *Maman* had brought her home from the hospital, I claimed her as "my baby" because I was so glad to have a sister and not another brother.

Esther sat on her bed with her arms crossed over her chest. She was always deep in thought, but I couldn't figure out why she looked so angry.

I sat beside her on the bed. "What's wrong?"

"Only bad people get arrested. Why did they arrest you?"

Taken aback at this unexpected remark, I answered without thinking. "I didn't do anything wrong. You'll find out when they arrest you too."

"They came with a truck and picked up people. They said they were bad people."

"They're not bad. We don't know where the Nazis take them. Do you think those people or I did anything wrong?"

Esther got quiet. Leaving her to brood, I walked toward *Maman* in the kitchen.

Maman had heard. "I'll talk to Esther later. Children have a strange way of showing their fears."

"I know." Pausing to regain some composure, I apologized. "I'm sorry I spoke so. I answered before thinking about her age."

"Age doesn't make any difference. In war childhood doesn't exist." *Maman* continued with the soup preparations and called Esther over to help her.

"I'm sorry," Esther said on her way over.

"Don't be sorry. I'm home. Things will be all right."

I hugged her and walked to the china hutch. I looked at the delicate cups and saucers that had once belonged in a richer setting. Before Papa died, our house had lacked for nothing. Papa had owned a successful *epicerie*, a fruit and vegetable store, and we had lived in an enormous house. He spoiled each of us, and I was his princess whose tears softened any deserved punishment, even when I should have been chastised for stealing my brother's motorcycle. I remembered that day as if it were a motion picture playing in my mind. It was when I was thirteen years old.

* * * * * * *

I revved the throttle on my brother's motorcycle. Adamantly my oldest brother Charles had told me not to touch it, but I would prove to him that I could drive it, even if he wouldn't teach me. I had watched him enough. Wearing a dress presented no problem; I simply tucked it between my legs. I knew I could handle anything. However, I hadn't calculated on the balancing part being so difficult.

I began to weave and got too close to Papa's store. I tried to swerve, but I fell off the bike onto the step. Glass exploded as the motorcycle crashed through Papa's plate glass window.

"Hurry! She's dead!" screamed my younger brother Jean.

Scraped and bruised, I lay there on the step of my father's wholesale grocery store. I was scared to open my eyes. A bit dazed, I finally peeked at the damage. The black motorcycle seemed alive with its sputtering motor and spinning rear tire. Glass covered the floor and shelves. At least the flying debris hadn't hurt any customers. Jean was crying, thinking I had killed myself,

When I moved, he ran over to me. He hugged me and tried to pull me up. Irritated, I brushed him away and retorted, "I'm all right. Don't tell people I'm dead."

Luckily, I hadn't broken any bones, but my leg was throbbing and bleeding. My parents were going to kill me for this. I was always getting in trouble and this was one more accident to add to my growing list of mischief. *Maman* ran toward me. As any teenager would do, I acted more hurt than I was to avoid *Maman*'s wrath.

When *Maman* got to me and saw the blood, she was convinced I had seriously hurt myself. *Maman* screamed, "Aaron, Sara's nearly killed herself!" Ignoring the broken glass, *Maman* bent down to cradle me in her arms. "Are you all right? What happened?"

"*Maman!*" I whined. "My leg hurts, *Maman*."

Carefully she checked me over and realized I only had cuts and bruises. Then I was in for it. "Sara, how could you do this?" she asked. "Didn't I tell you to stay away from your brother's motorcycle? I knew something like this would happen."

I shifted the blame to someone else. "Charles would never teach me how. I wanted to ride it and have some fun."

"Breaking your father's window is fun?" She dabbed at some of my cuts with her handkerchief. Then appealing to some heavenly intervention, she raised her hands in exasperation. "Oy!" she pleaded. "I wish I had ten boys for this one girl. Not one of the boys gives me so much trouble. "

By that time Papa strolled from the back of the store where he had been working with a customer. Looking at the mess, he put his hands in his jacket pockets. He covered his mouth to hide a laugh. This mild reaction set *Maman* off on one of her tirades.

Maman pointed at the glass and said, "Look at what *your* daughter did, Aaron." I was always my father's daughter when I had done something wrong.

With a smirk and a shrug of the shoulders, he said, "Now she knows how to drive."

Maman shot him an angry look. "Is that all you're going to say? Your only daughter did it again. She could have killed herself. Aaron, you've got to say more to her."

"Yes, she's my daughter and not yours," Papa said acquiescing. Then bending over to look at me closely, he asked, "Sara, are you hurt?"

"Papa, my leg hurts a lot," I said, tears welling in my eyes. Papa never got angry with me.

"That's all? I'm glad it's nothing serious," Papa said and hugged me. I clung to his neck for effect. Then he got me on my feet. When he saw I wasn't that badly hurt, he said to *Maman*, "Chana, take her home and I'll get someone to clean up this mess."

After turning the motorcycle's ignition key off, Papa picked up the battered bike. He brushed the glass off the seat and put the kickstand down. The front light was broken, the frame was bent, and the front tire would need to be replaced. Charles would kill me. This was the motorcycle he had bought with his own money to get back and forth from college.

A crowd of customers gathered around, watching the motorcycle, *Maman*, and me. Embarrassed, *Maman* said to them. "She's all right. When we get this cleaned up, come back." After she shooed the gawkers away, she turned on me again.

"This is not over, Sara. After we get those scratches cleaned up, you have a lot of apologizing to do."

Roughly, she brushed the glass off me and took me home.

* * * * * * *

Maman with Jean in front of the *epicerie*, the grocery store

This 1931episode in Brussels, Belgium, characterized my parents'
personalities in general. Papa was the easy-going one and *Maman* tried
to keep us out of trouble. It turned out to be a full-time job for *Maman*,
along with having children.

Maman's wish for "ten boys for this one girl" was almost granted.
She wound up giving birth to ten boys, but two died in infancy. We
Rozens were a close-knit family even with all eleven children. It
seemed as though *Maman* was always pregnant when I was growing
up. I was the third child and the only girl for sixteen years. Our
pecking order turned out to be Charles, Jules, and me; then came Jean,
Simon, Albert, Henry, Bernard, Esther, Jacques, and Mariette.

Every time *Maman* would come home from the hospital with
another boy, I was disappointed. I wanted a sister desperately. Acting
like a true brat one time and thinking she had control over the sex of
the child, I said to *Maman*, "If you bring home another boy, I swear I'll
kill him." At the time I meant it; thankfully, *Maman* ignored my
infantile comment.

Finally after sixteen years, she brought home Esther, and I was
elated. Immediately I wanted to put my earrings on her, but *Maman*
told me she was too young. With eleven children total, *Maman* was
fortunate that her marriage to Papa was a good one. The matchmaker
had done a great job when she selected Aaron Gedalia Rozen for
Chana Malka Goldstein.

Poor *Maman* had had very little time to grow up. In her day girls
were married at thirteen. By the time my mother was fourteen, she had
given birth to my oldest brother, Charles. When she was married, she
hadn't even had her first menstrual cycle. She played with Charles like
a doll.

Maman had the equivalent of a high-school education, but girls
back then weren't expected to attend college. She was expected to get
married and raise children. I'm surprised she didn't run out of family
names for all of us. We were named after deceased relatives to honor
their memories, a custom of our family and of most western European
Jews. Naming the child after a successful relative invoked the
protective spirit of that person. I was named after my father's mother.

I grew up quite a tomboy; having eight brothers until I was sixteen
years old made me one. When I was younger, I would climb greased
poles in a dress, slide down the banister, go sledding and ice skating,
and ski when we went on vacation to Switzerland. The rope pull
system on the slopes scared me, and I fell quite a few times, but I

learned to ski well enough to keep up with my brothers. I found out early in life that I had to stand up for myself in any situation.

The episode with the motorcycle wasn't the only time I drove poorly. A year later when I was fourteen, I wanted to drive *Maman*'s blue car. It was parked in the garage, and I thought I could back it out and take it for a spin. However, I put the car in drive instead of reverse. I hit the garage wall and then got the car into reverse. Next, I hit the door of the garage when I backed up. For several minutes I tried going forward and backwards, trying to maneuver it out of the garage. Soon my brothers heard what I was doing and came over for a closer inspection. I had dented the front and back bumpers, scratched the paint, and broken the left light. Jules had yelled, "*Maman*, Sara's made a mess of your car. Come see!" I got into trouble again, but as usual my punishment wasn't harsh.

In our twelve-bedroom house, each child had his or her own room. Papa's business had done well, and we lived a life of luxury. Papa saved the choicest delicacies from his wholesale grocery store for us children. As he said on many occasions, "My children come first."

Papa loved to dance and when I was fourteen, he took me to my first formal dance. *Maman* wore a black velvet dress with a blue sash down the back. She was so tall and beautiful in that gown. I can remember how women of her generation wanted a tiny waistline and wore corsets. Papa helped her pull that corset as tight as she could get it. He liked to show her off at dances. Proudly I danced with my good-looking Papa that evening.

We also had a menagerie of pets, ranging from cats to greyhounds. Jean, my brother one year younger than I am, used my love of animals to pester me at times. One time he lowered a dead mouse on a string outside my bedroom window. Dangling it there so that I was sure to notice, he was enjoying himself immensely. I was used to his tricks and ignored him. However, when he lowered my cat on a rope and dangled her outside my window next to the mouse, I screamed. The poor cat clawed frantically at my windowpane, trying to get in. I yelled for *Maman* to come quickly because I wanted her to see what Jean was doing. When she got to my room, naturally Jean had pulled up both the cat and the mouse. She thought I was seeing things and told me to quit saying things about my little brother. I marched up to his room and set the cat free. I looked for Jean to get even with him, but he had disappeared when he heard me coming. Jean the jokester got away with tormenting the cat and me that day. However, when he got into a fight one time after school, I told on him and he got a spanking. That was one of the few times my father ever spanked any of us.

My older brothers had friends over all the time; however, one time when *Maman* was not at home, they brought their girlfriends over. Curious all the time, I wanted to spy on them. When they closed the door to the parlor, I watched through the keyhole. They were kissing when Jules must have noticed my eyeball. He opened the door, told me to go away, closed it again, and stuffed his handkerchief in the keyhole where I couldn't see. I knew better than to pull the handkerchief out; he would have locked me in my room. Besides, I snitched on them later by telling my parents. After that, Charles and Jules "guests" were monitored a lot closer.

Nathan had been one of my brothers' friends. He was thirteen years older than I was and thought of me as a kid sister most of the time. I found out the hard way that Nathan would tell on me if he saw me doing anything wrong. One time when I was sitting on the grass in the park with my boyfriend, Nathan and Charles saw us. My boyfriend was just about to kiss me when Nathan and Charles gave us a look of disapproval.

As soon as they glared at us, my boyfriend ran away like a scared rabbit. He was afraid he'd get in more trouble, and Nathan and Charles were a lot older and bigger than he was.

"You don't have to watch out for me," I retorted to Charles. "I can take care of myself." I sounded brave, but I knew I was in big trouble again. Charles would tell *Maman*, and she would keep me on an even tighter tether than she had before. I thought I'd never get to go to a dance alone with a boy.

Sure enough, *Maman* found out. When I got home that same day, we had another one of our tete-a-tetes. I remember I told her, "You don't trust me with boys. Is that why you won't let me go to dances? Why do Charles and Jules get to go? Jean and Simon will get to go before I do."

"They're boys, Sara. Boys can do more at an earlier age than girls."

"*Maman*, I want to dance the fox trot and the cherry bomb as the other teenagers are doing, but you have Charles and Jules follow me."

"They're your brothers. They have to look out for you."

"Even Nathan tells on me, and he's not my brother. It's not fair," I whined. "I was just sitting on the grass with my boyfriend and Charles thought we were doing something wrong."

"Charles said it looked like your boyfriend was going to kiss you in public. You're only fourteen. It isn't proper. Next year you can go alone to a dance with a boy."

"I'm tired of going to dances with groups of friends. You're treating me like a baby."

"You're acting like one," she said. "Your curfew is 9:00, and you can't go alone."

Something raged within me and I said, "If I wanted to get pregnant, I could do it before 9:00. I know right from wrong."

"Don't talk that way to me!" *Maman* glowered at me.

I knew I had overstepped the bounds then. I ran to my room, slamming my door in defiance. Outraged that she would treat me this way, I threw myself on the bed

Later that evening I heard *Maman* telling Papa about my antics that afternoon. She said to him, "Aaron, she's willful. I'm afraid that if we don't let her go to some dances, she'll only get worse. Let her go. She's going to bring you a baby in nine months if you don't let her go. Even if she doesn't want it, she's going to bring you one."

During my teenage years I gave *Maman* so much trouble. I argued with her, challenged her opinions, and rebelled in various ways. When I look back on it, it's a wonder she put up with me. She truly had the patience of Job.

Mariette interrupted my reverie when she tugged on my robe.

"Can I get Guy up? I want to play with Gigi."

"Wait a little longer, and I'll get him up. You can look in on him, but don't wake him just yet."

"All right," whined a disappointed Mariette. To console herself, she snitched a sugar cube and popped it into her mouth before *Maman* could stop her.

"Mariettika, what have I told you about the sugar?" *Maman* warned. "It's hard to get."

"It's only one." Mariette twisted her blond curls in her fingers. Nathan didn't help the situation by laughing at Mariette's quick theft. Then she danced off to check on Guy, her "doll."

Maman shook her head with exasperation. "That little one will be the death of me. It's hard enough raising children without their father, but with the war, I don't know if I'll manage."

I laughed and let *Maman* continue with the soup while I got myself a cup of *ersatz* coffee, the weak brew that passed for coffee during the war. I looked at Albert's paintings near the china hutch.

Albert, my sixteen-year-old brother, was busy sketching at the table, as usual. He'd never let us see his works until he was ready. The most artistic in the family, Albert could play the flute and the piano as well as create wonderful oil paintings. Some of Albert's paintings were displayed in the palace. After all, Albert had been the godson to King Albert of Belgium because he was the seventh son born to our family. Two baby boys had died in infancy, making Albert the seventh boy.

I pointed to the dartboard hanging next to his painting and cautioned him that Henri or Mariette might hit the portrait of the nude lady. A dart sticking in her breast would ruin the painting.

He told me Henri had taught Mariette well and she never missed. He continued to sketch on his pad.

I walked back to the kitchen and leaned on the counter as *Maman* prepared the soup. "Where's Simon? I didn't see him last night and he's not here this morning."

Maman chopped the vegetables. "He spends most of his waking hours with his girlfriend Margaret. She's a Gentile. She lives across the street, and her parents love Simon."

"Does he still work with Nathan?

"Yes, when he's not out dancing with Margaret. I feel like I've lost him already. You know what they say. A son is a son until he gets a wife. A daughter is a daughter all of her life."

"Are they serious?"

"I'm not sure, but Margaret is a sweet girl. I like her."

"Well, I'm caught up on everyone except Charles. Where is he?"

"I don't want to talk about him."

I was surprised by *Maman's* abruptness. Charles must have done something awful to merit this response.

Maman pointed to the doorway of her bedroom. Mariette held Guy. He rubbed his sleepy eyes and looked around the room.

I walked over to Mariette and took Guy from her. I smoothed his hair and realized he didn't recognize me. My heart was killing me inside. My own child didn't recognize me. "*Cherie*, it's me."

Pulling back, he looked at me. "*Maman*, are you back?"

He used a complete sentence, and I was shocked. I had missed so much—his first haircut, his first sentence, and so many firsts. When I was arrested, he was barely walking. He had grown a lot.

"Yes, sweetheart, I'm back. I will stay with you all the time. I'm not going any place." I hugged him and cried. Returning to my seat at the table, I held him on my lap, something I had longed to do for eight long months. He had lost some of his baby fat, and he had more curly, blond hair since I had last seen him. Guy looked so beautiful! My baby was growing up.

He wanted to get down and play with my younger brothers and sisters, but I didn't want to let him go. When Guy saw Nathan, he squirmed on my lap and held his arms out to him. "Papa, hold me."

Nathan took him, and I ached inside. An insane jealousy made me want to snatch him back, but I knew I couldn't push for Guy's affections. They would come in time. Eight months was an eternity for a child.

Maman saw my pain and intervened. "Sara, help me in the bedroom."

I followed her. She closed the door, and I cried. *Maman* made me sit next to her on the bed. With *Maman* rocking me, I felt like a child.

"*Maman*, he doesn't recognize me. My own little boy...." I couldn't finish. I could only sob.

"It will take time." She smoothed my hair. "Remember he's a tiny child. He loves you."

"I know, but it hurts." I couldn't catch my breath as I choked back my tears.

"Shh, darling. It'll be all right."

"No, it won't. I can't get back the months I lost with Guy. I didn't see his first steps." Tears filled my eyes, blurring my sight.

"But you're alive, and you're back."

"I hate the Nazis." Seething anger spilled out. I grabbed a pillow from the bed and threw it across the room at the wall. "They took me away from my baby. Why?"

"I don't know. The Nazis hate people, especially us Jews. I've seen them kill people on the street."

"Oh, God! In Brussels?"

"Yes, here. We're not safe." *Maman* crossed to the window, closed the drape, and turned back to me. "You were safer in Paris."

"What do you mean?"

"Jews here in Brussels are being singled out. It's only begun. Already we've had to register. You'll have to register tomorrow."

"Why, *Maman*? They didn't know I was Jewish in Paris. A French guard at the prison found out I was Jewish, but he didn't tell anyone. I don't understand how he knew."

Thinking a moment, *Maman* said, "Maybe he was Byla's husband. You remember my friend Sammie who lived in our building? Her sister Byla is married to a Frenchman who works as a prison guard."

"That's possible."

"But, Sara, they have records here. They will catch you whether you register or not." *Maman* returned to sit by me on the bed. "Maybe it'll go easier on you if you register. The Jewish Council is cooperating with the Nazis by giving them the names and addresses of Jewish people throughout the city. Our names are on those lists."

"Jews are turning in Jews? You're joking!" I clutched a pillow to my stomach, knotting the pillowcase in my fist.

"No, I'm not joking. Jews who are on the Jewish Council cannot be trusted. They would turn in their own parents or the rabbi for some extra food or promise of not being shipped off to one of the work camps."

"Surely, the rabbis are safe from this."

"No," answered *Maman*. "They are treated worse than others."

"Can't anyone protect the rabbis or the temples?"

"The Germans have already closed one synagogue and burned it. They took the books out and burned them on the street. They burned the Sidis and the Torah. Our holy books mean nothing to them. They hate anything to do with the Jewish religion."

"*Maman*, where is God? Why does He allow them to do this? We are Jews."

"Honey, I cannot tell you. This is the way they are. We have to take care of ourselves."

"Oh, no. I didn't realize all this had happened." I dropped the pillow I had been clutching to the floor.

"That's not all," she continued. "We're not allowed to be out without proper identification." She picked up her purse from a chair next to the dresser and showed me her *Ausweiss*, her identity papers. I stared at the large "J" stamped on it in horror and disbelief. *Juif* was French for Jew. *Maman* continued, "They also promise if we register, we will find out information about our relatives in other countries. Then they promise us extra food stamps, but I think it's just lies."

"I didn't know it had gotten so bad." I gave the identity papers back to her. "I thought I was coming home where I would be safe."

"It's not safe here any more. They kick little children on the streets. Some of the Germans can be bribed, but we have no money. We haven't had money since your father died."

"I know, *Maman*."

"I wish your father were here to take care of us. We don't have the widows' fund from the government any more."

"Nathan and I will try to help as much as we can." I put my arm around her shoulder.

"I know. I thank God you're home." *Maman* paused a few seconds and looked at her folded hands in her lap. Then she asked what had been on her mind the whole time I was imprisoned. "Sara, what happened to you in the prison?"

Worry lines creased her forehead. "They didn't touch you, did they?"

"No, they didn't. All I had to do was laundry. No one hurt me."

She exhaled a breath of relief.

"Now tell me about Charles. And where is Jules? Are they all right? Where are they?"

"Jules is safe for now. He's still a waiter at the *Cirque Royal*. He, Agnes, and the three children are all right. It's strange how fate works. Your father was so upset over Jules dating a Gentile that he tore his clothing and said *Kaddish*, but now, because Jules is married to a Gentile, the Germans haven't bothered him as much."

"Why is that?"

"I don't know. I suppose since the children aren't being raised in the Jewish religion, the Germans aren't as concerned with Jules."

Guy appeared in the doorway and she picked him up and brought him over to me.

"That's all I thought about in prison—holding my baby again." I took him from her then and hugged him closer.

Guy winced at the tightness of my grasp and said, "*Maman*, you're hurting me."

I relaxed my hold on him. "I'm sorry, *Cherie*. I just love you so much."

I shifted Guy to my other hip. "What about Charles, *Maman*? You didn't answer before when I asked about him. Where is he?"

"When the Germans were coming into Brussels, Charles, Renee, and her family got out. I begged him to take the children and me, but he said there wasn't room in the car for us. Then I begged him just to take little Mariette, but he refused. There was room for all Renee's family, though. He drove off and left us standing there, knowing the Germans had taken over Belgium." Fighting back the tears, she continued, "I guess Charles made it across the border safely. I don't know."

"How could he do that, *Maman*?"

"In war we all have to make choices. He chose his wife's family over us."

"I can't believe it." Feeling like I'd been slapped, I stood there thinking how my brother could leave *Maman* and the children at the mercy of the Germans.

As she left the room to check on the younger children, I saw Nathan playing with Mariette. Too young to remember Papa, Mariette had taken to Nathan like he was her father.

Rocking Guy on my lap, I thought over *Maman*'s words. Having my son back in my arms was precious, but with Hitler's forces moving like they were, this moment would not last.

Within a week I found a two-bedroom second floor apartment just across the street from *Maman*'s. Her apartment was too crowded, though she would have let us stay as long as we wanted. When I would bring Guy to see her and play with my younger brothers and sisters, Guy would bounce on every step up to the third floor, saying, "*Bobonne*, where are you? *Bobonne!*" That was his way of announcing our arrival to his grandmother in French. Such a special bond had formed between them.

Shortly after finding the apartment, I called my nanny, Catherine. Before I had left for Paris, she had been working for Nathan and me, helping me with the baby. A lovely lady in her mid-fifties, Catherine loved our family. She had taken care of me when I was little, and now she was taking care of my child. While I was in Paris, she had returned to her suburb of Brussels. She came back to stay with us when I called her. Her husband had died, her daughter was grown, and we were now her family.

For the next few weeks it felt as if things had returned to normal. Nathan continued to work at the tailor shop, I took care of Guy, and Catherine helped me. However, the Nazi occupation overshadowed every aspect of our lives. Our peaceful time together was over too quickly.

Simon and Albert in Brussels, 1939

CHAPTER 5—AT THE MERCY OF A MADMAN

Early one evening Nathan and I stopped at one of the few clubs where Jews were still welcomed. This surprised me since Nathan didn't like modern dances, but I didn't question him. I assumed he had a good reason.

We found a small table covered with a white tablecloth. At one time it had been pristine, but with the war, washing tablecloths took second place to finding food. Customers didn't mind and ordered their liquor, an intoxicating escape for many. As long as people drank to dull their losses, little clubs like this could survive until the liquor ran out.

After our waiter took our order, Nathan said, "*Maman* told me this is where Jean was supposed to be, but I haven't seen him yet."

"Neither have I. Maybe he changed his mind and went somewhere else." I removed my black hat and gloves and put them on the table.

Nathan turned his head as he scanned every face in the room. He had never ignored me like this.

"What's going on?" I asked. "What do you know that you're not telling me?"

Nathan tried to recover by looking at me and smiling, but he couldn't hide his concern. "I wanted to see him dance the cherry bomb. That's all." He motioned to the gramophone as it blared out the popular swing music.

I wasn't convinced, but before I could ask any more, the waiter brought our wine. A few red drops added to the mosaic on the cloth. Nathan sipped his drink, but his eyes darted to anyone who entered the club.

Soon Jean and two other men hurried in. They were out of breath and sweating, their hair wind-blown. I squeezed Nathan's arm to get his attention and pointed them out.

Clearly angry with Jean, Nathan shot up from his chair and headed toward the three young men. Rarely did Nathan get angry, and I knew something was wrong.

Nathan pulled Jean aside by the front of his shirt. Nathan's face reddened, and the veins in his neck bulged. For a minute I thought he was going to hit my brother. Then Nathan released his grip and gestured toward our table. As Nathan ushered Jean between the tightly packed tables and chairs, Jean's friends disappeared into the crowd.

Nervously, I sloshed some of the wine onto my black skirt. I brushed it off and stood up to excuse myself to the ladies' room, leaving Jean alone with Nathan.

When I returned a short time later, Jean was already gone and Nathan was paying the bill "Where's Jean?" I asked him.

"This isn't the time or the place. We'll talk about it on the way home."

Though the streets that early December were relatively quiet with no German patrols in sight, we hurried home. No curfew had been enacted yet for Jews, but we dreaded running into any soldiers.

Once we were inside our apartment, I took off my coat. Throwing my gloves on the table next to the sofa, I unpinned my hat. "What did Jean tell you?"

"Jean is working with the resistance. He's been with the Belgian underground ever since the invasion."

"So that's why he's gone every night. He lied to *Maman* about all the girls." A mixture of pride and fear overwhelmed me. My eyes welled with tears, and I was afraid of what might happen to my brother. Nightmares of Jean being shot on the street in front of me kept me awake most of that night.

When I saw Jean the next day at *Maman*'s, I pulled him into the hallway where *Maman* kept the live fish in a tub until she was ready to cook them. I checked to make sure no one was coming because I didn't want the rest of the family to hear. "Jean, Nathan told me what you do every night. I'm scared for you."

"I'm careful, Sara. They won't ever take me alive."

"Jean, please don't say that. I don't want you to die."

"The Nazis are killing us Jews anyway. I saw a member of the Jewish Council shot dead. I was on the street when it happened. At least this way I'll die fighting."

"Stop it, Jean. I don't want to hear you talk about dying."

He looked at the fish desperately sloshing in the pan. "Surala, I'm not going to sit and wait for them to kill me. Promise me if something does happen, you'll tell *Maman* I died for my country. And promise not to tell anyone what you know."

I studied his determined face for a few seconds. "I promise, but be careful. I love you." Before we went back into the apartment, I hugged Jean.

I kept his secret and didn't tell *Maman*, but I feared for his life. If he were caught, he'd be tortured for information before they killed him. I didn't want my brother to die like that.

Since it was early December, we wanted to celebrate Hanukah as best we could. Like the Maccabees, we also prayed for deliverance from tyranny, but by the middle of the month, Henri, Esther, and Jacques came home early from school, looking like they had lost their best friends. *Maman* asked, "What are you doing here? School isn't out yet."

"We cannot go to school any more," Jacques told *Maman*. "We're not allowed. The teacher told us Jews aren't allowed in school. The other children started making fun of us and pointing. They said, 'This is our school. Get out!'"

What we had all been dreading had now begun. We would be separated from other Belgian citizens and singled out.

"This is Hitler's doing," said *Maman*, pushing a graying strand of hair back in place. "He's poisoned their minds. Not everyone can be nice, Jacques. Don't blame them."

"But they're the ones calling us names."

"Don't hate, *cherie*." *Maman* lifted Jacques' face toward her. "You don't know what they're being told."

"Maybe they're being forced to say these things. Their parents may be telling them to act like they hate Jews in public. If they act like they are friends, they could be next. It's not the children's fault."

"It's hard, *Maman*," Esther said.

"I know, but don't hate, Esther." *Maman* placed her hand gently on Esther's arm. "It's the war, not the children."

"Why, *Maman*? What did we Jews do for them to hate us so much?" Tears welled in her eyes.

"Honey, I don't know. What do you want me to tell you?" *Maman* hugged her, trying to protect her from the horrors of the war, but knowing she could not.

From then on, *Maman* helped the children with their reading, but with all of her sewing and trying to keep the family fed, not much spare time could be found. Jacques and Henri began to spend a lot of time on the streets. They avoided the Germans by hiding and learning to disappear quickly.

Over the next few months the Germans rounded up Jews and sent them off to work camps. My own uncle was arrested and taken away when he came to *Maman's* house. We heard about letters sent from the camps telling us things were not so bad. We would just be put to work; however, no one ever returned from these "camps." We didn't know what lay ahead.

Within a short time, I was pregnant again. Being pregnant should have been a time of rejoicing, but I felt uneasy about my baby's future. *What would the world be like for her? Would she be hated just for being born a Jew?* I didn't want that. I wanted a world of peace and love for my baby, one where she would be safe, but I wasn't bringing my child into such a world. I didn't know if my baby would have a chance.

The Nazis announced new edicts every day against Jews. Besides registering and having *Juif-Jood* stamped on our identity cards, Jews were now barred from the press, the radio, from legal professions and from becoming teachers. Jewish doctors and dentists could no longer practice legally. *Was this what my child had to face? What would be next?*

In April Nathan lost his job at the tailor shop. Jews weren't allowed to own a business any more, and Nathan's cousin, Mocha Gutteman, lost his tailor shop. We had saved some money and were able to stay in our apartment, but Nathan couldn't find a job anywhere. No one could hire a Jewish employee.

As the Germans secured their hold on Belgium, we lived in fear every day. We heard decrees against Jews being played on loudspeakers when the trucks passed through the streets. We were forced to wear the Star of David as identification by late May or early June of 1942. However, I was proud to wear it as a symbol of my faith. I would never be ashamed of the Star of David. The Germans made us buy the material for the stars with our own money.

My brother Simon did not feel the same way about having to wear the Star of David. He said he wouldn't wear it. Simon had already been turned away from the university and told he could no longer attend. He had been a part-time student who also worked at the tailor shop with

Nathan. Now he had no school and no job.

Though our Belgian neighbors could not help us Jews very much concerning the decrees and the deportations, they were not anti-Semitic. They resisted in whatever ways they could by giving Jewish people shelter and food.

However, our king, Leopold III, did little to stop the persecution. He surrendered to the Germans in the same month Belgium was invaded. He was not like his father, King Albert, who had never shown any anti-Semitism. King Albert had died in a climbing accident in 1934 near Namur. My brother Albert was as upset as if he had lost a member of our immediate family. I was glad our beloved king was not alive when the Germans invaded Belgium in May 1940. We felt as though we had no one in the government left to speak for us now.

I couldn't believe I had actually wanted to date Prince Leopold when I was a teenager. The king had invited our family to the palace on many occasions, and that's how I met Leopold. When he wanted to take me dancing, *Maman* had refused, knowing royalty would never be seriously interested in a Jewish girl. I'm just glad I never went out with him.

Since Nathan could not find work, he began to sell suits on the black market to buy food and pay the rent. We sold jewelry and furs Papa had given me for less than half of their value, but one cannot eat a diamond.

In the open-air markets with the brightly colored umbrellas the flower merchants suffered. Few people could afford to buy flowers. The green grocers, who sold vegetables, fared better than the lace makers. Expert lace makers can only make inches a day, but yards of it sold for less than potatoes. It took hours of scouring the vendors at the market to find decent prices.

Maman and I shopped at the closest market, one where Jews were still allowed to purchase items. At this market, which had been a source of livelihood for most people in our community, tragedy struck on July 2, 1942.

The all-too-familiar sound of trucks and sirens filled the air. I went down the flight of stairs to the front of the apartment. Germans surrounded the green grocer's and the entire block. Soldiers jumped from the backs of trucks. They shouted at frightened people, huddled together for protection. A woman fainted while her terrified daughter tried to hold onto her. Two soldiers grabbed her by the arms and slung her into the truck. The little daughter climbed in after her, more terrified of losing her mother than the sadistic guards. A cruel soldier shouted to an elderly person, "You're going to work, you worthless Jew-pig!"

The soldiers used their bayonet tips to prod those caught in the trap into the waiting trucks. They looked for any reason to jab someone who moved too slowly. Too many times I had witnessed a similar scene, and I didn't want to watch any more. I knew what would happen to any Jew at the market today.

At the time I was just two blocks away. I looked across the street where *Maman*'s apartment was and realized with horror today was when *Maman* had said she and Albert would buy groceries. I said a silent prayer she had changed her mind and wasn't at the market. Craning my neck to see the people they were putting in the trucks, I recognized some people from the neighborhood. All I could do was pray, "Oh, God, please help *Maman* and Albert! Don't let them be arrested."

I saw Josephine, a Gentile neighbor of mine, coming back from the store. Her pace quickened as she neared me. She grabbed me roughly by the arm and told me, "Sara, go back inside. They've just taken your mother and Albert. Get back inside."

"No! I've got to help them."

"Somebody may see you. You can't help them if they see you. Move!"

I stumbled back up the steps to my apartment. My hand trembled as I closed the door. *What would happen to my mother and brother? Where were the Germans taking them? What had they done to be arrested and herded into a truck like animals?*

There had to be something I could do. I went back to the door and opened it a crack. I hesitated. *What could I do?* A sense of helplessness engulfed me. I wanted to run out into the streets and thrash the men who were taking my mother and brother away from me. Instead, I closed the door and pounded my fist against it. "Not *Maman* and Albert, God, please not them!" I pleaded desperately, sliding down against the wall to the floor. Holding my head with my hands, I sat stunned, not knowing what to do.

Then I thought about my younger brothers and sisters. They were alone. I had to go to my mother's house and get the children. I didn't have much time. As soon as a person was arrested, the Germans would show up to find others and to take anything of value. I had to work quickly, but I had to wait until the trucks by the store had gone.

I had heard the Catholic nuns and priests would help Jews. I didn't know for sure if they would take my brothers and sisters, but I had to ask them.

Nathan was at Mocha's house. I called his house and his daughter Leah answered the phone. I told her to give Nathan the message that the Nazis had arrested *Maman* and Albert. We had to hide my brothers and sisters.

I got off the phone and watched the streets until the Germans left the area. I ran to *Maman*'s house. Esther was with Mariette. I asked her, "Where are Henri and Jacques?"

"They're at the park, and Esther is going to take me too," Mariette said.

"Sara, what's wrong? Where's *Maman*?" Esther asked.

"The Germans took her and Albert. We've got to leave here quickly before the Nazis come back. Now hurry!"

"But we can't leave without *Maman*," Mariette said.

"We have to, *cherie*. You have to come with me right now."

We hurried down the stairs without taking anything; there was no time. At the park we spotted Henri teaching Jacques a game. Jacques threw one rock and scooped up the others. From a distance I saw Nathan approaching. Mariette began to cry, and I held her while we walked toward them.

Nathan took her from me and held her. "Mariette, we have to get you to a place of safety. You do whatever Sara tells you and be a good girl." He handed her back to me and took Henri's hand.

"Where are we going?" Henri asked him.

"Sara will take the girls to the Catholic sisters, and I'll take you boys to the orphanage run by the priests."

"No, I don't want to go to an orphanage."

"Henri, there's no time to argue. You have to go now!" I said.

Henri stopped and stepped away from Nathan. "I'll take care of myself on the streets. I don't want to stay with any priests." He took off running. We had no time to chase him down.

"Sara, take the girls now," Nathan said. "I'll find Henri later." He took Jacques in the direction of the boys' orphanage. Jacques was only nine years old. I couldn't bear to think of leaving my little brother with strangers, but no other hiding place was available for a young child.

The Germans checked the orphanages on a regular basis, but the priests hid the boys when the searches were made. I had heard they had special places for them. Jewish boys were easy to spot because of their circumcisions. The Germans could easily identify them as Jewish by making them drop their pants. That's why the priests hid them if the soldiers conducted a raid.

Even though Jacques wasn't a tiny child, he was still risky to place. People would not take in older children whose boisterous nature would draw attention to them. We had no other choice of where to put him.

Mariette clung to me, crying, while Esther stood by me silent as a statue. We didn't talk while we walked toward the convent run by the nuns. I feared for my little sisters, but tried not to let them see it. I smiled at Mariette and took Esther's hand.

We reached the convent with its saints, lions and gargoyles positioned against the ancient gray stones. As we entered the wrought iron gates, I saw one of the sisters and asked her for help.

She led us into an office, blessing herself as she passed a statue of Jesus. Inside the office a large, older woman in the traditional black and white habit looked up from her desk. The wrinkles across her forehead gave away her age, but no lock of gray hair showed from around her tight-fitting headdress. She had kind eyes, and I felt at ease with her.

I told her we were Jewish and needed her help.

She asked me the names and ages of my sisters.

"Their last name is Rozen." I spelled the last name for her. "My name is Sara Hauptman." I paused again as she wrote down the information. "Esther is ten years old, and Mariette is seven."

The nun studied the girls and said, "Girls with light hair are easier to hide. I'm afraid we won't be able to keep them together though. If one were found, we wouldn't want her sister arrested too. You understand, don't you?"

"Yes, I understand."

When Mariette heard they would be separated, she bit her lower lip and her face turned ashen.

"Mariette," I said, "you have to stay with this lady. I cannot take you with me. It's not safe where I'm going. You will be safe here."

"Sara, don't leave me. I'm afraid. I want *Maman*." Mariette cried and clung to my neck. I could do nothing, and I had never felt so helpless in all my life.

"Why can't Guy be with us?" Mariette asked pleadingly.

"Because he's a boy. He can't stay with you. He's too young to stay here."

"Why can't we go to Catherine's?"

"We cannot let you stay together. If they find one, the others can be alive. Look at what happened with *Maman*. If Albert hadn't been with her, he wouldn't have been arrested. I can't bear to lose all of you."

Finally the nun intervened and picked Mariette up while I said good-bye to Esther.

"Esther, I love you and Mariette. Please understand this is the only way I can save you. *Maman* is gone. You have to be brave and take care of Mariette until they find you a place to hide. Can you do that?"

Still in shock, Esther nodded. I hated to leave her like this, but I had no choice. I kissed them both and nearly collapsed as I tried to walk away from them. Mariette screamed as I left. I will never forget her pleas. "Don't leave me, Sara. Come back." Those words drove spikes through my heart.

Blinded by my tears, I made my way out the door of the office. Somehow I got back to my apartment. I called the church where Nathan had taken my brother and talked with a priest to make sure he would be all right. He told me they would have to take him to an orphanage out of town. That way was safer.

Josephine, my neighbor who had warned me about the arrests, came over and made me some weak tea with a used teabag, trying to get me to calm down. Wild with fear, I couldn't stop crying all day. I felt so guilty for leaving my little brother and sisters with complete strangers. Josephine told me about other children who had been placed with the nuns and priests, assuring me my family members would be in good hands.

From the window I watched as the Germans ransacked *Maman*'s house, carrying away her belongings. My brother Albert was a good artist. Now the soldiers hung his paintings on the sides of a truck with little regard for their value. One soldier crammed the portrait of the nude lady between chairs; a nail caught the canvas, tearing it and ruining a beautiful piece of art. After that, I turned away, unable to watch any more.

When they left, I sneaked over to see if anything was left, but *Maman*'s apartment was completely empty. Only bare walls and floor remained.

Later I found out *Maman* and Albert were taken to a camp, Malines, near Mechelen, Belgium, located about twenty miles from Brussels. I prayed they were all right and were only being put to work.

As I stared out the window blankly at *Maman*'s apartment building, I asked Nathan, "Why are we so hated? What did we ever do to them?

Why would they want to hurt *Maman* and Albert?" I cried from the insanity of it all and covered my face with my hands.

I turned back to the window. The unbelievable scene of the Germans looting *Maman*'s possessions seared my memory deeply. I shook my head in exasperation and thought, *My God, we're at the mercy of a madman.*

Esther, Mariette and Guy on the Rue Marchet in Brussels

CHAPTER 6—A LIGHT IN THE DARKNESS

Daily the Germans raided public buildings and private homes to take away the Jews. Like *Maman* and Albert, people were arrested without any warning on the streets. They had done nothing wrong. Their only crime was being Jewish. Even the elderly weren't safe. Nathan's Aunt Esther, at age seventy-eight, jumped from roof to roof of four-story buildings to save herself from arrest.

From Catherine's apartment, which was across the hall from ours, I saw a pregnant woman kicked repeatedly by a Gestapo officer. Again and again he drove his boot deep into her abdomen, intentionally trying to kill her unborn child. She tried to get to roll into a fetal position to protect her baby, but he was too fast with the blows. If she managed to get her back to him, he would kick her as hard as he could, forcing her to expose her baby once again. Screaming from the pain, she pleaded with him to stop. "For God's sake, don't kill my baby!"

He just laughed at her and spat in her face. He punched her in the face until she was unconscious. Then he grabbed her by the hair and dragged her down the sidewalk. Her legs gave out from under her, and they looked like a rag doll's, limply falling in all directions. As they got further down the street, I could no longer hear any sounds but the clicking of the heels of his boots on the bricks. I don't know what became of that poor woman and her child.

I was pregnant at the time and wondered if my unborn child and I would meet the same fate. *Would I find myself in this woman's position? Would I one day walk out of my house and find myself face to face with a Gestapo officer looking for a Jew to murder?*

When Nathan got home that day, I told him what I had seen. Still trembling when I recalled the attack, I hoped I wouldn't give birth prematurely. I was only eight months along and wanted my child to have a normal birth, as if that were possible during a war.

"We have to separate, Sara," Nathan said. "It's not safe here. We have to see what we can do to save each other and the baby. I don't want you near those animals. Go to Catherine's house. Fewer Germans patrol out in the countryside than in Brussels."

"I don't want to leave you, Nathan. I need you now more than ever." I ran my hands protectively over my unborn child and imagined the torment of that poor woman as her child was bludgeoned to death.

"Lots of people are dragged away like that woman you saw," Nathan said. "You never even had to work at hard jobs before. I don't want you dragged off to some work camp or attacked in the street." Pacing the room, he rubbed the back of his neck. "If you won't go to Catherine's right away, then let Catherine take Guy to her house in the country and keep him. He'll be safe with her. After the baby is born, you go with her too. I'll stay with my cousin Mocha."

"Separate? I don't want to be in the country so far from you."

"Mocha's wife Leah is pretending to be married to a Gentile man. I can stay with them and be safe. I'll come see you when I can." He took my hand and led me to the sofa. After he helped me get situated as comfortably as I could in my advanced pregnancy, he ran his hands through his hair. His eyes, puffy from sleeplessness and worry, told me he had already thought this through.

"No, Nathan. It's not a life," I resisted. "If they take us, they take us together."

"No. I don't want to think of you being arrested. We'll try it a few days. It won't be long before you go to the hospital to have the baby. We must try and see how it goes."

"Nathan, if I stay indoors, I'll be safe. Our neighbors won't turn us in."

"What about Madame Francois? She has always been jealous of what we have. She'd turn us in to show what a good Nazi she is. She's probably the one who called the Nazis when your mother and Albert were arrested."

I thought about how this middle-aged Nazi sympathizer acted superior to everyone. Every day she flew her Nazi flag with its twisted swastika from her apartment. "You're right," I acknowledged. "She would. She'd turn us in to get our furniture." I looked at the dark French provincial pieces, the gramophone, and the leather chairs.

I couldn't imagine leaving our·home and not sleeping in my own bed. I wouldn't be able to take anything with me. We'd have to leave everything exactly where it was. If we gave anything to neighbors, they'd be under suspicion and could be arrested along with us.

"We have to stay in other places," Nathan continued. "For now you go with Catherine to Ardennes, and I'll stay with Mocha. We can arrange to see each other once in a while, but we can't stay together here any longer. I'll continue to look for Henri whenever I can. Mocha told me he saw him on the street yesterday, but when he called his name, Henri took off like a frightened rabbit."

After we had taken the other children into hiding, we had not been able to find Henri. He hid any time someone recognized him.

I knew I couldn't argue with Nathan about leaving our apartment. He was right. I didn't want to be separated from him, especially with me being eight months pregnant, but we had few choices. We could stay and wait for Madame Francois to turn us in, or we could go into hiding.

I walked across the hall to talk to Catherine about our plan. She agreed with Nathan and began packing her things right away. She was relieved to hear Guy and I would be coming with her. I returned to my house and started to pack the familiar little yellow suitcase. *How many times would I have to pack up my things and go away because of the Nazis?* At least this time German soldiers didn't watch my every move.

Nathan packed a small bag to take with him to Mocha's. He could easily hide it under his suit jacket if the need arose. He put many of his toiletry items in his suit pockets.

As I locked the door, I wondered if I would ever see anything in that apartment again. We couldn't risk telling anyone where we were going. The danger was too great that the Nazis could find a way to get them to talk. Then Catherine and Mocha's lives would be in danger too.

I stayed with Catherine and Guy in the country for a week or so before I called Nathan and went back into the city to see him. Contacting him was a danger in itself, but this week of separation seemed like two months. I didn't have him to hold me in the night and rub my back when it ached with the progression of pregnancy. Often he would insist on my eating more. I knew he gave me his portion of food, and he made up a story about eating a meal at Mocha's. I only ate his food for the baby's sake. My heart ached to see Nathan again.

After that phone call, Nathan and I arranged to see each other, only we stayed with friends in separate houses. We would pay a little to help with food, a treasured and hard-to-come-by item. If we could pay, people were more willing to take us in. Though, many would have taken us in whether we could pay or not.

When I went for an overnight visit, Guy would stay with Catherine, whom he called Nonnie. He thought of her like another grandmother. Her Belgian heritage and his blond hair would keep the Germans from being suspicious of them.

Whenever I could arrange a trip back to Brussels, I would sleep wherever someone could put me—on a concrete floor, in an attic, or in a basement to keep from being discovered. People tried to make me comfortable, but I woke up the moment the baby moved or if the weight pressed against a nerve too long. Rarely could Nathan and I stay at the same house.

A few weeks later on October 5, 1942, I stayed with a neighbor, Yvette. She lived on the main floor of the apartment, and she gave me a broom to knock on the ceiling if I needed help. I was far along in my pregnancy and knew the baby might come at any time. Around midnight I felt a familiar, warm gush. My water had broken.

Nothing would stop the baby from coming, and I knew I didn't have much time. Guy came twenty minutes after my water broke. I grabbed the broom and repeatedly hit it against the ceiling to wake up Yvette. *Was she such a sound sleeper? Couldn't she hear me?* I kept on jamming the broom against the ceiling until I thought I would knock the light fixture onto my head.

Finally Yvette must have heard me. She descended the stairs, knowing what had happened. She asked me about my contractions.

As I tried to tell her I hadn't had any yet, the words wouldn't come out of my mouth. I couldn't talk any more and had to grab onto a chair. All I could think about was the sharp pain. I felt my whole body spasm with the contraction.

When the contraction was over, she helped me into the chair.

Yvette ran back upstairs and told the hospital we were on our way. She also phoned Nathan at Mocha's and gave him the news. Luckily, she had a car and could get us to the hospital. She helped me into the back seat and took off for *Hospital Dieu*, the same hospital where Guy had been born.

All along the way I prayed we wouldn't be stopped by a German patrol. If I had a contraction in the back seat while they questioned us,

I wouldn't have breath to speak. I could only hope that we could get to the hospital without any problems.

Even though *Hospital Dieu* was Catholic, the staff still treated Jewish patients. Nathan would have to take a circuitous route where he could hide from patrols since he was violating the curfew. The Belgian hospital workers would let him in when he told them his wife was in labor.

When Nathan got to the hospital, they allowed him to see me only a few minutes. He would have to go to the waiting room with Mocha the rest of the time. I was in so much pain the only thing I remember telling him was, "This will be the last. No more."

He kissed my forehead and agreed this would be the last child. When the next contraction began, the nurse whisked him out of the room. If he had been close enough during that contraction, my nails would have left their mark on his shoulder. I grabbed onto the railing of the bed with a death grip.

The nurse gave me some chipped ice in a cup, but she wouldn't allow me any drinks. She also got me up and had me walk in between contractions. I thought I would drop the baby with each contraction, but this birth wasn't as easy as Guy's. *Maman* had been with me when Guy was born. *How was I to get through this labor without her?* I wanted her there desperately.

I did not receive any drugs. *Hospital Dieu*, as well as most European hospitals, believed in natural childbirth. I was in labor for fourteen hours until 3:30 in the afternoon of the next day. Finally our beautiful Monique arrived on October 6, 1942. Our gorgeous baby girl weighed eight pounds, two ounces. She looked so much like Nathan; she had his ears and nose. I was so grateful she was healthy with all ten fingers and all ten toes. She had a tiny bit of reddish-brown hair. All I wanted to do was cradle her close to me and smell that magical scent of my own child. Nathan and I named her Monique after Nathan's aunt, Mocha's mother, whose was also named Monique. Her Jewish name would be Malka, and Malka was also my mother's middle name.

I wanted to nurse Monique, but my milk never came in. The nurse tried a pump, but I didn't have any milk. The nurse made me stay in bed, but brought Monique to me at regular intervals to bottle-feed her.

Each day when Nathan would visit, he was only allowed to stay with me fifteen to twenty minutes. Hospitals were very protective of mothers and infants. During our short visits, we planned where we would go when I was released from the hospital. We would return to

Mocha's together. Then as soon as the baby was able to travel a little distance, I would return to Catherine's in the country.

Staying in the hospital eight days after a birth was customary for all Belgian women. Nathan was going to pick me up around nine o'clock on the morning of October 14. I sat in the room waiting for Nathan, and he was late. Nathan wouldn't be late, especially when he was picking me up from the hospital.

For hours I waited, growing more fearful with each passing hour. I made up reasons in my mind for his lateness. *Maybe he had to avoid some German patrols. Perhaps he couldn't leave Mocha's house. Maybe the Nazis were searching it.* It never crossed my mind Nathan wouldn't come for me.

About three o'clock in the afternoon Nathan's cousin, Mocha Gutteman, came in the room, twisting the brim on the hat he held in his hands. Mocha, heavyset and short, was generally full of life. I knew something was wrong. "What are you doing here? Where's Nathan?" I asked him.

"I'm sorry to tell you the Germans took Nathan at the hospital door when he came to pick you up."

My worst fears had come true. Nathan had been arrested. Feeling like I couldn't take my next breath, I sat stunned a few moments. I hugged Monique closer and asked, "Are we in danger too? Do they know about the baby?"

"I don't think so," Mocha said. "Nathan was smart. He told them he brought some clothes to donate. He told them his wife and child had been arrested, and he wanted the clothes to be used for some good."

"Where is he now? Do you know?"

"No, all I know is what the nurse told me. She saw him arrested and took the clothes from him. When I came in to find out what floor you were on, the nurse told me what happened. I was just coming by to see the baby."

"Where's Guy? Was he with Nathan?" I snapped.

"No, he's at home with Helen and Leah."

"Mocha, what are we going to do? What's going to happen to Nathan?" Almost sensing my fear, Monique began to squirm and cry. I reached for her bottle and tried to give it to her, but she pushed it away. I tried to force her to take the bottle and stop crying.

"Calm down, Sara," Mocha said as he took the bottle from my hand. He must have known I was transferring every bit of panic I felt to Monique. She wouldn't settle down until I did.

He continued, "The first thing we'll do is take you back to our place. Then I'll make some calls to find a safe house for you and the baby."

"What about Nathan?"

Mocha ran his hands through his dark hair and took a deep breath before he answered me. "You know there's nothing we can do. If we ask questions, they'll arrest us too. We hope he'll just be sent to a work camp. That's all we can do."

I sat silently, knowing Mocha was right. We couldn't call or ask for help from anyone. We were all helpless. No one could bring Nathan back. Clutching Monique in the baby blanket, I followed Mocha as he picked up my suitcase. Monique cried and I realized how tightly I was holding her. I wanted to cry too, but I knew I would only upset her more. We were leaving the temporary protection of the hospital for an unknown destination.

How would I manage without Nathan? Who would take care of us? How could I raise both Guy and Monique without a husband to provide for us? I felt utterly alone with such an awesome responsibility. This tiny new child depended solely on me to protect her and give her a decent life. *What kind of a life could I provide for her now?*

CHAPTER 7—IN HIDING

Mocha found Monique and me a place of safety with a Gentile friend. I contacted Catherine about keeping Guy with her again. She took him to Ardennes, a suburb of Brussels. I asked everyone I knew if they had heard anything about Nathan. All I could find out was he was taken to Malines, the same camp near Mechelen where *Maman* and Albert had been taken. Maybe they would see each other at the camp.

Months passed as I stayed with Mocha's friend. Never did I find out any more about Nathan, *Maman* or Albert. On occasions Catherine would come into the city to see Monique and me. She could stay at her room across the hall from our old apartment. The risk of staying in my apartment was too great. My neighbor Josephine told me Germans would stop by on a regular basis checking for us since we were Jewish. Luckily, they had not found where we were.

It surprised me the Germans hadn't taken our belongings. Madame Francois certainly wanted my French provincial furniture, the brown leather chairs, and the gramophone, but for some reason she was not allowed to take them yet. Perhaps our belongings were the cheese in the trap for us.

I made arrangements with a lawyer to give Catherine power of attorney with all my affairs because Jews no longer had any legal rights. Therefore, Catherine had access to my bank account and could continue to make payments on the apartment for me. Also if something did happen to Nathan or me, she would be the legal guardian for Guy and Monique.

Since I could not find out any news about Nathan, I decided to return to Ardennes with Catherine. I was reluctant to travel far with

Monique being so young. Catherine came in for a few days to help me until we could go back to her house. Guy stayed back in Ardennes with Catherine's eighteen-year-old daughter Susanna.

Whenever I could manage a discreet conversation with my neighbor, Josephine, she'd tell me whatever news she had heard.

"Where is your husband? He's never around any more," I asked Josephine.

"He's gone to Liege. The children and I are doing all right here, but with his politics it's better he's in Liege. He's made it clear he hates the Nazis and will do anything to sabotage their plans."

"Do you think Madame Francois said something to the Nazis about him?"

"Probably. When the war's over, the other neighbors and I will make sure she gets what's coming to her."

"Good!" I wholeheartedly agreed.

Josephine didn't stay long and went across the hall to her apartment. I felt a twinge of jealousy, knowing she could return to her house. I longed to be back in my own home with familiar things. I missed having access to my clothes, to put Guy and Monique to sleep in their own beds, to fix a cup of tea with my lovely teapot and cups, and so many things I took for granted before the Germans came.

As most days now, moments of reverie were always interrupted. While I was in Catherine's room with Monique, the Germans came into the building. They never knocked on doors. Like thugs, they would sling any door open and search the place. When Catherine saw them, she closed the door. They must have seen her and decided she wasn't Jewish. I waited in silence, listening for the sound of their heavy boots to pass down the hall. Again my good luck, my *mazel*, held up, and they didn't search her room.

"We need to go back to Ardennes," Catherine said after the Germans left our floor. "It's safer there."

"I can't stay in Ardennes long. I still want to find out what I can about Nathan."

"Sara, you saw how they come into houses without any warning. The next time they could find you. Then what would happen to the baby?" She took little Monique from me and cradled her.

"I can't sit around and do nothing." I walked to the window and stared out at the alley below.

"All right. I'll help you find a place to stay for a short time. As soon as you hear any news, you come straight back to my house."

Catherine found a place for Monique and me to stay. Most people would not risk having an infant in their houses. A lady named Sophie agreed to let us stay. I had to return to Ardennes to tell Guy why I was not going to be with him for a while.

When Catherine and I returned to her house, I was afraid what Guy would think. His *Maman* was going away again. I had already left him for eight months while I was in a Paris prison. Now I had to leave him again. *My God what insanity this war brought on us!*

When I held Guy and told him I had to go away again, he began to cry and asked, "Why, *Maman*?"

"It's war, *cherie*. I cannot keep you. I'm afraid the Germans are going to take us. I want to save you from the trouble they caused your father. You have to mind me. Please be patient. We're going to try and save ourselves. You'll stay with Catherine."

"When will I see you again, *Maman*?" asked Guy, tears streaming from his eyes.

"I'll come back every two weeks and check on you."

"*Maman*, you won't forget me?"

"Never, *cherie*! Never! Papa and I love you. Don't forget *Maman*." I hugged him and finally had to give him to Catherine. He managed a weak smile as tears continued to course down his cheeks.

I thought I would pass out as my heart nearly broke. Walking out that door and leaving my little boy again was so difficult.

As I hid at Sophie's house with the baby, I couldn't find out anything more about Nathan, *Maman*, or Albert. Nathan had been sent to Malines where my mother and brother had been sent. Because Albert was a godson to the late king, Queen Elisabeth of Belgium offered the Nazis the equivalent of $50,000 to free my brother. The Nazis refused her offer. A Jewish life was worth nothing to them.

The decrees against us Jews had become harsher and harsher. Jews were not allowed in restaurants, Jews could not listen to music, Jews could not dance, and we couldn't own bicycles or cars. The Belgian people were angry that they could do nothing for their friends and neighbors. Fear of reprisal kept them from protesting outright. They were forced to become bystanders.

However, they could save the children. Belgians began to hide more and more Jewish children. Madame Pascal was a name I heard connected with the Committee for the Defense of the Jews. This committee and many individuals saved thousands of Jewish children in Belgium. In spite of the efforts of such Gentile rescuers, I learned of atrocities being committed against Jewish children by the Nazis. Many were tricked into taking poisoned candy. The Nazis were demons without souls.

I warned Catherine about these poisonings and begged her to keep Guy safe from them. If anything happened to him or Monique, I wasn't sure I could go on. I wanted to stop these heartless fiends who poisoned children.

While I was in hiding at Sophie's, the Germans searched her house. I had been sitting in the living room having tea with Sophie, a blond-haired woman in her mid-thirties. She and a friend of hers, Madeline, hid us on different occasions. When Sophie heard a car pull up outside, she said, "Go to the basement. Don't move."

I scooped up Monique and made sure I didn't leave any evidence of my being in the room. Sophie whisked my cup and saucer away. She only left her cup; then the fact two people had been having tea wasn't so obvious. With a practiced move, she turned a picture of one of her relatives over to reveal a picture of Hitler. Often if the soldiers saw a picture of Hitler in a person's home, they would not search it, thinking the owner was a loyal Nazi. They would just say their *Sieg Heil* to it and leave.

When I got in the basement, I heard the boots above me and knew the Germans were questioning Sophie. One of them asked, "Are there any Jews here?"

"I believe in Hitler," Sophie loudly declared to the Nazis. "I'm loyal to the Germans. I wouldn't have a Jew in my house. I don't have anything to do with Jews."

I knew she was saying it loud enough that I could hear and know not to make any noise. I held Monique's mouth tightly. One cry would mean death for all of us. The Germans would send Sophie to a concentration camp as quickly as they would send Monique and me. I prayed they would leave. Then I could move my hand from Monique's mouth. Seconds ticked by like hours.

I prayed, asking God to spare us. Endless silence ensued, and I dared not breathe. Any sound would give us away. I craned my neck to hear the next word, but nothing now filtered though the dividing floor. At any second I feared they would come downstairs and find us. I held Monique's mouth tighter. Her face began to turn blue. I wanted to let go, but I couldn't. I couldn't let her cry. She had to be quiet. *Shh, shh*, I kept thinking. *Don't cry, Monique. Please don't cry.* I tried to uncover her nose to let her breathe, but I couldn't feel any air going in. *Oh*

God! My baby! Make the Nazis leave, dear God. Please make them leave.

"We don't like Jews," Sophie again vowed. "I wouldn't have one in my house." Finally she must have convinced them. I heard the boots resonate on the creaking floor above. Then the door closed.

With extreme gratitude to God, I sobbed as I heard the boots go out. I took my hand from Monique's blue mouth. *Please Monique, breathe!* I tried to blow air into her small lungs. She didn't respond. I tried again, but no response. *My God, I've killed my own child! Please God, no! Please God, help her.* I hugged her tiny body to my chest. I prayed again as I watched her beautiful face for any movement. I held my breath, waiting for a sign of life. I didn't know what else to do. *My God, I've killed Monique! I've killed my precious baby. She's dead. God, please don't let it be. Please bring her back. I don't want to live if I've killed my baby. No, no!*

Suddenly she gasped slightly for air and choked. I turned her on her stomach and gently patted her back. She coughed, and I turned her over again. She was breathing. *Oh thank you, God.* I bent over her, tears streaming down my face. My hands shook so badly I could barely hold her in my lap.

When I was sure she was breathing all right, I lifted her to my chest and hugged her gently. Had the Germans stayed another minute, I would no longer have my daughter.

On the way down the steps to the basement, Sophie said, "They're gone." When she saw me sitting and sobbing, she said, "Sara, are you all right?"

"I nearly killed her, Sophie. I nearly suffocated her."

"Oh God, Sara. Let me see." Sophie stroked Monique's face. "Look. The blue is going away. She has normal color in her face. She's breathing."

Monique let out a wail that was sheer music to my ears. She screamed from pain and fright. I said, "That's it, Monique. Scream and let it out."

"Sara, let me get you something."

"No, I'll be all right. Just sit with me a while."

She hugged both of us and rubbed my shoulders as I rocked Monique. I said, "If they had stayed another minute, she'd be dead."

"I tried to get them out as quickly as I could."

"It seemed like hours." Looking at Monique's face and wiping her tears, I continued, "I can't do this any more. I can't put her in this kind of danger. I have to give her to Catherine. Sophie, I don't want to kill my own child."

Looking at Monique's sweet face and stroking her hair, I said, "She's only nine months old. She deserves better than this. I want her to live. Sophie, your quick thinking saved our lives. If you hadn't been so convincing, we'd be on our way to a work camp or we'd be dead."

The thought chilled me. I sat shivering, but not just from our narrow escape. I realized my dress was soaked through. I let Sophie hold Monique for a few minutes as I wiped my sweaty hands on my dress. Until that moment, I hadn't realized I needed to change my clothes. I had never been so frightened in my life. Sweat had poured off me, and my clothes were drenched. I had lost control of my bladder and needed to change everything, but I couldn't move. I just sat in the basement unable to do anything for myself.

"Sara, I'll heat some water upstairs and bring it down for you," Sophie said after realizing I was frozen from fear. "I'll bring you a washcloth, towel, and a change of clothes. Can you hold Monique while I go up?"

"Yes, I'm all right now." We both knew better than to have me come out of hiding. The Germans would often return when they thought the Jews in hiding would come out. Sophie helped me get through the next few hours, but that incident convinced me I had to give Monique to Catherine where she would be safer. The thought of parting with my nine-month-old child was too much to bear, but after nearly killing her, I had no choice. I contacted Catherine the same day.

In the meantime Sophie said she would find me another place to hide, which she did. The Belgian people were very good about helping hide us. Sophie's house was no longer safe. She could not have Jews stay with her again. Now that she was suspected of helping us, she could not afford to hide anyone.

Catherine readily agreed to take Monique. When I would visit Catherine, her neighbors in that little ranching community assumed I was her daughter and my children were her grandchildren. I would ride my bike out to see them about every two weeks. Going past the brown brick farmhouses with their red tile roofs gave me a sense of the timelessness of the countryside. Even though Belgium was an occupied country, these little farms seemed to continue as they had for hundreds of years. The white cows still grazed in green pastures, the farmers still plowed their fields, and the land itself was unchanged.

With my frosted hair or a wig, people would not recognize me as a

Jewish mother. Whenever I passed a German soldier on the streets of the little town or Ardennes, I would greet him with, *"Guten Morgen* or *Wie gehts?"* I would act friendly as though I weren't Jewish at all. It was easier for a woman to pass herself off as not being Jewish, but with a man the physical evidence of a circumcision would betray him. With my last name being Hauptman, a Germanic name in origin, I was also a bit more protected. Even though I would visit the children and Catherine occasionally, I would never endanger their lives by staying with them for very long.

Every day I hungered for news of my children. *What had Monique done today that I had missed? Did Guy ask about me? Did he want his Maman to read him a story?* I'm sure Catherine reassured him every night when she tucked him in, but I wanted to be with my children. However, I also knew I had to do something to stop the Nazis. If I truly wanted to be with my children without fear, I couldn't sit by and do nothing. I had to act.

I talked it over with my brother Jean. He encouraged me to become involved with the underground. Jean worked with many people in the underground who had connections. In fact, Jean had whisked our younger brother Bernard off in the middle of the night to a castle in the Ardennes Mountains under the protection of Baron De Ryck. Bernard was now called Jean Bernard and posed as the Baron's nephew. Esther, Jacques, and Henri were now at a castle called *La Bas.* Henri had finally been found and was safe. Then Jean told me about ways I could help. I thought it over, but I had to make sure the children would be all right first.

When I saw Catherine again, I told her I would be staying in Brussels. She didn't ask me why. I think she knew. All she said was the children will know their *Maman* and Papa will be coming back for them some day. She must have had some premonition I would survive.

I continued to stay in different places for varying amounts of time, but never more than a few weeks at a time. Feeling like I had to do something and not wait any longer, I decided to contact a member of the underground. I would not be a bystander any longer. My brother Jean was a patriot who wasn't afraid to risk his life He was a freedom fighter who became my inspiration. I would fight back any way I could.

CHAPTER 8—RESISTANCE

I had to convince myself I was about to do the right thing by joining the resistance. *Was this really what I should do? Was I taking an unnecessary risk? Could I just stay with Catherine and the children and not fight?* I had to make sure before I went any farther.

I had already witnessed what happened to so many Jews who thought they could hide. When they were caught, the Nazis paraded them to their cars like some Roman gladiator's captured slaves. The other neighbors would watch their humiliation. I had already been in a prison for eight months. I would rather fight than be locked up again. One last trip to Catherine's would convince me.

As I sat with the children, playing with them and watching them run in the yard, my mind would constantly drift to seeing them behind bars with me, cowering and being slapped. If some Nazi touched Guy or Monique, I'd kill him. I don't now how, but I'd find a way to kill him even if it were with my bare hands.

Susanna, Catherine's daughter, must have been watching me. When I brought the children in and got them settled on the bed for a nap, she had me come into the kitchen for some coffee. As she put the pot on the stove, she asked me, "What have you heard about Nathan or your mother or Albert?"

"Nothing new. No one seems to know a damn thing or else they're not telling." I sank into a kitchen chair and refolded the napkin several times.

"I might know of a man who could tell you something."

"My God, why haven't you told me before?"

"It's not as easy as it sounds. He works with the underground.

There's always a risk."

"If he can find out something about Nathan, tell me how to contact him." I leaned closer to her. "I don't care if it's risky. Tell me."

"His name is Jean Marie Moortgat, the chief of police of the southwest section of the city."

"Do you mean St. Gilles?"

"Yes. He has several people helping him at the courthouse."

"How do they help?"

"They make false papers and make arrangements so people can get to Sweden."

"Could they get papers for Simon? He'd be safe in Sweden. I know how much you like my brother. Could they help him? Where he's staying is not a good place."

As she considered my request, she poured the coffee into the cups. "I can't say for sure, but I can arrange through a friend of mine for you to meet Jean Marie."

"Call your friend, Susanna."

Susanna started to take another sip of coffee, but I placed my hand on her arm and said, "Call your friend right now."

She put her cup down and headed for the telephone table in the living room. I could only hear bits and pieces of the conversation, but it sounded like Jean Marie would meet with me tomorrow. When she returned, she said, "It's all set. Jean Marie will expect you tomorrow. Go in the front entrance. His office is on the main level."

After our conversation, I went in to check on the children. Catherine was sitting in the middle of the bed with them playing peek-a-boo with Monique. She loved my children. I knew if they could not be with me in the city, this is where they would be in the best possible hands. I spent some time playing with them and finally said goodbye.

The next day I took the tram to St. Gilles for my appointment with Jean Marie. I wasn't going to play any games. I would tell him right off I was Jewish and needed his help. If I could convince him I was serious and reliable, perhaps he would help Simon get out of the country and also tell me something about Nathan.

I followed Susanna's directions and arrived fifteen minutes before the appointment. I wanted to make sure I could find his office and also give a good first impression of my reliability by being on time. I had never been inside the St. Gilles courthouse before. I knew that was where criminals were kept overnight before being transported somewhere else, but that was all.

On the main floor from the many offices I could hear the sound of typewriters clicking in their efficient staccatos. I entered his office and told a man working there who I was. He tapped the shoulder of a young man in his late twenties with medium brown, curly hair. I never imagined such a young, handsome man would be the chief of police. I expected someone much older. However the intensity in his eyes told me he could size people up in one breath.

He came over, introduced himself, and ushered me inside the smaller office, away from the bustle of the outer one. His 5'8" frame towered over me. He shut the door and offered me a chair. After he was seated behind his desk, he asked me, "How can I help you?"

I came right to the point. "I have a brother who needs false papers to get to Sweden. Susanna probably told you he's Jewish and can't stay where he is much longer. He and the other teenagers with him are in danger. Can you help them?"

His keen eyes studied me before he answered. "Yes, I can."

"Thank God! Can you also tell me anything about my husband who was arrested in October? His name is Nathan Hauptman."

He leaned back in his char and glanced out the window before looking back at me. "It may take a while. The Germans take the people to a holding camp north of Brussels at Malines."

I leaned across the desk. "I've heard that much. Can you tell me any more?"

"The trains take people out of the country, and we don't have any information what their destination is. It may be a work camp in Germany."

I swallowed hard and closed my eyes for a moment, digesting the news. "Thank you for telling me, *Monsieur*." I looked down at the floor and then back up at him. "What do I need to do to help my brother?"

"Tell me where he is hiding, and I'll have someone contact him."

After I told him, I picked up my handbag and got up to leave. I had done what I set out to do. Simon would be on his way out of the country soon.

As I turned to go, he asked me. "Do you want to help even more?"

I was more than willing. I wanted to do anything I could to hurt the Nazis and save Jewish lives. With Nathan gone, I had to do whatever I could to help others avoid his fate.

"Yes," I answered. "What do you want me to do?"

"Follow me." We started down to the basement of the courthouse.

On the stairs he said, "Catherine told me about you too."

Surprised, I asked, "Catherine told you about me?"

"Yes, Catherine told me you would be a good worker. Can you type?"

"Yes. I was trained as a nurse, but I can type very well."

"Good. This is where you'll work." He opened the door to a small office with a typewriter, a desk, and several file cabinets. The room had no windows and only one overhead light.

"What kind of work will I be doing?"

"Making false papers. The first one will be for your brother, so learn the process carefully."

Picking up a stack of papers, Jean Marie showed me what to do. I would take the identity papers of someone who was deceased and change the dates and ages by using a special typewriter. The work wasn't difficult, but I knew if I were caught, I might be killed. I was willing to take the risk to get Simon and others out of the country. My own safety wasn't as important as the work I was doing.

I worked the entire day in the basement. I had no concept of time passage until Jean Marie came down to tell me to go home. Another worker was behind him to replace me. She knew the routine and went to work right away. I didn't have to explain where I left off; she knew after a quick glance and began typing.

From then on, I worked in the small room in the basement in the daytime and other resistance workers would relieve me at night. I was the only Jewish person working in the courthouse. Many of the resistance workers lived in the nearby town of Leon de Waterloo. Napoleon's famous place of defeat became a rallying point for the Belgian resistance workers to make another stand, only this time against the Nazis.

I got to know Jean Marie very well as we worked together on the false papers. He would tell me the type of papers he needed and I would make sure I found the right match. Though Jean Marie was only around twenty-seven years old, he had a wife and son. We talked about our children occasionally. He showed me a picture of his son, Robert. Even though he had a family, he was never reluctant to engage in dangerous activities. The opposite was true. Because he did not want Robert to grow up under the Nazi rule, he fought all the more for freedom. Like me, he was willing to risk his life for his child's future.

Jean Marie was a good-looking man, and that's probably how he got his code name Cupid in the underground. He liked to smoke a pipe and was very friendly with everyone except the Nazis. At one time he had a mustache, but he shaved it off. He was an impassioned man who knew what he was doing. People trusted him and respected his leadership.

Five months passed rapidly working with the underground. Often I would sleep in the courthouse. We were working night and day to get people out of the country. I forged the visa for my eighteen-year-old brother Simon. His papers were those of an 89-year-old man who had died. He and many others escaped to Sweden.

I also began using a false name now, my sister-in-law's name, Agnes De Vos. I changed my birthplace and date from Laskagef, Poland, on August 15, 1918, to match Agnes's. Jules and Agnes became extra cautious about her name being on more than one identity paper, but they were willing to help without asking too many questions.

While I worked at the courthouse, I heard of other ways Belgians were helping to save Jewish people. A Gentile would marry a Jew to get him or her out of a camp if an arrest were made. The Gentile would vouch the Jewish religion was not being practiced in the home. Sometimes this "white" marriage was enough to get an official to release someone from a camp. White became a code for Gentile.

These "white" marriages were performed for many Jews. My husband's cousin Mocha and his wife were able to save themselves and their daughter with a "white" marriage. Helen "married" a Gentile to protect her family. The Gentile man moved out of his house and allowed Helen, Mocha, and their daughter Leah to stay. One time when Helen heard the Nazis were coming to the Gentile man's house, "her husband" came over to answer the door when the Germans arrived. Leah and Mocha were hiding when the Nazis knocked on the door. The Gentile man told them he was married to Helen. One of the Nazis asked him, "Why did you marry a Jew?"

"She's not Jewish," the man told the soldiers. "She's Catholic. Don't bother us." He pointed at the crucifix hanging on the wall. That must have been enough for them because they did not enter and search the house. Helen, Mocha, and Leah all survived because of this generous Gentile man's willingness to help. In fact, when the Gentile man passed away after the war, he left his belongings to Helen.

Jean Marie trusted me with more duties after several months. He had me deliver some messages for him. On one of those errands, I met Maurice Gilbert, another Belgian resistance worker. Before Maurice retired, he had been a lawyer and served on the Belgian Supreme Court. He was a wealthy man who had a large estate on the edge of the city toward Waterloo. The estate, located about thirty minutes away from town by bus, was large enough for horses and all sorts of animals. When I rode a bicycle, it would take me between forty-five minutes and an hour, but I didn't mind the trip through the lush, green, rolling hills of my homeland. The pastures dotted with the black and white cows momentarily made me forget we were at war.

Though a grandfather at the time, Maurice was quite active in the resistance. Maurice had a distinguished look to him and was still attractive with his gray moustache and penetrating eyes. He knew Jean Marie well before the war and had dealt with him on many legal cases.

Maurice's daughter and older granddaughter Tinca were also messengers. I had made Tinca's false identity papers, as well as hundreds of other false papers. After he got to know me, Maurice suggested I dye my hair blond so I wouldn't look quite so "Jewish." So I bought some peroxide and changed my hair color. As a "Suicide Blonde," I was freer to travel, to deliver messages, and to help the resistance.

Maurice also had a younger ten-year-old granddaughter, Amy. She was too nosy whenever I would come around, so we sent her out of the room when we had messages to exchange. Her mother would take her around town on the trams or on long walks while people were being brought up to the third floor attic to hide. In those days the Germans would trick children into revealing secrets about their parents by offering the child candy.

In addition, a desire to re-educate the Belgians in Nazi idealism took hold. Children would be "invited" as an "honor" to attend a Nazi Youth Camp. The principal would call the parents and tell them how wonderfully their child had performed and ask to send their child to one of these camps. Of course, instilling Nazi ideals was the number one objective of such a camp. Many parents resisted, even to the point of removing their child from public school and using illness as an excuse. Amy's mother removed her from the school on Rue de Bordeau because of her "invitation" to one of these camps.

Jean Marie's family lived across the street from this school and his son, Robert, attended it too, but Amy's mother was afraid of what was being taught. Even Amy's tutor, Miss Nitz, was suspected of being a Nazi collaborator. At first Amy was instructed at Miss Nitz's house, but later on Miss Nitz insisted on teaching Amy at home. The Nazis were masters of invading privacy. With children being so indoctrinated, even making eye contact with people on the street was risky. No one was above the scrutiny of the Nazis. Therefore, Amy was never present when people were brought into Maurice's home. He hid Jews, resistance workers, and downed Allied fliers in his attic.

To transport the false identity papers to Maurice Gilbert, I used different methods. Sometimes I would put them under my skirt, down my brassiere, or under my wig. I had four wigs—a black, two brown ones, and a blonde one of a different length than my own—supplied to me by the resistance. I would change clothes at the courthouse, using the clothing and wigs they supplied. Sometimes I would wear glasses to cover my identity while delivering papers or messages.

If I only had one or two identity papers to deliver to Maurice, one paper might fit under my bicycle seat. Putting them in a pocket, in a purse, or any outer garment wasn't wise. I needed an easy way to dispose of the papers without the Germans noticing. I could shake one loose from a slip if needed. Whenever I made my deliveries, I watched every person I passed.

The fear of being followed was a constant shadow. Some German soldiers came to Maurice's door once when I was in his living room, but whatever he said to them at the front door was enough that they didn't enter. I breathed a sigh of relief when they left. They hadn't been following me. When he returned, he said, "From now on, come later. The Nazis might get suspicious if they see you here during the morning when you don't live here."

After that I would give him the papers at the door. If he needed more papers, he would tell me. Usually I would go to his house a couple of times a week. My signal was to knock twice at the door. Maurice would always answer the door. Amy's mother would whisk her out of the room when she heard the knock. That way Amy knew nothing.

Tinca, Maurice's older granddaughter, once came to the house where I was staying, and Amy was with her. She delivered the message and left quickly, but that one visit was enough for Amy to remember me. Yet Amy knew me as Agnes De Vos, not Sara Hauptman. Amy would not learn my true identity until fifty years later.

A few months after I began delivering messages, I thought my cover had been blown. I was on a tram and the Germans were routinely checking identity papers. When they approached me, one commanded in German, "*Ausweiss!*" Without hesitating, I handed him my papers

that had my sister-in-law's name, Agnes de Vos. I had made the papers
myself and trusted they would pass his inspection. After all, this wasn't
the first time my papers had been checked.

"You look Jewish. Come with me," he said after he looked at the
papers and at me again. For some reason he decided to detain me. The
Wehrmacht soldiers regularly detained people. I knew I had to stay
calm and trust my true identity could not be discovered.

At the next stop I was roughly ushered off the tram by this soldier.
He directed me to a phone at a near-by building. Smugly, he looked at
my papers and asked, "When I call your home, who will answer?"

"My son Guy," I answered. Agnes and I had discussed the danger
of her answering the phone with her real name. If she answered
"Agnes de Vos," I would immediately be thrown into a cell and
interrogated. I didn't want to be put in the position of revealing what I
did in the underground.

He dialed the number and waited, looking at me with one eyebrow
raised. I held my breath and prayed. I could hear my nephew, also
named Guy, answer. Trying to conceal the sweat under my arms, I held
them to my sides and held onto my purse in front of me. Luckily when
Agnes's oldest son replied, he said, "*Maman* is not at home. She is
out."

Annoyed, the soldier dropped the receiver back into its cradle. All
he said to me was "*Los*," which meant go. He believed I was the Agnes
who was not at home and let me go.

I put my papers in my purse and left as quickly as I could. Waiting
for the next tram seemed like an eternity. When it arrived, I found a
seat and slumped into it, staring out the window and thanking God for
my delivery. Though I had been scared, it didn't deter me from my
work at the courthouse.

On one mission Maurice Gilbert gave me a strange package to take
care of. I asked him, "Maurice, what is this?"

"A parachute. Take it to the courthouse and tell Jean Marie what it
is. He'll know what to do with it."

"It's so large. I'll have to pretend it's laundry I've picked up for
Jean Marie. If anyone asks, I'll tell them it's a blanket for the jail."
Holding the package to check its weight, I asked, "Do you have some
rope to tie it on my bike?"

When he left the room, I looked up at the ceiling and listened for
any noises. Only the ticking of the clock on the mantle broke the
silence. The downed Allied fliers were up in the attic, knowing their

very lives were in my hands and Maurice's. *Were they American, Canadian, or British? Were they young men my age or older?* I often wondered about the people hiding in Maurice's attic, but never seeing them was safer. Then Maurice returned with the piece of rope.

"Tell Jean Marie we couldn't get one of the parachutes before the Nazis came. It became entangled in the tree and our men were unable to get it down. At least the Nazis will be looking for one flyer, not seven. Tell Jean Marie we have three pilots and four crewmen here."

I was surprised so many were housed in one place. "I'll tell Jean Marie, but that parachute was a dangerous sign to leave behind. How soon do you think the Germans will be searching for its owner?"

"They already are. Now go quickly and have Jean Marie take care of this. Tell him a second parachute will be delivered to him by another courier."

I handed him the false papers he had requested and left. I took the parachute wrapped in brown paper and tied it to my bike. On purpose I took a route by a dry cleaner. If I were stopped, the soldiers would have no reason to suspect the package was anything other than laundry. When a German patrol did pass, I smiled and waved to them as though nothing were wrong.

I delivered the parachute to Jean Marie in the basement. Late that night Jean Marie had someone bury the parachute. No one ever found the buried parachute, and as far as I know, the fliers, dressed as working people, made it safely out of Belgium.

I never met the people for whom I made the papers. The less I knew the better. If I were caught, that would be one less piece of information I would have. I saw people coming out of Maurice's house and getting into a car one time, but that was the only time I ever saw anyone whom he hid.

The highest number of identity papers I had to deliver to him at one time was twelve. That time I hid them in every conceivable place. Usually I got a request for only three or four. His message would have how many were needed by number and gender and a time of delivery. I'll never know exactly how many people Maurice and Jean Marie managed to save from the Nazis.

Whenever people associated with the resistance movement or Jews were arrested and held temporarily in the police station, Jean Marie would try to get them out. If the Germans had already counted the exact number of people, smuggling some of them out was impossible. When a resistance member had an urgent message to pass on, he would slip a note in a cow bladder and put it in the refuse pail. The Germans didn't bother to look through the pail of human waste. Although they meant to demean Jean Marie by forcing him to empty the slop buckets, the Germans didn't realize he was sometimes receiving messages this way.

Jean Marie called me to his office and told me one of our men had been arrested. He had to get us his information before they tortured him. "He's written it on a paper and put it in the waste pail. Can you pick it up for us?"

"Yes, but how can I get into the men's section? They won't allow a woman in."

"You won't go as a woman. I chose you because you're so short someone would think you were a boy, especially when you wear this." He held up a boy's clothes and cap. I knew I could tuck my hair up under the cap and pass as a boy.

I put on the large shirt, jacket, long socks, and knickers. The shoes were a little too big and I stuffed the toes with tissue. The leather jacket would hide my bosom. After washing my cheeks to remove any rouge, I checked my appearance in a mirror and was satisfied. I tried to sound like Henri as much as possible by lowering my voice some, and I was confident my disguise would work.

Jean Marie gave me a final approval before I left. The jail was in the same building as the courthouse, so I didn't have far to walk up some stairs to the upper level of the building. As I approached a German guard, I shoved my hands into my pockets and looked disgustedly as a little boy would do when he was told he had an onerous chore to perform. I had seen my brothers act like this every time *Maman* gave them a job to do. I said to the *Wehrmacht* guard, "I have to empty the waste pails. *Monsieur* Moortgat sent me."

Unconcerned, the guard unlocked the iron gate to let me pass. Then he opened the door to each cell on that floor as I went in to empty the buckets. The prisoners looked at me with little interest. Bruised and bloody, each man looked as though he had been through the first phase of torture. I took the bucket from each one and disappeared down the hallway to empty them into a flushable toilet on the lower level. I tried not to look at the contents and scrunched up my nose to avoid the smells. Blood and a tooth knocked out by the Nazi interrogators topped one pail.

I saw no sign of the cow bladder under the feces, but I was sure I would find it in one of the buckets. I carried the buckets at a distance from my body, trying not to spill any of the vile contents on myself. When I got to the toilet area, I carefully poured out the contents and found the bladder. I rinsed it off in the sink and slipped it down the front of my pants. Then I washed out the sink and flushed the toilet.

I finished the rest of the cells above and later gave Jean Marie the message. Afterward, I changed my clothes back to being a woman again. My breasts still had imprints from the cloth I had wrapped around me to flatten my breasts and make me look like a boy. Putting on my own clothes made me feel like myself again. I rearranged my hair and put on a little rouge. However, I washed my hands all day long, never feeling like I quite got the contents from the waste pails off.

At times my co-workers in the underground would have to kidnap a collaborator or a Nazi and torture him to talk. It sounds barbaric to say the people I worked with resorted to such tactics, but it was war. Though I personally was not involved in interrogating people, I knew such tactics were used. Those who collaborated with the Nazis got what they deserved for sending thousands of people to their deaths. If we did not get the information, more innocent lives would be lost. We had to stop the Nazis, and the resistance used whatever means were possible to obtain information.

The resistance also listened to the German movements and plans by radio. Possessing a radio was illegal, but Maurice Gilbert kept one hidden in his attic. We all took many chances, but peaceful cooperation with the Nazis would only allow them to kill more people.

We heard about fellow members of the resistance who had been caught by the Germans. Some were shot, and others were tortured before they were shot. We heard about the victims' fingernails being ripped out or the tendons on the wrists being exposed and brutalized. These were just two of the hideous ways of getting people to talk. Some knew they would crack under pressure and would kill themselves just before capture.

Jean Marie gave me a pill filled with poison in case I were caught. I kept it in my purse only a week and decided I wouldn't take it even if I were arrested. I was also afraid that Guy or Monique might find it in my purse and swallow it when I went to visit Catherine. I flushed it down the toilet and told Jean Marie. He said it was my decision. Some people liked the assurance the pill gave them, and others prayed they wouldn't crack under interrogation.

The Nazis would use any means to kill Jews. At one point they urged Jewish parents to bring their children to clinics to receive inoculations. A few moments after the inoculation, the child would die in the mother's arms. I thought about my own babies and how I could protect them from these inoculations. The next time I visited Catherine I warned her. The relentless Nazi campaign to annihilate us gained momentum. I would do everything in my power to stop them.

Living under these conditions where tyranny ruled every aspect of one's life made friendships rare. You could trust few people. I couldn't tell anyone about my activities because if I were arrested, my relatives would be the first ones they would question and torture.

I slept at the courthouse or at friends' houses, those friends whom I had made before the war. I delivered all sorts of messages and packages. I became a master of disguises. Jean Marie also felt I could pass myself off well and he asked me about taking my involvement a step further.

"I need someone to be a watcher for another underground worker. He's going to drop a grenade into a window of the building commandeered by the Nazis. It's close to the *Palais Royal*. I need someone to make sure no one is watching and warn him by blowing a whistle if there's some trouble. Would you be willing to do this?" Jean Marie asked.

Although I agreed, I was filled with trepidation. Trusting Jean Marie, I knew the assignment was critical.

I took a bicycle from the courthouse and peddled toward the Nazi-occupied building. The narrow street was empty. When I was a few yards away, I stood the bike against another building around the corner from the intended target. I walked along the rutted brick sidewalk and waited for the other underground worker to appear on his bicycle. Double-checking my watch again, I made sure I was on time. Every nerve in my body tingled. I jumped at every shadow or sound. Then I saw the cyclist. He fit the description Jean Marie had given me of a man wearing a black jacket and cap.

He reached into his jacket and pulled out the grenade. Tossing it perfectly into the open basement window, he sped on his way as though nothing had happened.

I raced around the block back to the side street where I had left my bike. All the while I waited to hear the explosion. With trembling, icy fingers, I grabbed the handlebars. I thought to myself, *Hurry up! Get out of here now!* I disappeared as quickly as I could. I wobbled as I tried to keep the bike straight on the ancient brick inlay of the street.

Seconds later the grenade exploded in the building. Even a block away, I could feel the force of the explosion. Debris clattered onto the street. Voices cried in agony. Other voices shouted commands. I knew some of the Nazis inside were dead or would be dying shortly.

I returned to the courthouse and reported to Jean Marie. With a nod of affirmation, he accepted my account of the incident. Jean Marie knew lives had been taken, but he did not gloat as the Nazis did. Knowing he had ordered another person's death was a burden. His actions protected our country and many more lives. If we did not resist, no one would be left to stop the Nazis from carrying out their annihilation. However, what happened next made me refuse to be a direct participant again in such missions.

Within the hour the Nazis rounded up twelve innocent people off the street and shot them. I felt responsible for their deaths. They hadn't done anything to deserve death. They had just been on the street at the wrong time. We members of the underground had killed the Nazis, not these twelve people. When I heard what had taken place, I told Jean Marie to use someone else.

"I can't do it. I can never forgive myself for their deaths." I handed him the whistle, sank into a chair, and tried to wipe from my mind the image of the twelve people being shot. *Who were they? How many children wouldn't have a mother or father coming home? How many young people with their promising lives ahead of them were in the group? How many lovers would grieve over their loss? Who were these twelve who died for something I did?*

"You didn't kill them, Sara. The Nazis did. You were simply following my orders." Jean Marie put his hand reassuringly on my shoulder.

"It doesn't change the fact I saw what happened."

"Don't think that way. The Nazis kill people whether some of their own have been killed or not. Don't blame yourself."

"I can't do it." I handed him the jacket and cap.

"Sara, I'm sorry this happened, but I still need you to work for us."

"Of course, I'll keep working. Just don't ask me to help this way again. I can't." As I left his office, I wondered if the person wearing the black jacket felt as guilty as I did at this moment.

Jean Marie encouraged me daily and had me continue to work with the false papers. That part I could do. I felt as though I were saving lives that way. Still the deaths of those twelve people haunted me day and night. I could not get them out of mind. I would wake up in a sweat in the middle of the night, seeing members of my own family in front of a firing squad.

After the bombing I worked at the courthouse by going through the files in the basement.

A week or so later some SS men came in to look around—three in front, two at the door and two more. I was so nervous I was visibly shaking. I was afraid they had found out I had been an accomplice in the grenade incident. Even if they only found out I was making false identity papers, they'd arrest me or shoot me on the spot.

One of the SS men asked me to pull a file for him. Two of the policemen who worked for Jean Marie came over and stood by me to give me reassurance and to hide my shaky movements from the German. I handed him the file and all of them left to check the cells upstairs. They didn't ask me anything. I had escaped this time, but how long would my luck hold out?

Jean Marie had told me what he had planned to do if we were ever caught together He said, "You're Jewish. You'll be sent to a work camp instead of being shot."

"Do you really believe those letters sent back from the camps are true?"

"Probably not," he honestly replied. "I'm sure they're being worked hard."

"What will happen if we're caught?"

"They won't kill you. They'll kill me, but not you. If they catch us together, this is what I'll say, 'I don't want to die with a Jew. You take her away. I want to die by myself.' Then I'll sing the Belgian national anthem. I'll tell them, 'I don't want her next to me. I'm Catholic.'"

"I hope you never have to test that plan."

"So do I."

Maurice also had a similar plan if it were ever needed. Fortunately, neither one of these resistance workers had to denounce me as Jewish.

Keeping busy with the resistance gave me a new purpose in life. I had hoped to hear news about Nathan, *Maman*, or Albert while I worked with the underground, but I heard nothing. Like Jean Marie, I knew of the danger I faced while working with the underground. However, knowing the kind of a world the Nazis would create for my children outweighed the dangers.

Sara as a "Suicide Blonde"

CHAPTER 9—THE JEWISH LION TAMER

After my episode of nerves at the courthouse when the Nazis asked me for papers, I told Jean Marie I needed to work somewhere else. I would still deliver messages, but I needed to get away from the courthouse for a while. The stress of remembering those killed in retaliation for what I had done was too much. Every day I worked at the courthouse I kept thinking of them. I needed a change of duties.

Jean Marie found me a job as an usher at the *Cirque Royal*, a large stone entertainment center a few blocks from the main market place. Many shows and exhibitions, such as the circus, boxing matches, and other sporting events, took place at the *Cirque Royal*. The arena's red velvet seats provided unexpected comfort for spectators. The Germans especially enjoyed the boxing matches. A large turn-out could always be expected, and I took advantage of this by overcharging them an extra hundred francs for better seating. The Germans knew I overcharged them, but they teased me by calling me *Kleine Teufel*, little devil. I didn't like their flirting with me, but I knew better than to make a scene about it. I just took their money and went about my business.

My brother Jules also worked for the *Cirque Royal's* popular restaurant as a waiter. By working at the *Cirque Royal*, I could see Jules, make some extra money, and keep up my work in the resistance too. While I worked as an usher, I still received orders for identity papers. I would deliver them between work hours.

A young German soldier had been flirting with me shortly before a messenger from the underground gave me a small paper. Just as I was about to read the message, the soldier started back toward me. Without a second thought, I swallowed the paper. I'm surprised I could get it down my throat without any water, but I did. Luckily, he was only jealous of the male messenger and came over to find out who the man was. The soldier said, "Is that your boyfriend?"

"No, I don't have a boyfriend." I thought to myself, *No, I don't have a boyfriend. I have a husband. He'd kick your scrawny tuchis if he saw you flirting with me.*

"I'll be your friend." Awkward and fidgety, he looked to be only a few years younger than I was and probably had not talked to girls much. "What time do you get off work?" he asked as he fumbled with a piece of chocolate and nearly dropped it as he offered it to me.

Germans used chocolate to get what they wanted because sugar was in such demand. Even here in Brussels, a city known for its fine Belgian chocolates, the sweet delicacies became harder to get. Knowing I could use this chocolate to trade for other items, I pocketed it without any hesitation. Then I lied about the time I got off, smiling all the while.

My brother Jules also saw what was happening and came over to help me. "What do you want with my sister?" Jules asked the soldier.

"Nothing," the soldier said. "I just want to talk to her."

"She's working. She doesn't have time to talk." Jules gave him a move-along gesture with a white linen napkin still in his hand. "After work if you want to talk, you can find her."

For Jules to make a scene over me was too great a risk. The owners of the bar and restaurant knew he was Jewish since he had been working for them for years. However, they were taking a chance just to keep him working for them.

The soldier walked away disappointed, but he didn't leave the *Cirque Royal* completely. He was waiting for me. I told some of my fellow workers what was going on. They covered for me, so I could leave through a back way an hour earlier than I had told the soldier.

The messenger told Jean Marie what had happened, but Jean Marie wasn't worried about me. He trusted I could take care of myself because he had trained me well. Still he was smart enough not to use the same male messenger to me ever again.

Another man, an usher at the *Cirque Royal*, was a resistance worker too, though we tried not to communicate very much. In addition, one of the can-can dancers, Juanette, was with the underground. We had to protect each other's identities as much as possible. Therefore not to put them in danger, I tried not to be seen with them socially. If a group of people from the *Cirque Royal* were going out to have coffee or tea, we might be together.

The Germans were constantly watching every movement. We could not openly communicate any messages from the underground, but we learned to use gestures and certain speech. For example, if I scratched my hair, it meant Germans were approaching. If one of us would mention a place in conversation and winked, it meant we were to meet at the location that night. I would say something like, "I met Francois there yesterday at eleven." That would mean the meeting was for eleven at the place I mentioned when I winked. We would constantly change meeting places for fear the Germans would catch on.

The German soldiers were drunk a lot of the time when they had leave from their units. They would flirt with all the Belgian girls. It sickened me to have a German come close to me. One time a soldier's flirting went too far. I kept telling him I was on duty, but he persisted in following me and getting closer each time. He had dark hair and a smug face covered with acne scars. Although he thought he was a ladies' man in his uniform and tall black boots, he looked more like a thug from a gangster movie. He stood so close to me I could smell the beer on his breath.

"Come have a drink with me," he said. "I can show you a good time."

"I'm working now. I'd get fired if I left." I moved away.

"No one will fire you if I tell them not to. I'm a soldier of the Third Reich. People who are smart cooperate with us."

I hated the way he emphasized "cooperate." The sexual overtone was too strong to miss. It made me want to vomit. I thought to myself, *If he touches me, I'll kill him.* I said, "I told you I can't leave."

Juanette, one of the can-can dancers, saw what was happening. Wearing a tight, red dress that accentuated her perfect figure, Juanette could catch every man's eyes in the arena. When she walked up, the soldier gave her his full attention.

"Buy me that drink," Juanette said. "I'm better than she is." She took his arm and led him away to the bar.

Jules, waiting tables, glanced over at me every chance he got. He couldn't leave to rescue me this time. He sighed a breath of relief when the soldier left with Juanette and signaled me to take another section of the arena. I traded with another usher to make it harder for the same soldier to find me again.

Even Leonard, the ringmaster of the circus, would protect me sometimes by telling the Germans I was his girlfriend and to leave me alone. One time when the Nazis were scrutinizing identification papers, Leonard took me out a side entrance under the pretense of checking the tigers' cage. He didn't know my papers were good. By then I was using the false name of Sura Miodownik. Leonard may have guessed I was working for the resistance, but he never said anything. He had his son and daughter in a car waiting to take us to the courthouse until the Germans were gone. He was very protective of me. I was aware of women being raped in wartime. I was lucky to have people like Jules, Juanette, and Leonard looking out for me.

Jules was worried about me. He even asked Leonard point blank once, "Are you having an affair with my sister?"

Leonard, who was sixty-nine years old, smiled. Even though he had salt and pepper hair, he was good-looking enough for many young women to have an affair with him. In fact, I thought he was better looking than his sons. Leonard shook his head and said, "No, Jules, we're not having an affair. I love her like a daughter. I like to talk to her. That's all."

"I'm sorry for asking, Leonard, but I have to watch out for her."

"Then you've got your hands full."

Jules may have suspected I was working for the underground, but I wouldn't tell him for sure. After I had gone dancing one night, he asked me the next day, "Where do you go in the middle of the night?"

"I went out dancing." Since I was only twenty-two years old at the time, he may have believed me, or at least he never questioned my alibi. One didn't say certain statements during war, and questions were not truthfully answered. His not knowing about my activities was better.

One time when I actually was out dancing with some friends, the Germans started checking everyone's papers. My friends wanted to sneak me out of the dance. I told them, "It would look suspicious. Calm down and act normal."

"But Sara the Nazis are checking papers," Pierre said. "We should go."

"No, that would single us out for their attention. Don't let them see you're nervous."

Pierre lifted his glass, but he sloshed the contents. I knew I had to do something to get his mind on something else or he would give us away.

"Pierre, come dance with me." I took his hand.

He put down his glass and looked at me as though I had lost my mind, but my assurance gave him confidence. Holding his hand, I led him to the dance floor, threw my high heels off, and we began to do the jitterbug. I loved this dance and Pierre was a good dancer. In no time at all, he was concentrating on the dance moves and not the German soldiers. Pierre threw me over his shoulder and swung me around. Soon the soldiers tired of checking papers and left. They never asked any of the people at our table for their papers. Confidence was a key element when dealing with the Nazis.

In those days high cork heels were the fashion and since no silk hosiery was available, we used make-up on our legs. Being Europeans, we didn't shave our legs, but we did use make-up on them. The make-up industry flourished during the war for this reason.

Also I was surprised we weren't arrested just for dancing the jitterbug. The Nazis didn't approve of such music. Swing music was banned in Germany, and jazz was considered low class. The Germans liked marches and music by German composers,

I also enjoyed listening to Edith Piaf, who was a great French singer during the war. Because she had a hunchback, she sang behind a curtain while her boyfriend played the piano. Luckily, the Germans didn't censor her music or arrest her for being handicapped. Germans considered people with any handicap to be "life not worthy of life."

I missed going to the movies and seeing some of my favorite actors and actresses, like Maurice Chevalier, Bing Crosby, Bob Hope, Grace Kelly, Joan Crawford, John Wayne, Clark Gable, and Gene Autry. Belgium had been "invaded" by the American film stars before the war, but now American films were *verboten*, forbidden.

Something of a show-off in me made me want to act and be a star. I got bored with my job of being an usher, so I began to look around for another one at the *Cirque Royal*. I had watched all the performers and knew I could be in the circus. Also by performing in the ring I wouldn't have to deal directly with the Germans. One of the underground members suggested to Leonard that he should allow me to try out for the job of the lion tamer. I was scared to work with the lions and tigers at first, but I figured if someone would train me, why not?

About a week before I began my training as a lion tamer, I was traveling on the city tramway between the *Cirque Royal* and the house where I was staying. The main boulevards of the city were covered with Nazi uniforms. Like a cancer, they spread to every part. Feeling confident with my good set of forged papers and thinking about my new career, I wasn't paying too much attention to the other passengers. All of a sudden a Jewish man named Jack recognized me, even though I had blonde hair. A member of the hated *Judenrat*, he would betray his fellow Jews to the Nazis for his own safety and personal gain. My family had even helped this man when he first came to Belgium. They had supported him and given him a house. I despised him for the traitorous way he was repaying their kindness. This was the same man who had probably turned in Nathan and now he was going to betray me to a German soldier on the tram.

"I saw her at a nightclub," Jack said, pointing at me as he spoke to a German soldier. "She's not really blonde. She's Jewish. She's Chana Rozen's daughter."

I wanted to kill him. I glared at him and thought about cutting out his tongue so he couldn't betray more people. However, I could speak fluent German, which I had learned in school. Knowing I was an actress, I said in perfect German with confidence, "Who is this Rozen? You dirty Jew, get out of here!" I stepped behind the soldier as if he were protecting me from this unwarranted attack. I took out my papers and handed them to the soldier as proof of my innocence.

The German soldier looked at my papers and believed me. He told Jack, "Go down, you Jewish *schwein*. You dirty Jew pig, get off the tram." He tossed Jack off the electric tram like the sack of garbage he was. Then changing his demeanor to one of concern for a damsel in distress, the soldier turned to talk to me.

Batting my eyelashes at him and smiling, I told him I worked for the *Cirque Royal* and invited him to a show. I waved an energetic good-bye to him as I got off the tram. Later he came, saw me working there, and was convinced I was just a Belgian and not a Jew. The Nazis never believed you could be both.

After that episode I decided to dye my hair brown again. Leonard, our French ringmaster, told me the job would begin sooner than I thought. The lion tamer was leaving to return to Paris and he needed his replacement immediately. Leonard said, "You're little and cute. People will love you as a lion tamer."

"Who will train me?"

"The other lion tamer, of course. And I will watch everything to make sure he does a good job. How about it?"

I thought it over and said, "All right. When do I start?"

"Tomorrow we'll start your training. You'll start by feeding them and brushing them. After they get used to you, we'll start with the act. While you're training, I may have you fill in with the elephant act and as one of the can-can dancers."

I overcame my fear of the big cats by rationalizing if I could take a risk by working with the underground, surely I could go into the ring with lions and tigers.

When Jules found out about my new career, he was surprised. "Sara, why are you taking this job?"

"It pays more and I won't have to work by the Germans."

"You were a devil when you were younger and just look at you now," he said. "You climbed a greased pole in a dress, you rang all the doorbells in the apartment building, you stole Charles's motorcycle, and you scraped the fenders on *Maman's* car just backing it out. I know you're a daredevil, but you're so tiny. Aren't you afraid to be in the cage with the lions and tigers?"

"No," I assured him. "Nazis and animals are a lot alike, and the animals are more predictable."

So there I was center ring. The Jewish lion tamer. However, no one in the audience knew I was Jewish.

During my training I was given a whip, a chair, and some cookies or biscuits to reward the big cats. I learned to call their names to bring them into the ring. A co-worker with a pistol would stand by the entrance and let the lions out of their cages as I called them. The big cats ran from the entrance to the gold-painted enclosure where I waited for them. This short distance was called the lions' walk. We were never afraid one of them would bolt and run toward the audience. Of course if one ever did, the man with the pistol would take care of it. That was such a remote possibility that we never considered it a danger.

Nine big cats at one time shared the ring with me. I had them walk around the cage, roll over, jump from stand to stand, and even jump through a ring of fire. I'd have five lionesses in the cage during the ring-of-fire routine. A man standing near the ring would light the ring and bring it to me. The lionesses growled in a trained response to the fire, but they weren't truly afraid of it.

All of the lions and tigers were well trained already. All I had to do was learn the routine. As part of it, one of the lionesses, Mitzi, would pretend to maul me just to get the audience wound up. She would growl, paw at me, and act as if she were going to rip me to shreds, but her ferocity was just an act. Mitzi never even scratched me, but the audience didn't know this. I'd use the chair and the whip to pretend to get her back into line.

I'll never forget my first performance when the ringmaster called my name. Swastikas. Bright lights. Roars. Intense beams blinded me, and I could see nothing. The deafening cacophony made my heart race. Leonard pinched my cheeks so I wouldn't look so pale. I raised my arms above my head and tried to stay calm. The animals must not smell my fear. Acid bile from my stomach burned my throat, but I willed myself not to throw up. Placing one foot in front of the other, I gritted my teeth as I became the center of attention. I wanted to break and run the other direction, but I knew escape was impossible because the crowd had already seen me in my white sequenced outfit. With a fake smile of confidence, I looked at the throng of people. Then I braced for the second wave of nausea. I told myself, *You can do this, Sara. You've faced worse than this. Keep acting.*

Lights followed my every move as I ran into the ring. Holding my upstretched arms wide to the audience, I heard their applause and exclamations about my size. "My God, she's only a child!" "She's so tiny." "Look at her!"

When I looked at the Nazi symbols everywhere in the audience, I remembered some of the humans outside the ring were more vicious than the animals inside it. Still shaking, I opened the cage door and made sure all the platforms were ready for the lions and tigers. I closed the cage's metal door behind me, picked up my whip, signaled the gatekeeper, and prepared for the running entrance of the first lioness.

Mitzi growled and pawed at me with practiced ferocity. I snapped the whip at her, and she sat on her assigned stool as the other lions and tigers entered the enclosure. I felt safer with them surrounding me than the Nazis watching from the audience. I could only hope they would never find out I was the Jewish lion tamer.

The lions and tigers went through the routine of jumping from one platform to another, growling and pawing at each other at appropriate intervals. Then without the audience noticing it, I'd give the big cats their reward of a cookie for performing so well.

Receiving applause for each trick made me more confident. Before the ring-of-fire trick, I had all but five of the big cats exit the cage. Still a bit anxious about the fiery rings for the lionesses to jump through, I was afraid I might catch my outfit on fire or I wouldn't hold the ring just right and the lionesses might get burned. However, with confidence I held the lit ring between the two platforms. The five lionesses jumped through without so much as singeing a tail. The applause after that trick made my ears hurt. I put out the fire, bowed, and then had four of the lionesses exit the ring. I kept Mitzi with me.

She jumped off her platform and ran at me as she was trained to do. She swiped the air at me and looked ferocious to the audience. I got the chair and the whip and got her back into line. Afterward, I slipped her a cookie for being such a good lioness. That's when the audience jumped to its feet, applauding and roaring with approval. I sent Mitzi from the ring and bowed with satisfaction. I relished this limelight.

Leonard congratulated me when I came from the ring. "Sara, I would never have guessed this was your first time. You're a natural at it."

"Thank you, Leonard. I was nervous at first, but I just remembered your instructions and things went smoothly."

"The audience loves you. I've never heard such applause before."

"Really?"

"Go take another bow. They won't stop until they've seen you again."

I took another bow and basked in the audience's thunderous response. I loved it. I came back literally glowing. I told Leonard I wanted to brush the lions and tell them how good they had been. He smiled as I grabbed the brush and headed for the cages.

Actually I grabbed the brush and headed for the toilet. I was so nervous I had to throw up. Afterward, I went in to see the lions and tigers to give them some more cookies and brush their thick, coarse fur.

The lions and tigers were always very good, like children. I liked them and they liked me too. When they licked my arm with their rough tongues, I knew they had accepted me. I respected them and never forgot they could be wild animals at the slightest provocation. I never startled them or changed the routine.

Two lions and two tigers bred future cubs for the circus. When the female lion, Mitzi, gave birth to four cubs, I helped her with them. The firstborn cub was a female and the other three were males. After Mitzi gave birth to the female cub, she pushed it toward me for safekeeping while she gave birth to the males. Even though this was Mitzi's first litter, she was a good mother and took care of her cubs by washing and feeding them. She wouldn't let anyone else near her cubs except me. I could play with them because Mitzi trusted me completely. Leonard was surprised. He said he wouldn't have believed how Mitzi trusted me with her cubs had he not seen it with his own eyes. As proof, he took a picture of me holding the little female cub.

I would wear different wigs, my short skirt, a tight-fitting blouse with sequins, and short boots to perform every night at 7:00 p.m. On Saturdays we had two shows, one at two in the afternoon and one at seven at night. Sundays we only gave one show at two in the afternoon. I had three outfits for performances, one white, one blue, and one red. Because I wanted to keep these outfits, I paid for them out of my own pocket; otherwise, the circus would provide the costume for performers who did not wish to keep theirs.

I also rode the elephant in another act after the lion tamer portion was over. The lion-taming act was always in the middle of the show and the elephant routine was in the finale. Two other girls and I would make the elephants sit down, stand on two feet, and bow. The elephant raised me on its bristly trunk so I could get on its back and ride around the ring. Being short was an advantage for me to jump onto the elephant's back from its trunk and cross my feet to ride. The ten elephants raised their front feet and put them on each other's backs for a dramatic line-up. I'd tightly hang onto the head harness when this part was done since I didn't want to fall off under all those pachyderm pounds. In one part the elephant held my leg in its mouth and spun around the ring. Surprisingly, I never got dizzy. I wore a different costume for this act, a belly dancer type outfit made of flowered blue and pink cloth.

The other two girls performed more daring tricks with the elephants than I did, but my act could still get the audience wound up. The most exciting part of the elephant act was when the elephant pretended he was going to step on me. I lay under its foot and the gigantic beast pretended he was going to stomp me. The audience went crazy then, screaming at the handlers to save me. Of course I was never in any danger, but the audience didn't know. I trusted the elephant because I worked with him, and he knew me as well.

I worked for the circus and stayed in the hotel with the other circus people. People from all over Europe worked for the circus. Performers from Yugoslavia, Greece, Bulgaria, Russia, and even China had acts. The Chinese performed a tumbling act, the Greeks performed on the trapeze without a net, and a Russian pair performed a knife-throwing act. The Bulgarians performed an acrobatic routine wherein they stood on each other's shoulders, used a springboard for height, and made spectacular catches. Three children were in this act. A lot of the acts included entire families. Sometimes up to eleven or twelve people from one family were part of the act. Often several generations were represented.

The horseback riding act was one of these and also one of the best. The Russian rider, dressed as a Cossack, had four horses running around the ring in unison while he stood on their backs. A child in this act circled under the horse's belly as it galloped around the ring. The entire family, which included two men, two women, and the little boy, were gifted equestrians.

In the dog act the poodles dressed in costumes danced, pushed baby buggies, and made spectacular jumps. This is probably where I got my love of poodles. All of the acts awed the audience with daring stunts or cute tricks.

The circus traveled to various cities and countries occupied by the Germans. On one trip we were allowed to travel by train to Antwerp, Holland, Luxembourg, and Paris. Antwerp always held a special place in my heart because that's where Nathan took me when we eloped. At times the flood of memories threatened to drown me, but I managed to keep going. The road trip took about eight weeks in all. We stayed in Antwerp one week, in Rotterdam in Holland two weeks, one week in Luxembourg, and about a month in Paris.

Leonard was originally from Paris and his wife lived there. She was an invalid and could not travel with the circus. Paralyzed from the waist down, she was confined to a wheelchair. While we were in Paris, Leonard took me to meet his wife, Amelia. She had wanted to meet me. Perhaps she was afraid I was his mistress, for Frenchmen often had mistresses then.

When I met her, I wanted to assure her I was not his mistress. For the visit, I bought some flowers for her. Amelia was a lovely, but very ill lady. A maid pushed her wheelchair into the room, adjusted her clothing and pillows, poured a glass of water and set it on the table by the wheelchair before she left. I noticed how slowly Amelia moved her arms and how emaciated the flesh had become. Feeling somewhat awkward about handing her the flowers, I offered to place them in a vase for her.

After arranging the flowers and placing them on a nearby table, I continued the conversation by telling her about how I joined the circus, about conditions in Belgium, and about traveling on the trains. She seemed preoccupied, but polite. I didn't know if her illness was affecting her attention or something else was bothering her.

"Sara, I'm a sick woman. I love my husband and my husband loves me, but I don't mind if he has girlfriends. I can't be a wife to him anymore."

So that was what was bothering her. She thought Leonard and I were having an affair. "I'm not his girlfriend," I asserted. "Don't worry. I'm too young to have an old man on my body."

At that she laughed and said, "I love you, Sara." I could tell she was relieved to find out I was not Leonard's mistress.

"Besides I'm married and have two children." I made it clear I had no interest in her husband as a lover whatsoever. We respected one another. After that she eased into pleasant conversation about raising children.

Later she offered, "If you need someone to take care of your children, Sara, they could come here and stay with me. I have a large house with enough servants to take care of them even though I am an invalid." Obviously Leonard had said something to her. Perhaps he suspected I was Jewish or he may have been concerned about my children. He must have noticed how I had acted whenever Susanna, Catherine's daughter, brought Guy to the circus.

I was touched that Leonard's wife would offer to take care of Guy and Monique. "Thank you for your kind offer, but the children are in a safe place. I can see them more often in Brussels."

"I understand." She smiled at me and asked, "Would you like to come for tea tomorrow? Leonard and my sons will be here around four. I want you to come too."

Picking up my purse to go, I said, "I'd like that. It's been good to meet you. I look forward to tea tomorrow." I hugged her and left.

The next day Leonard, his sons, Amelia, and I were at tea. One of the sons, Francois, said, "You should see Sara, Mother. She's a great performer. She looks so tiny in the ring with the big cats, but she holds the whip and chair without any fear whatsoever." Leonard's other son, Joseph, was nodding in agreement with Francois' assessment of my performing abilities.

"Mother, I was afraid to do that act," Joseph said. "I was glad when Sara took it. Then I could keep being a clown." Both Joseph and Francois were good clowns and entertained the children.

Besides Leonard's two sons, his daughter and his granddaughters also traveled with the circus. His daughter performed in the can-can, and his granddaughters performed in a trapeze act, not the Greek family one though. Since Leonard was in his sixties, the fact some of his family members could accompany him was good.

Having tea with them and feeling some degree of family was pleasant, although it made me want to see mine again desperately. Seeing Leonard and his sons hang on every word Amelia spoke made me realize just how ill she really was. They knew she didn't have long. I could tell Leonard wanted to stay, but he moved on with the circus. He had to run the business, and how long she had—a year or a few weeks—was uncertain. Sadly, Amelia died a few months after our visit.

When we traveled by train, I shared a compartment with Josie, one of the girls in the elephant act and the can-can. She was from a lower class family in Belgium and ran away from home to take this job. A slim blonde who wore glasses, Josie had a lot of boyfriends.

We slept on the train, and special buses took us from the train to the arena where we performed. When we arrived in a new place, Leonard would have our pictures published in the papers and on posters to advertise our arrival. Unlike some of the show bills Americans used, Europeans did not sensationalize the acts. The entire crew of the circus was photographed together; one act was not given preference over another.

On these road trips I would call Catherine and the children whenever we reached a new destination to let them know where I was and how I was getting along. I would always address Catherine as *Bobonne*, or grandmother, to make sure anyone who was listening assumed she was my children's grandmother.

The Germans wanted our circus to travel throughout Germany, but Leonard had no desire to go there and was able to make up some excuse to avoid them. No matter where we went crowds of people turned out to pay their fifteen francs to see the show. The circus was a rare form of entertainment allowed by the Nazi government.

After traveling through the Bordeaux region of Belgium, we returned to Brussels. On our return Catherine's granddaughter, Susanna, again brought Guy to the circus to see me, though we couldn't communicate openly. I did manage to buy some ice cream for them. I wanted to hug him and talk to him, but I couldn't. The danger of the Nazis being around was ever present. Susanna had also warned Guy not to say anything to me. He later told me, "*Maman*, I was scared to death. When I saw you with that whip and chair and the lions jumping through the fire, I was so scared."

So my time at the circus was rather exciting, considering I was still working secretly for the underground whenever they needed me. During the off season for the circus, I worked at resorts as a hostess, but the circus was my main cover. As a natural-born show-off, the circus was a great place for me until the spring of 1944. That's when Simon returned unexpectedly from Sweden, and I did the most regrettable thing of my life.

CHAPTER 10—CAPTURE

In the spring of 1944 I got homesick and went back to my old apartment to see how things were. I checked on my belongings occasionally, but never stayed overnight at the apartment on the Rue du Prague. When I arrived, I found my brother Simon hiding. I thought he was still in Sweden, safe, but there he was.

"What are you doing here? You're supposed to be in Sweden."

"I got homesick for you, Nathan, the family, and my girlfriend Margaret."

"That's stupid! It's only been six months. You were safe in Sweden."

"Don't lecture me, Sara. I got tired of that woman in Sweden always throwing herself at me. I didn't want to go to bed with her."

Stunned someone would think of my little brother like that, I softened my tone. "So you're here." I dropped the lecture and hugged him. "It's not safe here. It was probably risky for me to come here too. We need to go."

I looked out the window with a conditioned response. "I'm staying with the circus at the *Cirque Royal*. Come with me there for tonight and then we'll find you a place to hide." I started for the door, expecting him to follow me.

"No, I want to stay in the house. I don't want you to pay for a place in a hotel for me."

"You can't stay here. The Nazis know Nathan and I are Jewish and we lived here. They might come back at any time."

Reluctantly he agreed to come to the *Cirque Royal* with me, but he wouldn't stay long. He watched the show and then returned to the apartment even though I begged him not to go back. I didn't realize how stubborn Simon could be, but he insisted on staying where he chose, not where his big sister wanted him to stay.

For about two weeks he stayed at the house. I suppose some time during that interval he saw Margaret again. Things must not have gone very well as he never mentioned her again. My younger brother Jacques suspected Margaret was cooperating with the Nazis and may have turned in *Maman*. We'll never know for sure.

I went back to see Simon and pick up some clothes. Stupidly, one night I stayed over. Being back in my house felt good, but it was dangerous. I kept hoping since nothing had happened to my belongings all this time we would be all right to return. I was wrong.

Around three o' clock on a Tuesday afternoon while Simon and I talked, we heard cars and tanks on the street outside. That sound was one we had grown accustomed to hearing, but it made us nervous no matter when we heard it. Looking out the window, I saw they had surrounded our building. Madame Francois could finally pat herself on the back for turning in some more Jews.

Simon and I looked at each other, not having to voice the fear we both could taste. I felt sick to my stomach as I swallowed to keep the bile from coming up my throat. I tried to think of some place to hide Simon, but no place existed for us now.

"Do you think they're coming for us, Sara?" Simon asked quietly. We could both hear the steady rhythm of boots thudding on the staircase below.

"I don't know. Have your papers ready." I took the identity papers from my purse.

Simon fumbled in his pocket, taking his out. Our papers were good since I had made them personally, but this sounded like more than an identity check.

When they started pounding on the door, I decided not to open it. If they had found us, they'd have to work to take us away. After evading the Nazis for so long, I knew this was it. I tried to swallow, but I had no saliva left in my mouth and licked dry lips. I looked at Simon and gave a pretense of assurance we would talk our way out of this.

The pounding of the rifle butts on the door finally splintered the wood. All we could do was wait. Six brown-uniformed men broke down the door completely. Four stayed outside, and two came inside. They were Gestapo—all blonde, typical Aryans. As they entered, one shouted, "*Jude!*" A third one from outside came in and grabbed Simon by the collar. He hit Simon over and over with his gloved fist.

"I'm not Jewish. I'm Belgian," Simon kept repeating. Futilely, Simon tried to hand him his papers, but the Gestapo agent ignored him. Not looking at Simon's papers, the Nazi threw them on the floor.

"Look at his hair," I yelled. "He's Belgian. Jews don't have blonde hair." I picked up Simon's papers, trying to show them. The Gestapo agent gave me a disdainful look and shoved me away.

Repeatedly he punched Simon's face. Blood from his mouth splattered on the carpet and walls every time he was hit. Simon fell, but the Nazi grabbed him and hit him again.

"Stop it!" I screamed. "Quit hitting him. We're Belgian." I pleaded on my knees with him, but he ignored me completely.

Almost unconscious, Simon fell into the brown leather chair. His face was a pool of blood. The other two Gestapo men went outside and left the one inside to torture Simon. This Gestapo agent had special training in how to torture people into confessing whatever he wanted from them.

"Stop it," I pleaded again. "He hasn't done anything. Why are you hitting him?"

It didn't do any good. This man knew tactics to get people to talk.

Simon's front teeth were gone. He was bleeding and bruised all over. The skin on his face was black and purple, smeared with the blood from his mouth and nose. I couldn't see Simon's eyes, and I thought the Nazi would kill him in front of me.

"He's Jewish. Stop hitting him," I confessed to him after I couldn't stand it any more. "We're Jewish."

Simon's face was bloodied all over. The soft skin under his eyes began to swell, and where they had knocked out his teeth blood spilled down his chin and throat onto his white shirt. Slumped into the leather chair, Simon was totally unconscious. Red blood filled the cushions, and I couldn't see the brown color of the chair.

I stood against a wall. Relieved the Nazi had finally stopped hitting Simon, I tried to go to him, but the other Nazis forced me back. "Please let me help him."

"Shut up, Jew *schwein* or you're next," yelled one of the Nazis.

I thought admitting we were Jews might save Simon's life. If they started to beat me, they might torture information from me about my underground work and contacts. I had made my decision and had to live with whatever it might bring. They already suspected we were

Jews; hopefully, they wouldn't suspect I was an underground worker as well. I kept quiet.

The Nazis ripped up floorboards and wallpaper. They thought we had valuables hidden in the house.

Sinking to the floor, I said, "We don't have any valuables. Anything of value we've already sold."

"All Jews have jewels hidden. Where are they?"

"I told you we don't have anything. It's all gone."

Disgusted, the Nazi joined the others, searching for the elusive cache of jewels they were sure I possessed.

Of course, I wasn't going to reveal the location of the safe. I had a few pieces of jewelry, but telling them the location wasn't going to lessen Simon's torture. They would only have beaten Simon more for my keeping information from them.

"Get your bag. You're coming with us," one of the soldiers said.

Another Gestapo agent told us, "Take anything of value or importance. Those items will help you in the work camps." Then the two of them laughed and said something in German to each other that I couldn't hear.

I threw some clothing in a suitcase—dresses, nightgowns, underwear, shoes, a shawl, a sweater, and my coat. The macabre scene resurrected the memory of the time I was arrested in Paris, but after seeing what they had done to Simon, this situation was a thousand times worse. Simon's suitcase, the one he had taken to Sweden, was still in the house. I took that too. All we could take was one bag each.

After what seemed like hours, they dragged Simon, limp as a dead body, to a black car and threw him in. Climbing into the back seat with him, I wiped the blood from his face with my handkerchief, but it continued to pour. I held the cloth on his gums and hoped he wouldn't choke. During the car ride, I watched Simon and didn't notice where they were taking us.

After a short drive we wound up at a Jewish holding center still in Brussels. Simon did not regain consciousness. They yanked us from the back seat, and Simon was dragged inside. They separated us into different rooms. At least I could see Simon, but I couldn't go to him. Someone put ice on his battered face.

While we were waiting to see what would happen next, other Jewish families were brought in. Crying children clung to their mothers. Men's faces were beaten and bloody like Simon's.

As I sat in the room I hoped Jules would realize what had happened to us when I didn't show up for work. Maybe he and Agnes could get some of our belongings out of the house before the Nazis liquidated it. I knew the Nazis would probably take the antique furniture. Jules and Agnes could not get anything as large as furniture out. Madame Francois finally could have what she wanted now. My only hope was Jules could empty the safe, get some photographs, clothing, or the beds for his children. Maybe he could save some family heirlooms.

We spent one day at this center before we were taken to Malines, where the Nazis had a camp, like a ghetto, set up. It took about forty minutes for the truck we were in to reach Malines, located near the town of Mechelen. Three women about my age, two babies, and about a dozen older people were in the truck with Simon and me.

Malines was a temporary detention center and work camp. It had a huge brick hall for the prisoners to stay, which looked like an old fort. Thin mattresses covered the floor where two to three hundred people, both men and women, were crowded in. We had to provide our own form of a blanket for cover, but we were allowed five-minute showers, *ersatz* coffee and bread for breakfast, soup for lunch, and a supper.

An outward semblance of normalcy pervaded Malines. This camp turned out to be a front put up by the Nazis to convince the Belgian people all the camps were like this. No guard towers nor barbed wire ringed the area. They gave the illusion the camps were places to work. They had people sewing, working in the kitchens, doing custodial work, and performing other forms of regular labor. We Jews were even fooled into thinking these really were work camps at first.

Simon and I were together at Malines. He had been able to clean up from his beating, but his top front teeth were gone. The German guards here allowed Simon to be bandaged.

At Malines I was overjoyed to find my friend Frieda and her mother Eva. When I saw them in the crowded hall, I pushed my way through the people to them. As we reached each other, we hugged and cried.

"Frieda, I can't believe you're here. I thought you had a good place to hide."

"We did, but the Nazis found all of us anyway just a few days ago. Someone must have told them where to look. They never would have found it by themselves."

"Do you know who turned you in?"

"No, but the Nazis knew exactly where to go. We had been in the basement with a hidden entrance. The Nazis came right to the cabinet's hidden door and broke it down."

"Did they only arrest you and your mother?"

"They got all twelve of us. Mother and I haven't been sent out yet. My father, brothers, older sister, and the others were sent on transports away from here."

"Where did they go?"

"No one knows. Names are posted on a list and they're taken out. No one has come back from wherever they're taken." Frieda stepped across several people to sit next to Eva.

I hugged Eva and found a place to sit down. Mother and Eva had been good friends. Frieda was a few years younger than I was, but we had grown up to be good friends. Seeing someone I knew was comforting. At least they had survived this much.

"Have you heard anything about Nathan, my mother or Albert?"

Eva shook her head sadly. "No, I haven't. They're not here though. I've checked. They were sent out some time before we arrived."

Disappointed, I looked down and sighed. "I wish I knew how they are doing or where they were taken."

Eva touched my cheek, empathizing with my pain. From the look on her face, I knew she had more bad news to tell me. "Sara, did you hear about Jean?"

"What about him?"

"I found out from a kitchen worker he was arrested. He was here at Malines too."

"Jean? Not Jean too! How did they arrest him?"

"I don't know. I only heard he was here. Some friends from our old neighborhood told me when I asked about your mother."

"Has he been sent out also?"

"Yes," replied Eva. "That's all we know."

I knew I shouldn't tell anyone about his connection with the resistance. The fewer people who knew, the better.

"I was hoping I would see Nathan or *Maman* here." Looking at my intertwined fingers, I began to cry. Eva and Frieda tried to comfort me, but I couldn't stop crying. "I miss my family," I mumbled.

"I know," Eva said. "We'll stay together as family as long as we can."

Simon had noticed me talking to Eva and Frieda and came over. We continued to talk to them about other people from our neighborhood, but they were the only ones who hadn't been shipped out.

For weeks we stayed in the large hall doing jobs around the place.

Somehow the conditions at Malines were nothing like we expected. New people would arrive at intervals and others were sent out, but we never got to see them leave. Names would be posted and they would be taken out, but that's all we knew. Simon was assigned to sew clothing at Malines. After all, he had learned to be a tailor. I was a custodian, cleaning up different places wherever I was directed.

We were allowed to keep our own clothes, talk to others, sing, and the children could play outside. We weren't allowed to have any religious services, but at least here we weren't treated as badly as we thought we would be. Members of the Belgian SS would use any action as an excuse to whip someone, kick us, or call us names, but I never saw anyone beaten to death at Malines. The German soldiers guarded us, but the Belgian SS treated us worse than the German soldiers did.

We befriended a little thirteen-year-old girl whose parents had been taken on a transport. She seemed so young and helpless to be alone. The Nazis didn't care if they separated families like this. I just hoped Simon and I could stay together.

While at Malines, Jean Marie tried to communicate with me, but unsuccessfully. A Jewish man I knew from Brussels told me he had seen Jean Marie on the other side of the fence. A German guard ordered Jean Marie to go away. Jean Marie may have been trying to get a message to me or someone else in the camp, but I'll never know.

In addition, Leonard and Maurice Gilbert appeared at Malines, under the guise of trying to arrange a circus performance at the camp. The Nazis told them to go away; only Jews who didn't deserve any entertainment were in this camp. Maurice had posed as the business manager of the circus, and Leonard had even brought along some of the posters from the circus, one of which included me as the lion tamer.

Leonard told them I was the best lion tamer he had ever had and that I was a Belgian Gentile. They must have arrested me by accident, and he needed me back.

The Nazi officer assured him I had confessed I was a Jew.

Leonard persisted by telling them my last name was Miodownik, a Gentile circus performer.

I had made the set of identity papers myself using the last name of Miodownik and had made a set of papers for Guy with the same last name.

Leonard puffed indignantly at the Nazi overseers. Appealing to their stereotype, he said, "She can't be Jewish. She's a good worker." He tried, but he couldn't get me released.

As I was leaving the area with my fellow prisoners, a girl working at Malines slipped me a message from Leonard. "I'm sorry I failed. We can arrange a 'white marriage' for you to get you out."

"Don't do it," I answered through the same girl. "Too risky." My heart pounded. *Would the Nazis connect me with the resistance? To Maurice Gilbert and Leonard?* I didn't want anyone else arrested.

Months passed while Simon and I continued to work. New arrivals from neighboring countries, such as Holland and Luxembourg, came and went. Some didn't know they had Jewish ancestry. They practiced Christianity, but they were treated the same as we were.

Every six days the Nazis called out names for a new transport list of people leaving Malines. Where they were sent was a mystery. One thing was clear though—they never came back.

When I heard the name I had used on my papers, Sura Miodownik, called out, my jaw dropped. My hand flew to my mouth, and I closed my eyes. Lowering my chin to my chest, I stemmed the flood of tears long enough ask Frieda and Eva if I had heard the name correctly. Frieda's and Eva's names were called out too, but not Simon's. Transport number twenty-six was scheduled to leave that very day, July 31, 1944. The Germans told us to get our belongings.

After the SS soldier finished the list and instructions, Simon put his hand on my shoulder. "I'm going too."

"No, you're not. You're only nineteen years old. Stay here."

"I'm not going to let you go alone. What happens to you will happen to me. Jean is gone. Albert and *Maman* are gone. Nathan is gone. Maybe we'll see them over there." He was trying to sound optimistic, but it didn't work.

"No, let me go alone. You've got a good job here."

"Nothing doing. Where you go, I go."

"With all the bombers flying over, maybe the Germans are losing. Later you can find us."

"No, you're not going alone." He walked away from me, and I had a hard time keeping up with him.

"Where are you going? What are you going to do?" I clutched his arm, but he shook free and strode ahead. Grabbing at his sleeve over other people, I tried to reach him.

Then he strode off toward the SS soldier. He maneuvered among the crowd faster than I could.

I wanted to scream, *No, don't listen to him. He doesn't know what he's saying.* But I couldn't stop what he had put into motion.

When Simon returned to me after speaking to the SS soldier, he said, "We're going to another work camp like this one. Don't you remember the letters? They said not to worry."

"We have no way of knowing if the letters are real. The underground warned us if family members were taken, we would probably never see them again."

"Things will be all right. If I have to work in a mine, I can handle it." I could tell Simon's mind was made up. He refused to listen to me any more.

The Nazis encouraged us to take our jewelry, our clothes, and our suitcases. I had my wedding ring, my watch, my coat, a light sweater, and a small suitcase of clothes. Since it was summer, I wore a plaid pleated skirt and short-sleeved white blouse. Also I had the a rubber band around my wrist. The underground told me always to keep one because it was useful in emergencies.

Simon had his suitcase with the same items he had taken to Sweden. I desperately wished he were still in Sweden where he had been safe.

Then on that Wednesday morning the guards called our names. A silent dread pervaded the hall.

At 12:30 in the afternoon Simon was separated from me, and we were forced into lines by gender. Only women and children were in my line. Eva and Frieda were with me, but I lost sight of Simon.

We left the main hall of Malines, carrying our suitcases with our names printed on our luggage. As we prepared to board the transport, German guards took our suitcases away from us.

When we walked to the tracks, a stunning jolt ran through the line. Our "transports" were cattle cars. Hundreds of people were being crowded in. The Nazis lowered and aimed their rifles at us. They shouted, "Run to the cars."

People bottlenecked at the door to the reddish cars. No step stool or gangplank offered assistance. The Nazis threw people into the cars and shouted orders to move the line faster.

The guards manhandled us like we were no more than garbage to be thrown away. Eva, Frieda, and I were in the middle of the line to be loaded. Together the three of us inched our way toward the wooden slats of the walls of the car. The only opening inside the car for air was the small space between the boards. By being close to one of these, we could breathe a little.

Women of all ages and children crammed into the tightly-packed enclosure. Since hundreds of Belgians were in this transport, we recognized a lot of people in our car. Even rich people were on the train. They had hidden in good places, but the Nazis found them anyway.

The Nazis forced more and more people on top of one another, but no more room existed.

We stepped on each other as we tried to find space to stand. Being short, I kept getting shoved toward the floor. If I fell, I would be trampled. Frieda, taller than I, held onto me to keep me from falling. I struggled upward. All I could see were people's backs and chests. Arms were shoved into my face. I pushed back.

I felt like my ribs were splitting from all the bodies jammed against me. We held onto each other and pushed others away to keep them from crushing us. The compression of hot bodies and the lack of airflow suffocated us. A cold wave swept over me. Even though it was a summer day, I felt chilled. My blouse was drenched with sweat. I felt light-headed and thought I would faint. I held onto Frieda more tightly than before.

I barely managed to whisper to her, "Where are they taking us? Why are they trying to kill us?"

People shouted through the boards, "Let us out! You're suffocating us!" The hundreds of people in the car cried and screamed. Babies wailed, old women groaned with mortal terror, some shouted obscenities, and voices screeched in high-pitched anguish.

The guards poked their bayonets through the openings to silence us. Women jerked back with gashes. Blood streamed from gaping wounds. When others saw the blood, they tried to climb over the backs of people, but there was nowhere to move. If a woman happened to be by a slat, she had no escape. Some were stabbed repeatedly and finally sank beneath the tide of screaming women.

Packed worse than sardines, we shuffled to find space for both feet while the next cars were loaded. People got sick and threw up. Vomit splattered onto people around them. Cursing, the people near the sick one tried to inch away, but it was impossible. We stood in other people's vomit. Urine ran down people's legs as terror caused them to lose control. Women cried for water for their little children, but no water was provided anywhere.

The train whistle blew, signaling the beginning of our hellish journey. Jerked like rag dolls as the train lurched forward, we fell into a chaotic tangle. Arms and elbows smacked into tear-stained faces. Every time the train changed pace, we tried to keep our balance. It was useless. In the beginning people apologized for stepping on each other or falling into another, but as the tortuous day progressed, all courtesy disappeared.

Women, tired and emotionally drained, pushed back as hard as they could. Someone screamed at a young mother, "Keep that damn baby quiet!" She couldn't give the baby anything.

"Leave her alone," I screamed back. "She can't help it." I was glad Guy and Monique were not with me. I thought, *This is hell*. Then it sank in—this was only the trip *to* hell. More horrors would await us *in* hell.

On the way we stopped three or four times. I recognized the station at Antwerp. I hoped they would open the door, but they never did. We stood in the cattle car, awaiting our fate.

I held my urine as long as I could. My stomach cramped. After hours of pressure, I could stand it no longer. Like everyone else around me, I had to let go. There wasn't room to squat down or remove underwear. I wanted to die of sheer embarrassment as the warm liquid ran down my legs and into my shoes, but it didn't matter. Everyone else had to go in the same way.

The stench of human waste, urine and vomit permeated the car. I tried to hold my nose or breathe close to my shoulder to keep the stench from overpowering me. Whiffs of air only came through the slats when the train was moving. When we stopped, the suffocating air engulfed me, cutting my breath to short gasps. People fought to get near a slat. We had learned to keep quiet when we stopped at a station. I hoped the Nazis wouldn't use their bayonets on us as they had the others.

Two elderly women became swollen and died. Dehydration, lack of food, not being able to use the toilet, or simply the terror of their situation could have killed them. We begged the soldiers to take the dead bodies out, but they only mocked us. With the heat the stench of decomposing bodies was beyond description. I had never before smelled anything so bad. People stood on the bodies. Trying to move them to one area of the car was useless.

Eva, Frieda, and I protected each other for the next three days of travel from Malines to Auschwitz. My parched throat became so dry I couldn't talk. My tongue swelled to three times its normal size. My throat burned, and my lips peeled from lack of moisture. I chewed on the rubber band, causing my mouth to salivate a little, but it wasn't enough.

The entire time we were never given water or food. Some women had hidden food and we shared what we had, but it was never enough to go around. Cursing and hitting always resulted.

Little children had it the worst. Children whimpered as mothers tried to comfort them. They begged for water and asked their mothers, "Why can't we have something to drink? Where are we going?" These little ones could only see darkness as the mass of humanity pressed in on them.

During the night we jolted through northern Germany to Berlin. Germans jeered at us as we passed. Some women begged the guards to shoot us and end our suffering, but the Nazis only laughed at us.

From Berlin we traveled southeast. Twenty people died in the cattle car, but the Germans wouldn't remove their bodies. We begged the soldiers to remove the corpses, but all we were told was, "*Macht das Mund zu!*" Keep your mouth shut was their reply to every request. "*So vas?*" characterized their attitude. They didn't care. To them, we were already dead.

CHAPTER 11—THE RINGS OF FIRE

On August 2, 1944, in the late afternoon we arrived at Auschwitz. As soon as the train stopped, we heard guards yelling, *"Raus! Raus!"* Stepping into the fading daylight, we squinted. At first I thought my eyes had not yet adjusted because a smoke hung over the area. For miles we had smelled a strange odor, but we thought it might have been the train engine's exhaust or some odor associated with battle. This horribly strange odor, much like the smell of teeth being ground in a dentist's office, only a thousand times worse, engulfed the entire area. I tried to cover my nose with my hand, but the odor permeated every breath. I did not realize what this terrible smell was at first, but soon I learned.

Barbed wire was everywhere. Armed guards in towers surrounded the compound. Smokestacks loomed in the distance, discharging a foul ash.

Pushing and pointing their guns at us, the guards separated the men from the women. We stood in designated areas by the tracks. All the workers were yelling, *"Schweigt!* Be quiet! Don't look around!" I didn't know what would happen to us. Frieda and Eva stood close to me as we held hands.

Cars ahead of ours were emptied. On one car only one little girl about seven or eight years old had survived. I don't know what the others died from—perhaps dehydration, starvation, or some other cause. Later on people said gas had been used on that car. If that were the case, the only way the little girl survived was by putting her face between the slats of the floor. I don't know for sure, but she was the sole survivor. We saw her run up to the SS man in charge and begged him to let her live. She said, "I'm strong. I can work. Please let me live."

The tall, slim, clean-shaven man with light brown hair wore the dark uniform of the SS—black boots, riding pants, and white gloves. He wore glasses, and he carried a black whip. Smiling, he told her to go play with a ball. As she ran in the direction he indicated, he shot her in the back. He showed no emotion when he fired the gun—not a smile of pleasure or a twinge of regret.

Blood spurted from the girl's back as the bullet pierced her tiny body. Even the hardened SS women recoiled at this murder, but quickly recovered their stoic expressions.

I stared at the little girl's body. *What had she done to deserve being shot?* My whole body shook as tears stung my eyes. I clinched my fists as hate raged inside me. Jewish workers warned us not to cry or react. *How could I not react to cold-blooded murder?* I wanted to take the gun and shoot that devil as he had shot the little girl.

Later we found out the murderer was Josef Mengele. Like Satan, Mengele had a nice outward appearance, but a heart of pure evil. *How could a man who looked so normal be so monstrous?*

Then the Nazis told us to take off our clothes by the railroad tracks. At first people were reluctant to obey the commands. Many people from Belgium could understand German, but the command seemed ludicrous. *Why should we take off our clothes?* When rifle butts slammed into people's cheekbones, smashing them beyond recognition, we obeyed without hesitation. Everyone in unison began to take off shoes, dresses, slips, and even underwear. When a few people hesitated to remove these final pieces of clothing, again the rifle butts crushed bones. Workers in blue-striped uniforms gathered our clothes in baskets and took them away.

Some could not stand the humiliation. Mothers were forced to disrobe before their children. Older people of the community were exposed before hundreds of strangers. It was too much for them, and a few died of heart attacks on the spot. We were not allowed to help any of them, nor were we allowed to ask questions. Constantly the SS soldiers yelled, "*Los! Jetzt! Schnell!*"

Along with Mengele, we saw other Nazi SS and the German shepherd dogs. SS members, male and female, stood by Mengele as he looked at each person and then pointed which direction to go. The older people and the small children were directed to the left. Women with children were told to give their children to the older people. At first they thought they were just going to be sent to another location.

Jewish people, who had been coerced to work with the Nazis for a little extra food, were called *Kapos*. They did the Nazis' dirty work for them. The Nazis thought themselves too good to touch a Jew. To them, we were vermin, rats to be exterminated. Therefore, the *Kapos* took the young children from their mothers to put them in a line going to the left with the older people. Some mothers could not bear to be separated from their children and followed them within inches to the left. If anyone tried to go to another line from what was indicated, the SS or Mengele himself, with gloved hands, dragged the person by the hair back to the selected line, or Mengele shot the person.

Sometimes the SS guards unleashed the attack dogs upon the person who changed lines and let the dogs finish the victim. I had never seen such brutality. These dogs were vicious beyond belief. When they would go for the person's throat, instinctively the person put up an arm in defense. But the dog tore the flesh on the person's arms until the victim could no longer fend off the brute. With a woman, the dog went after her breasts as she tried to keep the animal's fangs away from her throat. The woman was helpless to keep the beast from ripping her chest to hanging shreds of flesh. Once the dogs tore at the throat, it took only seconds for the person to die. The powerful jaws crushed the windpipe or tore it away.

Sickened by the sight, we tried to turn our faces away. The SS guards told us, "Look at what will happen to you if you try to change lines." They delighted in this savagery and patted the dogs' bloody muzzles for a job well done.

During this "selection" we saw many middle-aged women being sent to the left. Frieda and I decided to keep Eva in between us and hide the fact she was older. Frieda was around nineteen, and her mother was in her forties. By my standing in front of Eva and Frieda standing closely behind her, Mengele could not see her age as easily. He allowed her to pass with us to the right.

The left line stumbled away as the guards poked at them with bayonets, and the dogs lunged against their leashes.

In all, nineteen women from Brussels stood on the right side of the "selected." We looked at each other in confusion, but didn't dare speak.

Our jewelry was confiscated. I lost the wedding ring Nathan had given to me and my watch. These were the only pieces of jewelry I had with me.

Then the *Kapos* herded us together to be shaved. First they shaved our heads. Using scissors to cut the majority of our hair, the *Kapos* threw the hair in piles by color. Then they dipped a razor in water and scraped our scalps, leaving some odd-shaped tufts at intervals. Our heads were bleeding where crude slashes took part of the scalp with the hair. Even our eyebrows were shaved off. Then the *Kapo* knelt down to shave our pubic area. With a rough drag or two of the razor's dulled edge over our privates, every hair on our bodies was removed. It didn't matter to the Nazis if a man were shaving a woman or a woman shaving a man. They took away every shred of pride and self-esteem. We weren't human beings to them. We were being processed as animals before the butcher.

Though we thought the people sent to the left were taken to barracks, we found out later that they were taken to the gas chambers. The *Kapos* knew what going to the left meant. The *Sonderkommando* took the dead bodies from the gas chambers to the ovens. They knew.

One *Kapo* urged a young woman with a baby to give the baby to an elderly lady and go in the right line. Some mothers may have guessed what lay ahead and preferred to die with their children. They instinctively knew. Heartbreak leaves little hope. The elderly and the children were taken away, but we stayed where we were.

Years later in doing research I learned our transport had 563 people from Malines. After the selection 223 men and 138 women were admitted to the camp. The remaining 202 people, 47 of whom were children, were sent to the gas chambers.

The *Kapos* ordered us to open our mouths and if anyone had gold teeth, the teeth were pulled with pliers, without any regard for the pain inflicted. I had four gold teeth in my lower jaw yanked from my mouth. The paroxysm of pain made me shiver and shake. I had to stand still, while blood pooled in my mouth. I spat the red saliva and blood on the ground. Any intake of air across the holes where my teeth had been made me wince. I wiped the blood from my chin and resolved I would not succumb to the pain.

I couldn't get warm and felt as though a fog surrounded me. It seemed like everyone moved in slow motion. I could see their lips moving, but the sound was delayed. A sense of distant detachment set in, as though this were happening to someone else, not me.

Somewhat disoriented, I stood for what seemed to be hours. I wasn't sure exactly how much time passed because they had taken my watch. I kept thinking, *Is it possible to take this much pain? How can they do this to us?*

Then about a hundred or more women from various transports, including Eva, Frieda, and me, marched to the showers. One *Kapo* said, "You're going to have the water." At first I didn't understand what he meant. They didn't give us a towel, a bar of soap, or anything. We were crowded into a cement square room where we could see shower nozzles mounted at the top of the walls. When the guards went outside, we screamed hysterically. We didn't know what would happen next. Then the water came on.

The cold liquid sloshed away the numbness. We drank mouthfuls of the cold water, the first drops we had had in three days. I wiped off as much blood from my mouth as I could. Swirling the water around the holes where my teeth had been made me shake with pain. Then I washed off the sweat and muck from the cattle cars. The cold shower didn't last very long, but we were grateful to have water at all.

After the shower a female *Kapo* took what looked like a rag from a basket and threw one at each of us. These rags turned out to be torn dresses to wear. I had a dirty, thin nylon dress with a hole over my breast. That was all I was given. No one had underwear. The thin dress with its red and pink rose pattern was more of a rag than a dress. Frieda's striped dress was many sizes too large for her. Luckily, Eva got a skirt and blouse. We weren't given striped uniforms to wear as some prisoners had been given. We were also given rough wooden clogs for shoes, even though usually we were given two left shoes or two right shoes. Rarely did anyone get a pair that matched or were the right size. Without socks, keeping my shoes on was hard, and right away I got splinters from the rough bottoms scraping against the soles of my feet.

Then we were marched about a mile and a half to Birkenau, the sister camp to Auschwitz. Auschwitz consisted of the gas chambers and the ovens, the death factory. Birkenau was where the workers were housed. We passed electrified wires and were put into Barrack B with two hundred other women. The men's barracks were about three blocks away, but separated from our section by barbed wire.

Barrack B was a large hall with bunks on both sides. Bunks is hardly an accurate descriptor, though. Our beds were just planks of wood built tightly on top of one another. We had to share the bunk with a dozen other women. Frieda, Eva, and I pushed our way into the middle of a row.

As soon as we entered, the onslaught of comments began.

"This is the end of your life," one woman said in Polish. "I've been in Birkenau since 1941. There's nothing to go home to."

"That's not true," I replied in French. "I'm going home. I have two children to take care of. I don't care what you say." I could understand most of her Polish, but I didn't know it well enough to answer in Polish.

When the other women heard my French, they circled us Belgian women like a pack of wild dogs about to attack. "Why do you come so much later than the rest of us?" a Polish woman asked. "We've been here for two years. You French people think you're such big-shots. You come so late. French whores!"

"Is it our fault you've been here two years? Don't talk this way to me." I wasn't going to take it from her and had formed a fist, ready to fight her if necessary.

The Polish woman backed off, and the rest returned to their bunks. We climbed into our bunks to escape the barrage of comments. Lines of nationality divided the barrack. The Nazis had succeeded in getting us to turn on each other. I knew the only ones I could trust were the other Belgian women.

Our bunks were so crowded that we could only lie on our sides. No one had room to lie on her stomach or back. During the night if we turned over, the entire row turned in unison, with much complaining and moaning. The ones on the end of the row sometimes were pushed off the rack entirely and hit the floor. Then she would climb back up and push the others to regain her spot or sometimes try to pry her way in between others in the middle of the rack. We learned to lie as still as possible, but when we felt someone else move, we moved with the others as best we could.

We didn't even have a toilet in the barrack. We had to go outside to a wooden outhouse where a plank of wood had holes cut out as toilet seats. A dozen such holes with no privacy served as our latrine.

I tried holding my breath or breathing into my hands to avoid the toilets' stench, but the odor overpowered everything. I had gotten used to the smells at the circus, and animal dung didn't bother me, but the smell of human excrement was far worse. A lot of time people wouldn't make it to the toilet and defecated wherever they stood or even in their bunks. No toilet paper was available. Some people used straw from our bunks, but others didn't wipe at all and developed skin sores. A few used the hem of the dress they wore. Since there was no running water anywhere, the dress remained soiled. Some women got to the point they didn't care any more.

Down the middle of the barrack was a three-foot wide brick strip where we had to sit in the mornings. Then a *Kapo* would blow a whistle and come through the barrack yelling, "Everybody up!" For breakfast two people brought in the food. We grabbed a cup for a dirty watered-down version of "coffee." Real coffee didn't exist for us, just dirty water. Our piece of bread, about three inches by three inches, was heavy because sawdust was used more than flour.

We went back to our bunks or planks to eat, crowded together like starving animals. Some women saved their bread for later. I learned not to hide it in the barrack because someone else would find it and eat it. If I planned to save the bread for later, I kept it with me at all times. Women had been reduced to the lowest level.

After "breakfast" we went outside for roll call. If someone were missing, we stood for hours until the person was accounted for. Often someone may have died during the night or if some woman couldn't take it any more, she committed suicide by touching the electric fence.

The women who had been there longer had jobs, but we Belgian newcomers were not assigned any type of work. We sat outside in the dirt most of the day. Then for lunch we passed around a chamber pot with soup. We took sips from the same pot. Soup was not a true name for this watery mixture of potato peelings and leaves or grass that pigs would refuse to eat. Occasionally some beans would be thrown in. The Nazis' attack dogs were fed better than we were.

We all suffered in various stages of starvation. My head ached constantly, and my stomach growled so loudly that everyone around me could hear it. It didn't matter, though, because theirs growled too. I grew weak, and my muscles didn't seem to respond to my mental commands. Sometimes I would think so much about food that I began to hallucinate. I thought I was eating some delicious morsel, only to realize, through pain, that I had bitten the inside of my mouth. Others were worse off than I was. Some people looked like their faces had completely sunken in, and only a thin layer of skin stretched across their cheekbones. Their eyes took on a sunken, hollow appearance as they moved like zombies in a trance.

Fights broke out sometimes over how much soup one person had taken. A teaspoonful was all I got at times. I was determined I was not going to fight about an additional teaspoonful of watery soup. This soup and the "coffee" were the only liquids we were given all day. Without running water anywhere, women begged for urine from someone else to drink or even beg for imaginary food. The Nazis were systematically making us feel less than human and act like animals.

I did not see any rats in our barrack. Had I seen any, I would have found a way to eat them. I would have taken meat wherever I could have found it. Even though we were reduced to this level of thinking, not one Jewish prisoner I was around ever resorted to cannibalism.

Never had I realized how hunger could make people act. When you're hungry, you'll steal, lie, cheat or do anything you can for food. Hunger drives you beyond all civilized boundaries. Starvation is unimaginable until it is experienced. Missing a meal or going a day without food is not the same as the endless longing for sustenance to continue life. The awful, gnawing pain drove us to madness. That's all I could think about—staying alive for my children.

Survival became my only goal.

Birkenau barracks and electrified fences

CHAPTER 12—THE DEATH CAMP

Even though no water pooled near our barrack, the mosquitoes were horrible. We could never be rid of them. Luckily, we did not have lice here. Since our heads and bodies had been shaved, we had no hair for the lice to infest. That wasn't the case at other sections of the camps. Eventually the hair on my shaved head began to grow back, but my eyebrows never did. Sometimes the *Kapos* shaved our heads again just for the humiliation of it. It became a sense of hope when our hair began to grow back. They wanted to take that away too.

During the day we nineteen women from Belgium cried, talked about our families, and sometimes sang. Most of the women in the barrack spoke Polish, and some spoke Yiddish. I could speak French, Flemish, Dutch, and German. From Nathan I had learned a little Polish. To survive and communicate, I quickly learned more Polish and even a little Hungarian. I learned enough of these languages to defend myself from the other women.

When I talked to the other women in the barrack, I would try to find someone who knew what had happened to my family members. I asked many women if they had heard of Chana Rozen, my mother, but no one had.

When I asked the *Kapo* in our barrack about my mother, she casually pointed to the smokestacks.

"I don't believe it," I told her.

After her heartless response, I hated the *Kapo*. She had better food and clothing. When most of us had nothing but a thin dress, she had a jacket. This Polish woman would be a thorn in my side. In spite of the

Kapo's cruelty, I held onto the hope I would find *Maman*.

Another woman in the barrack told me about an incident where a Jewish girl and man escaped. It seemed incredible. Supposedly she and this man escaped by wearing SS uniforms, went to a nearby town, were married, and spent some time together, but were caught in the town. Other versions say they were caught trying to cross the border into another country. This story gave us hope we, too, would be free someday. After they were caught, the Nazis executed them in front of the inmates of the camp. I heard the girl slashed her wrists to prevent the Nazis from killing her. She resisted them even to the end, and I admired her courage.

After the war I found out this incident was true. The girl's name was Mala Zimetbaum and the man's name was Edek Galinski. Like me, she had been born in Poland and her family had immigrated to Belgium. She had lived in Antwerp, and today her house bears a marker telling of her courage and her death at Auschwitz.

We tried to hold onto our faith even when it seemed God had forsaken us. Some women tried to observe holy days by lighting a match and saying a prayer at sundown on Friday evening, but if the *Kapos* caught anyone, it meant a trip to the gas chambers. We could mentally pray or think about a special religious rite, but we didn't make a show of it for fear of the *Kapos*.

Every day the *Kapos* would "select" people to be removed from the barracks. They never returned. People were sick all the time with diarrhea and vomiting, but we didn't know what to call the disease or condition. After this initial phase, the sick person couldn't eat or move. Getting sick meant death. I suspected this illness was typhus.

Three to four hundred people were selected each day to go to the gas chambers. The *Kapos* would come around, touch people with a broomstick, and tell them to get out. That was their death sentence. If a person refused to move after being touched, the *Kapo* would beat the person to death with the broomstick. Even if someone moved too slowly after being touched, the *Kapo* was on her in a minute, swinging the broomstick and smashing the person's skull like a melon. When the *Kapo* was in a rage, she wouldn't stop hitting until the person was dead. Female *Kapos* were quite capable of this brutality. They had no hearts. *Kapos* were worse than Nazis because they turned on their own kind.

The Nazis also forced musicians to play for them. They would have music playing as though there was nothing going on. Hearing the beautiful music was eerie, especially when we knew people were dying by the hundreds and thousands every day. We could hear the people going by and hear the music, but we could not look outside the window. That was an act punishable by death. Anyone looking out would be shot. I didn't want to find out whether this was rumor or truth.

We might be called to go outside at any time of the day or night. Being called outside three or four times during the day or night for a head count was not unusual. A *Kapo* would yell, "Everybody, out!" That meant someone was missing. On occasions we stood all night long. In the freezing weather, we had to stand in our thin, flimsy dresses for hours without any coat or blanket. Even if it were a man missing from the men's barracks, we women stood for roll call until he was found. It may have been anywhere between three to six hours before we were allowed to go back inside. One time when a man was missing, they finally found him in the toilet. He had thrown himself in the toilet, hoping they wouldn't look there. All of us suffered if any person were missing. The entire camp was punished for the actions of one person.

About two weeks after we arrived, the Germans gave us a tattoo on our left forearm as a means of identification. We were taken to a room where a person seated at a table grabbed the left forearm. They would use one needle to tattoo the numbers of a thousand to two thousand people before changing the needle.

As usual, I was the first before Frieda and Eva. The person at the table recorded my name before picking up the needle. Encrusted with blood from people ahead of me, the needle looked as though it dripped with infection. He dipped it into some dark solution and began on the letter A on my arm. At the first puncture I jerked, but he held on tighter. Gruffly he said, "Don't move. It only makes it worse."

Gritting my teeth, I tried to steady my left arm with my right and squeezed the muscle. Blood dribbled down my arm and onto the table. The person tattooing me didn't seem concerned and kept puncturing my arm with the rest of the letter A. Dip and puncture. Inject the stinging dye. Dip some more. He repeated this process over and over.

As a nurse I had given shots before and I knew this man didn't have the least notion of how to puncture the skin without causing a great deal of pain. He didn't care how much he was hurting me. It felt like a thousand angry bees had swarmed on me. I gasped for air whenever he dipped the needle in the inky solution. Then I'd brace for the next set of punctures. Dip, stab, inject. Dip, stab, inject. Finally the rest of the numbers were in place.

My identification was A24130. I would no longer be known by my name. To the Nazis I was only a number. Frieda was given A24131, and Eva was given A24132. All the numbers were in sequence. I didn't know what the A stood for and didn't know if the numbers meant over 24,000 people had been in this line before me or what significance the numbers had. Now this number became my identification. Sara Hauptman was gone, and A24130 stood in her place.

The dirty needle caused my arm to swell up twice its normal size. It looked like I had a football under my skin. No infirmaries or hospitals were built to treat us, and we had been warned by others to stay away from the hospital. It was a death sentence. The only form of medicine we could manage was our own urine. The acidic portion of the urine acted as a crude antiseptic.

Cradling our sore arms in front of us, we returned to the barrack. The other women had all been through this same torment and showed no concern for our misery. Most of them had been tattooed the same day they arrived. I don't know why the Nazis waited almost two weeks before giving us our numbers.

We also heard of atrocities that had happened to others upon their arrival at Auschwitz. I heard of an instance when a nine-month old baby was taken from the mother and thrown onto a fire. The mother had to stand and watch her child burn.

The smell of bodies burning was unmistakable. We now knew what that putrid odor was we had smelled from the train miles before we arrived at Auschwitz. We could see the chimneys, the smoke, and the fire. The ash would cover us, and we knew it might be the ashes of our loved ones. Over fifty years later I can still smell it.

CHAPTER 13--STERILIZATION

Whenever the Germans would come around during the *Appell*, or roll call, we were quiet and tried not to draw attention to ourselves. Being noticed might mean a death sentence. Mengele came by us sometimes during these roll calls, looking for people to use in whatever he did in his hospital. We avoided direct eye contact with his icy stares. Anyone who touched him would be killed, and it seemed anyone he touched also died. After a woman had given birth to a child, he took the child, kept it in his so-called hospital, and let it starve to death. He wanted to take notes on how long it would take. When the woman heard her child crying so pitifully, she wanted to die. The women in my barrack said they knew the woman and saw the baby. The mother prayed, "Please, God, let my baby die. Don't let him suffer." Nothing was too cold and calculating for this murderer. That's how Mengele received his title, the Angel of Death.

After knowing what had happened to this baby, other women didn't want to carry a child to term. Most women were sterilized or stopped having a menstrual cycle due to malnutrition and whatever the Nazis put in the soup. Those who got pregnant may have been the victims of a *Kapo* raping them, but others gave themselves willingly to a *Kapo* in exchange for food. A few women may have come into the camp early in a pregnancy and weren't showing yet. All of these were the women who had not yet been sterilized by Mengele. Many of them would try to abort the fetus because they knew what the fate of the child would be if it lived. It meant the gas chamber for a woman who turned up pregnant, and Mengele didn't want her for an experiment.

We hated the *Kapos* for their cooperation with the Nazis and for their treatment of their fellow Jews. These beasts could go into various areas of the camp. Male *Kapos* could enter the women's barracks. Affairs went on between some of them, and when they wanted to be together, the entire barrack was sent out into the yard, no matter the weather. Some raped women or threatened them with the gas chambers if they didn't have sex willingly. I never thought a fellow Jew could sink so low and defile his own people, but it happened. We only had Jewish women in our barrack, but we heard about other barracks with political prisoners, a special section for Gypsies, a family section, and other parts far worse than ours. We also saw twins in the barracks close to ours. I didn't know at the time how Mengele experimented on them, nor what experimentation he planned for others.

As part of the Nazis' Final Solution, Jews were to be sterilized. They didn't want our genes being passed on since they considered us *Untermenschen*, sub-humans. Thus they began a system of mass sterilization. Murder wasn't enough for them. They had different methods of sterilizing women using massive doses of X-rays or drugs.

One day my number was called to report to Mengele's hospital, and I was terrified. Most of his victims did not live. I couldn't force one foot in front of the other and nearly stumbled as I tried to move. Frieda was also on this list of about twenty-five women. We held onto each other as we were herded to Mengele's building. We had no idea what he had in mind for us.

As we entered the room in the hospital, workers shoved us into a large room with tables. We were told to lie down and put our knees up. I didn't know if we were going to be raped, cut open, or some other hideous thing performed. Frieda was as scared as I was.

Mengele and another doctor were preparing syringes. Then Mengele himself inserted something into our uteruses. No one told us what we were being given.

I wanted to scream and run from the room, but I couldn't. If I made any sound, I would be killed. Gripping the side of the table, I shut my eyes. I felt like my insides were on fire. I looked at Frieda. Mengele did the same thing to her and the others who were with us. Then he watched our reactions and took notes.

Horrible cramps and swelling followed the insertion. Mengele watched with sadistic pleasure as we writhed in pain, but he never showed us any compassion. We were test animals in his scientific experiments. When Mengele grew tired of watching us, he told us to go back to our barrack.

Doubled over, I could barely get off the table or walk. I held my stomach and reached for Frieda's hand. Trudging through the mud on the way back to the barrack, Frieda asked me, "Sara, what did they do to us? My insides feel like they're on fire."

"Mine too. I don't know what they did."

"Did he take my virginity, Sara?" Frieda asked. "Is that what it's like?"

"No, Frieda. That's not sex. Even if he punctured you, you're still a virgin. You've never been with a man."

Then Frieda asked what all of us were wondering. "Do you think he made us pregnant? Are we going to have babies?"

"Whatever they put inside us won't be a normal baby," another woman said. "Who knows what kind of a monstrosity he implanted in us!"

"Why would he want us pregnant when they kill women who turn up pregnant?" I asked her. "That makes no sense."

"Does it have to make sense for Mengele to do it?"

I knew she was right. Nothing they did made sense. Having people move a pile of rocks from one side of a road to the other all day long made no sense. Killing innocent people in the gas chambers made no sense. Burning their bodies and using the fat to make soap made no sense.

I could only hope we weren't pregnant. "We haven't had our periods in months," I said to Frieda. "Not since we arrived. I doubt we can be pregnant. It must be something else they did to us."

Days of nausea followed. I thought I was dying. Frieda was as sick as I was. We couldn't eat, but we had to get up. If we stayed on our bunks, we would be selected for the gas chambers. Counting the days after we had been given the drug, we showed no signs of pregnancy. Frieda asked me, "Sara, what was the first sign you had when you were pregnant with Guy?"

"Frieda, you're not pregnant. This isn't what pregnancy feels like. I had morning sickness with Guy, but this is not the same."

Finally after time passed, and we showed no signs of gaining weight, Frieda's fear of being pregnant subsided. Although the thought of what exactly he did do to us gnawed at us day and night.

CHAPTER 14—THE DEPTHS OF MISERY

Male *Kapos* could enter the women's section any time they pleased. I recognized one as a man from my old neighborhood of Anderlecht in Belgium. Abram Bolka had lived on the same street. He had been a heavyset, nice-looking guy in his early thirties with brown hair. Now he was a lot skinnier, but not as skinny as the regular inmates. *Kapos* got better food than the rest of us. He gave me a potato, which seemed like a feast. I hadn't eaten a real potato in months, but I would share it with Frieda and Eva later. I talked to him about what he knew in the camp and about the fates of Belgian people we had both known.

"Bolka, what do you know about my mother?"

"Chana was holding Rosa's child when she went through selection. Mengele sent her to the left."

I began to cry so hard that I couldn't think straight. Gripping my sides, I bent over. "*Maman!* Oh God, not *Maman!* Why? She was only forty-four years old and in good health?"

"Had she not been holding Rosa's baby, she may have lived. When Rosa found out her child died with your mother, she couldn't stand to live any more. She went to the wires."

Electrified wires surrounded the compound and many times people who couldn't take the torment any more committed suicide this way.

"And Albert?" I tried to hold back the tears. "What happened to him?"

"Your younger brother Albert went with your mother to the gas chamber. He might have survived, but he chose to go with your mother to the left. They didn't know left meant death."

Swallowing hard, I managed a reply. "Albert would never have abandoned *Maman*. Even if he had known, he would have gone with her."

"You saw what they do to people who switch lines. I couldn't warn your mother to put the child down and get to the right side. The dogs would have been all over her and Albert. My own father was sent to the left with your mother and Albert. I couldn't get him to the right side either." When Bolka spoke, he showed no emotion. How could he talk about his own father's death so matter of factly?

My mind reeled as I thought about *Maman* and Albert going into that gas chamber. Their bodies burned with the rest. No grave. No remembrance. No *Kaddish* said for them.

Squeezing my eyes shut with grief, I didn't want to hear any more.

"There's more," Bolka continued.

"What do you mean?"

"I heard your brother Jean was shot by an SS soldier when he ran from the train on its way to Auschwitz. At least his was a quick death."

"No, not Jean too." I almost collapsed with grief. I didn't want to ask about Nathan. If he were dead too, I wouldn't want to live. Finally, I mustered the courage to ask him.

"What about Nathan?" I braced myself for his answer.

"Nathan's alive. He's been put to work as a tailor here in the men's section."

Sighing with relief, I was thankful Nathan was alive. "Can you get a message to him? Tell him I'm here."

"I'll try, Sara. I don't know if I can get a message to that part of the camp, but I'll try." Bolka left without offering any consolation. Civilized people, not the near-animals of Auschwitz, consoled each other.

I sat in the dirt overwhelmed with grief. I doubled over, clasping my hands over my eyes. Down on my knees with my arms on the ground, I sobbed. I didn't want to accept that *Maman*, Albert, and Jean were dead. I couldn't stop thinking about them. I couldn't believe they were gone.

I'd never see *Maman*'s smile again or her hands always so busy. Gone was her gentle voice that read to the children. My brothers and sisters had no mother, and my children would never have their *Bobonne*. She was gone.

I felt so empty and lonely. I ached inside wanting to talk to her as we had done so much in the past. Losing my mother was losing my best friend. *Who would guide me now? Who would give me advice on raising children or listen to my day-to-day worries?* She was so full of life and had so much to offer. No one could ever fill the void left by her death.

Jean and Albert were so young. They had never fallen in love, they had never been on their own, and they had never really lived. They would never have wives or children. The world would never know how great a painter Albert could have been. I would never hear Jean's voice as he joked with me. Dying so young wasn't fair.

I wanted to shout at God. *Didn't God listen to my prayers any more? What had my mother and brothers ever done to deserve such a death? Why didn't God intervene? Why did He let them die?*

Then I thought about Nathan. I felt guilty to be happy Nathan was so near. If only I could see him. To be so near, yet so far, hurt me physically. I hadn't seen Nathan in almost two years. I missed everything about him—his smile, his green eyes, his caress, his Polish love songs to me, his joking manner. *What did he look like now? How was he doing?* He had no idea I was so close and thought I was safe in Belgium with the children.

A few weeks later I saw Bolka again. He chewed on his lower lip when he walked in.

"What's wrong?" I felt something horrible had taken place. "Something's happened, hasn't it? Is it Nathan?"

"Nathan was taken to the gas chamber."

"Oh God, no!" I closed my eyes and prayed it wasn't true. My body swayed. I caught myself to keep from falling. I didn't want to live if Nathan were gone.

"How do you know?" I hoped he was wrong.

"He couldn't walk, Sara. He only weighed about eighty pounds. His teeth were rotten. He was selected when he couldn't get up. No one could do anything for him."

My knees buckled underneath me, and I fell to the ground as he told me more. I just wanted this to be a horrible dream from which I would wake up, but I knew it wasn't.

"I asked Nathan for his piece of bread, but Nathan kept his bread with him and said, 'I'm not going to die with an empty stomach.'"

"Nathan said that? He would give away everything if someone asked him. This doesn't sound like my Nathan." I kept hoping he was mistaken. Someone else must have made that statement, not Nathan.

"I swear to God it was Nathan, Sara. I'm sorry." Bolka wasn't mistaken. He had known my family ever since we had gone to school together.

I couldn't believe Nathan was gone. I was so angry I wanted to hit something. Then I cried, put my face in my hands and thought, *No, it can't be true. No, God please, not Nathan.* When I could cry no more tears, I just sat there red-eyed with dry heaves.

Frieda and Eva came over to console me, but there was no consolation knowing Nathan was gone. I wanted to die with him. I felt numb and hopeless. Nothing mattered any more. I thought about going to the wires. Their siren song of death enticed me to come closer. *So what if I died? Who would care?* I figured it might be my time tomorrow. Auschwitz is a death camp. We were all going to die sooner or later.

"Where is God?" I said out loud. "What kind of a God would let us die like this?"

From that point on, I was so angry with God I couldn't believe He even existed. A loving God would not let His people go to the gas chambers and the ovens. Why didn't God spare Nathan? Nathan was a good man. He had never hurt anyone. Where was God? I gave up praying because my prayers fell on deaf ears. Or God didn't exist at all. That day I became an atheist. For me there was no God.

Then I thought about Guy and little Monique. They would never see their father again. Would they see me? I was alive by chance alone. Now I only had the children. For the children's sake I had to survive. I got up and made sure I got my portion of soup that night. That day something in me began to change. A callousness started to build up. I knew I would do whatever it took to survive and see my children again.

I tried not to get involved in other people's problems. If a fight broke out, I walked away. If someone found another woman's piece of bread under the straw, it didn't matter to me. The stupid woman shouldn't have left it in her bunk. I only cared about my Belgian friends. If something happened to one of them, I reacted.

One day a Polish girl pushed me too far. She was a girlfriend of the same *Kapo* I hated, and she stole Frieda's shoes, the rough wooden shoes like Dutch clogs.

"This is not right," I said to Frieda. "You haven't done anything to her. I'm going to get your shoes back."

"It's all right. I don't want to fight over shoes." Suffering from severe malnutrition, Frieda no longer had the strength to fight.

"No, it's not right of her to steal your shoes. You need those shoes. I'm going to get them back."

I went over to the girl and asked for the shoes back. She said something in Polish and gave me a go-to-hell look, so I punched her in the stomach. My brothers had taught me well how to fight. The Polish girl doubled over and threw up. When I took the shoes back, she reported me to her *Kapo* girlfriend. The sadistic *Kapo* came over to defend her lover. She hit me and called for a male *Kapo* friend of hers. He held me back as she comforted her lover. "Let's see how you fight with the gas chamber," she said.

I'm surprised the male *Kapo* didn't kill me right then. Instead he and another male *Kapo* decided to teach me a lesson about defying a fellow *Kapo*. They took me in front of a gate between the barracks and the kitchen. They forced me to kneel down on black charcoal and hold two bricks, one in each hand.

"If you drop one," one of the *Kapos* said, "you'll get two more. You will stay here until I decide you've had enough."

I knew better than to ask any questions. I have no idea how long I remained kneeling on those rocks with the weights in my hands. The muscles in my arms began to knot, and the circulation to my arms seemed to stop. I stared straight out in front of me watching the wind blow the weeds in the distance beyond the barbed wire. I couldn't see any birds or animals, but I watched for some sign of life.

All the while I thought about the block elder and her girlfriend. The girlfriend was the one who should have been punished. She was the thief. I was simply getting back what belonged to Frieda. From now on Frieda will have to sleep with her shoes under her head to protect them. These women think nothing of stealing. At first I thought they would steal only food, but they would steal whatever they want. The only law here was survive any way you can.

That cold morning I had nothing more than the flimsy dress, but this time my anger must have kept me warm. I kept thinking of ways to get even with the girl I hit. She was a small person and I could take her easily, but her girlfriend protected her. Her *Kapo* girlfriend carried a broomstick and would use it on any hapless person who got in her way. She wouldn't hesitate to beat me to death as she had others in our barrack. I would avoid her while I plotted my revenge.

I knew it was foolishness, but imagining the *Kapo* in my place gave me satisfaction. I would survive just to spite her. They were using me as an example to the new women to break their spirits and to break my own, but I knew I would not give in. If I gave in at this first punishment, far worse ones would follow. I had to maintain my resistance or lose my sanity.

After a while I couldn't feel anything except the black rocks digging into my knees. I looked down and noticed they were bleeding. The jagged edges of the rocks knifed into me as I tried to keep my balance and not fall over. Every time I shifted my knees a little the dagger-like stones only ground in deeper.

I grew tired and kept swaying. My back didn't support me very well and ached like someone squeezing my spine in a vise. My muscles in my arms, thighs, and back were rigid. I hoped I could hold up.

As the day progressed, it got warmer. Then I wished the coolness of the morning would return as the sun beat down on me. Beads of perspiration rolled from my forehead into my eyes. I tried to wipe them on my shoulder, but it did little good. I tried hanging my head down, but I was afraid I'd fall flat. Raising my head again, I stared into the field beyond the wires.

Ash from the crematoriums fell on me, coating my outstretched arms. I couldn't wipe the ash from my face or eyelashes. I tried shaking my head to get the ashes off, but it only helped a little. Every time the ash mixed with my perspiration black streaks smeared my dress sleeve. Rubbing my face against my shoulder, I succeeded in getting some off and could only imagine what my blackened face must look like. I probably resembled a golem or banshee.

After what seemed to be hours my arms shook from exhaustion. Through sheer will I kept them up. I kept imagining they were my children, and I couldn't let them fall. I couldn't let Guy and Monique down. I had to protect my children. Bowing my head a little, I summoned all the strength I could muster to keep my arms from falling.

Afraid my fingers would go numb, I tried flexing them around the bricks to keep a bit of circulation going. My greatest fear was I wouldn't be able to hold the bricks. I wanted desperately to let them go and fall over. They felt like a hundred pounds. The longer I kneeled the heavier they got. Collapsing onto the jagged rocks would release me. I shook that thought from my head. That way of thinking was deadly.

In my mind I silently repeated words to songs I knew. Anything to keep going. I couldn't fall over. I had to keep my mind occupied with any trivia—dates, teachers I had in school, the alphabet, numbers, past holidays. Then I thought about Papa, *Maman*, Nathan, Albert, and Jean. With delirium, I imagined talking with them.

Closing my eyes, I saw Papa's face. Through a daze I heard him say, "You can't play rough like the boys. You're a young lady, Sara." I shook my head again realizing I was hallucinating. It scared me to think I had lost touch with reality. Papa was right though. My hitting the *Kapo's* girlfriend got me into this mess. I had to obey or I'd die.

When the *Kapo* finally came to get me in the late afternoon, I was totally spent. I didn't have the energy to stand on my own. He told me I could drop the bricks. My arms didn't obey the command from my brain. I couldn't drop them at first. It felt as though my hands and the bricks had become one. Disgusted with me, the *Kapo* grabbed my right arm and dragged me to my feet. "I'm surprised you made it," he said. "Most people don't. You're lucky you're here and not in the gas chamber."

I didn't say anything. Somehow I stumbled back to the barrack where Eva and Frieda helped me onto the bunk. Frieda rubbed my arms and Eva rubbed my legs to get the circulation going. They tried to get some of the black rocks from my knees, but many were too deeply imbedded. All I wanted to do was let my arms remain down. I didn't care I had no food or coffee that day. I had endured, and that was enough.

It took weeks before I was able to get all the tiny, black pieces of rock out of my knees. I picked at them with my fingernail until I worked the slivers from under my skin. Using my own urine to put on my knees, I hoped they wouldn't get infected.

In the end, Frieda got her shoes back and the *Kapo's* girlfriend didn't bother either one of us again. She was afraid of me. The others left us alone too, and I learned to be wary of those who cooperated with the Nazis.

I was surprised about the lesbian relationship between the *Kapo* and her lover. I had never imagined such a relationship existed between women. At first I thought it was laughable, but when I saw them kissing and acting like lovers, I realized it was no joke.

Three months or three years in a death camp seemed the same. Passage of time meant nothing to me. One day was like the next. We had no means of keeping track of the time, and I was never sure of the month, day, or hour. The only thing that kept me going was the thought of my children. They needed me. I repeated to myself, *You're not going to the gas chamber. Live for your children*

Every day we waited to die. We waited for them to come and pick us out. Some prisoners would hang themselves. Every day someone couldn't take it any more, but we who were still alive suffered too. We had to stay in the cold and wait until a *Kapo* found the body. All this time I didn't want to have anything to do with anyone. I kept to myself. I didn't fight openly any more, but I was biding my time to get even.

Within the same week that I was punished, Bolka told me about a transport going to Dachau in Germany. "Go there."

"I cannot. Out of the hundreds of people who came from Belgium with me, only nineteen of us women are left. I cannot leave them and go. We're sticking together."

"All right, I'll try to take you all together. I think they need people in Dachau. I don't know if you'll get the gas or the water, but you have to take the chance."

I don't know why he helped me to get to Dachau. Maybe he felt sorry for me. Maybe he wanted to prove he had some humanity left. Whatever his reason, he was successful in getting all nineteen of us women on the list of over three hundred people going to Dachau, an unbelievable miracle.

We were given a shower and a blanket. Then we walked for miles. Many people didn't have shoes, but we walked. We were walking out of Auschwitz. I didn't care what lay ahead. Leaving Auschwitz was enough.

As we were walking, we began to itch and opened our blankets. They were full of lice. I had never seen so many lice in my life. In our barrack we didn't have a problem with lice because no one had any hair. Now we were being eaten alive by lice.

I had an idea about how to get rid of the bloodsuckers. "Let's turn the blankets to the outside," I said to Frieda. "Maybe the lice will fall off or freeze." We tried this, and it helped some.

After our long walk we were taken once again to a cattle car. The car was headed to Dachau in Germany. Maybe two hundred to five hundred people were crowded on this train. Sometime in the fall of 1944 we left. I had no idea what our fate would be when we arrived, but at least we were leaving Auschwitz. Anything had to be better than Auschwitz.

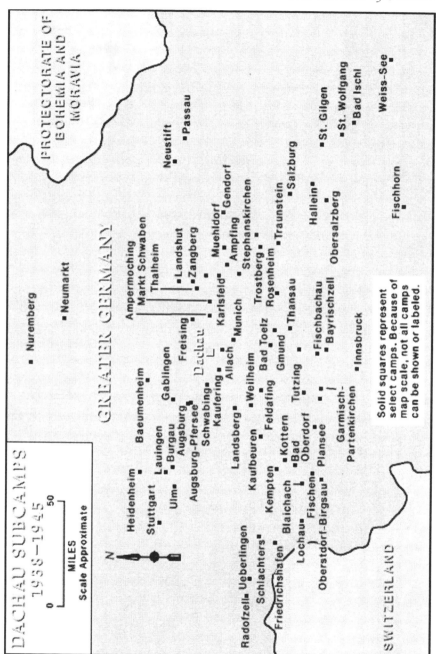

Map of Subcamps of Dachau
Courtesy of United States Holocaust Memorial Museum

CHAPTER 15—THE LION'S DEN OF DACHAU

We arrived at Dachau at night. I had no idea what day or month it was, though I knew it was 1944. Later research showed I arrived October 27, 1944. This concentration camp, the first one created by the Nazis, was located in a forested area of southern Germany although farms and houses were located nearby.

Dachau had an iron, latticed-work gate with the familiar slogan, "Arbeit Macht Frei" centered in a square in the middle of the gate, unlike Auschwitz's slogan which was on an arch above the entrance. Both were the Germans' idea of cruel irony. Work would not make us free. The only way out appeared to be through the smoke of the ovens.

Dachau had ovens, but we didn't see any gas chambers. On arrival, we were separated, men to one side and women to another. The barracks and camp looked better than Auschwitz. Grass grew around the buildings. Thirty-four wooden barracks, seventeen on each side, resembled the ones at Auschwitz, but inside there were no tiers of bunks. Only one row of bunks lined my barrack, and we had straw to sleep on. I was put into Barrack 11 along with Frieda and Eva and the others from Belgium. Luckily we were kept together.

Dachau was a huge complex of camps with over thirty subsidiary camps. Many prisoners from a variety of countries worked on armaments. Not all the prisoners were Jewish here. Some were political prisoners, including Catholic priests who had openly opposed the Nazis.

Soon after our arrival when we were in the yard of the camp, a starving skeleton of a teenager or maybe a man came up to me. Determining the age of a person was difficult when starvation had taken its toll on a body.

"I'm hungry," he told me.

I took pity on this poor soul and gave him my soup. I could do no less.

While he was eating, I realized he was one of the Bolka boys from Brussels. The Bolkas had rented an apartment on the fourth floor from my parents years before my father died. Their father bought from my father's wholesale grocery business for their grocery store. I knew this kid from the neighborhood. Papa gave him red candy when he came to the store. I figured I could give him my soup, and maybe he would survive another day. His brother and Jean had been friends. The boy told me his brother and Jean had both been partisans with the resistance. Jean had also worked with the Lifshitz brothers in the underground.

"My God, I saw one of your brothers in Auschwitz," I told this boy.

"I heard he was a *Kapo*. I don't want anything to do with him."

"He's your brother."

"I don't care. If he's a *Kapo*, he's dead to me. He's not my brother."

I felt so sorry for this boy. The only thing I could do for him was give him my soup, but I had no idea giving away food was forbidden.

The next morning two *Kapos* and a German SS man came into the barrack. The *Kapos* held the Bolka boy between them. The *Kapos* carried whips and a strange bench-like device. I had no idea what was going on.

"Who gave this man some soup?" the German SS man asked.

I didn't answer because I didn't understand what was wrong with giving my soup away. I waited for a minute, confused.

"Who gave away the soup?" he repeated. He looked as if he were going to hit the starving teenager.

I stepped forward. "I gave him my soup. It was my soup. I can do with it what I want."

The German advanced on me like an enraged demon. "That soup is yours to eat. If you don't want it, throw it on the ground, but you are not allowed to give it to anyone."

"It was my soup," I said, looking him in the eye. "I can do with it as I see fit." I refused to be scared.

"It's not yours." The German towered over me and yelled, "Nothing belongs to you. You cannot give anything away. You will be punished as an example to the others."

Then I was scared. I remembered only too well the punishment I received at Auschwitz. How did the German find out I had given away my soup? To be whipped for giving away a watery bowl of turnip soup was beyond belief. I knew saying any more was risking certain death, so I stood, waiting for the inevitable.

The *Kapos* with the whips and the bench-like device came forward. One of the *Kapos* told me to bend over and stretch my arms forward as he held them. They were going to beat me with the whips on my backside.

"Count each lash," the German told me.

"I cannot. I will pass out from the pain."

"Count!" His face turned red and his eyes narrowed to slits.

I knew I would not be able to count to twenty-five. I didn't know if I would survive the first few blows.

"We'll count," whispered one of the *Kapos*.

As I bent over, waiting for the first stinging lash, I wondered who had betrayed me. When the first blow landed on my back, I screamed from the skin-ripping pain. My back and buttocks were bleeding already. When the second blow fell on my backside, I passed out.

Later when I woke up in the infirmary, lying on my stomach, one of the Jewish workers told me to lie still. Alcohol was poured on my open, gaping wounds. The intensity of the alcohol made me scream. After that I don't remember much. Sometime later, I woke up again, but could not roll over. I lightly touched my wounds that were about three or four inches wide. They were still oozing and raw.

The SS doctor told me what happened. The *Kapos* finished counting for me. Frieda and Eva brought me to the infirmary to have my wounds treated.

As I lay there, the doctor said, "I've noticed in your records you were training to be a nurse. I could use a nurse in here. Do you want to work here?"

I didn't want to work indoors. I didn't want to give the illusion of helping people I knew were beyond help. This was not a true infirmary. I had been there long enough to see the young boys coming in who had been raped by the *Kapos*. They were torn up. They would trade sex for a piece of bread. I heard that some fathers prostituted their sons for food. I could do nothing for these boys, and I didn't want to see young children used this way. Most importantly, I had experienced firsthand the brutality of Mengele, an SS doctor. I wouldn't work for this man either.

"No, I want to return to where I was. I prefer to work outdoors."

"All right, but you know you can come here if you change your mind."

After four days, I returned to my barrack. I knew I couldn't stay in the infirmary too long. Those who did turned up dead. To work was to live.

"Who turned me in?" I asked Fried when I returned.

"I think it was the Hungarian woman. She seems too friendly with the Germans. Watch her."

"I'll do more than watch her." I drew my hand into a fist and headed toward her.

"Sara, don't think about retaliation," Frieda said, holding my arm. "It will be worse for you. Not yet."

"She'll get what she deserves some day."

Months later my prediction came true, but not by my hand. The Germans killed the Hungarian woman who had betrayed me. Apparently her closeness to them had been noticed and to keep her quiet, she was shot. Now she would betray no one else.

The Nazis took a number of us to work at the subsidiary camp of Kaufering. I was assigned to a *Fixkommando*. We replaced the train ties bombed by the Allies. Our commander, a soldier in the *Wehrmacht*, was in his thirties and wasn't brutal like the guards in Auschwitz.

We worked in shifts with about eighty people in each work detail. I was on the night shift with Frieda. We went out at approximately eight o' clock at night with our lanterns and worked until sunup. Then we went back to the barrack and slept. Other shifts worked during the day. Eva, Frieda's mother, was on a day shift and worked in another area, but she was in the same barrack as we were.

Since we were working, we received better food than at Auschwitz. Yet, they didn't give us adequate clothing for working outdoors at night. I asked for better shoes for us. Taking a risk, I spoke to the *Wehrmacht* soldier in charge because I thought he would listen. I realized they needed our labor; things weren't going well for the Third Reich.

"If you want us to work better, give us shoes. We cannot work like this," I said.

"You're going to work," he said.

"No!" I stood my ground. "If we don't have shoes, we're not going to work. It's too cold and it's freezing. If you want us to do a good job, we need shoes."

Three days after I spoke out, he gave us real shoes to wear, not the wooden clogs like we had in Auschwitz. These were real leather shoes.

This subsidiary camp of Dachau was far better than Auschwitz. Here they allowed us to shower once in a while, and we weren't afraid gas was going to come out. We actually had soap and towels. Our hair was allowed to grow back, but with that came the lice. Lice covered everyone, and we were constantly itching and bleeding from their bites.

At Kaufering, we mixed with other types of prisoners, not just Jewish prisoners. Some were here for political reasons, for refusing to join the Nazi army, for Communist affiliations, for homosexuality, for helping Jewish people, or for any reason the Nazis wanted to imprison someone. If a man didn't join the army willingly, he was accused of being a homosexual or a Communist and sent to the camps. Many men joined Hitler's army not because they were avid Hitler supporters but to avoid going to the camps,.

A Catholic priest in his fifties was in the group. Father John was tall, bald, skinny, and had a scar on his chin. Assigned to the same work crew, I often talked to him.

"Why are you here?" I asked. "You're a priest. Of all people, why would a priest be in a concentration camp?"

"First they told me I was arrested because I had a Jewish ancestor somewhere in my lineage, maybe as far back as ten generations. Then when they couldn't prove that, they accused me of being a Communist."

"So now the Nazis are arresting their own priests?"

"I don't consider the Nazis Christians. What they are doing is not Christ's teachings."

"How were you arrested?"

"I spoke out against the Nazis in church during Sunday mass. See this scar on my chin?"

I nodded.

"The same SS soldiers whom I had baptized as infants arrested me right after the service. They pushed me down the steps of the church. That's how I got this."

This priest was a good man, but speaking out was dangerous.

I got to know Father John better and jokingly asked him a question I had wondered about since I was a child.

"What do priests wear under those robes?"

He looked at me, surprised and amused. "Underwear. We do wear underwear. Mischievously he started to pull up the hem of his robe. "Do you want to see?"

"No, no, of course not," I answered somewhat embarrassed. "I was just curious. Now I know." Never shy, I wanted to know. I'm glad my curiosity didn't bother him.

The guards were more lax here than at Auschwitz. While we worked, they would sit in a guardhouse, drink coffee, and listen to music on the radio. They didn't care if a German man came over and talked to us. Concern about one of us escaping never entered their minds. If even one of the crew disappeared, we knew they would shoot the entire group.

When our crew worked during the day, we met a young German farmer named Heinz who lived with his mother and father on their nearby farm. He seemed to be a decent person who just wanted to help us. He was short and husky with blond hair, rosy cheeks, and wire-framed glasses. A nice-looking guy who dressed in the traditional farmer's clothing of overalls and a shirt, he had a friendly smile. He brought us fresh milk, soup, bread, and occasionally an apple. What a treat that apple was! We hadn't seen fruit since we were arrested. We each took turns, getting just one bite of apple. Sometimes up to twenty people got a small bite from the same piece of fruit.

Even Heinz's mother and father, who were in their fifties, came out to meet us and bring us food. His father, a heavy-set rancher with graying hair, and his mother, who always wore a long dress and scarf, were nice people. They were not like the other townspeople who watched us go by and made fun of us. Some of the townspeople sat on their porches and insulted with ugly names as we walked by to work on the tracks. After the war, these same townspeople denied they knew what was going on in the camps. They saw us walking by daily and insulted us every evening.

Thank goodness Heinz and his family were not like the others. Whatever food they gave me, I would share with others. I took some back for Eva in the barrack and for others I knew who did not have a chance to work outside and get food. Heinz and his family also loaded milk pails full of soup for the workers and guards.

The guards always got better food than we did. One time I switched the pails. We ate their soup and when the guards tasted what we had to eat, they spit it out. Heinz worried about what they would do, but I told him I would play innocent and cover it up.

I knew the middle-aged guard was basically a nice man. He had never beaten us and was decent in all his actions. He had three stripes on his sleeve and was in charge of this group. We did good work for him, and he respected us. He let us sing, got us shoes when we needed them and got us coats too. I knew I could probably get away with the switch with this guard. When the soup switch was discovered, this middle-aged guard called me over.

"What did you do? Did you switch the soups?"

"The pails look the same," I lied. "I couldn't tell which one was yours. We ate yours by mistake."

"Do you expect me to eat this pig slop? Couldn't you tell the difference?"

"No, except yours was delicious. It was a good dinner. If you don't want me to get the pails mixed up, next time put your name on yours."

Surprised by my outspokenness, he just shook his head and said good-naturedly, "*Kleine Puppe!* You're such a little doll. Even if you were sent to the fires, you probably wouldn't burn."

He let me get away with the switch, and we all enjoyed a great dinner that night.

Heinz, the farmer, was very good to us. He asked me once if I wanted to escape. By the way he talked, I suspected he had done this before and helped others to escape.

"Sara, I can get you out of here. I can get you false papers and take you away from here."

"I cannot disappear. If I do, everyone on the crew will be shot."

"The end of the war is near. Let me help you."

"If the end is near, I'll survive in the camp. I can't risk the lives of others just for myself."

"Sara, I love you. You could come with me, marry me, and I'd take care of you."

"Heinz, I'm a widow," I answered, somewhat surprised. "I have two children waiting for me to take care of them. I can't run away with you."

"Then just pretend you are married to me. You don't really have to marry me. I want to save you. Let me take you out of here."

"No, I can't let you take the chance of being killed or the others being shot. What about your parents? It's not good for them. They might be tortured if we disappeared. I don't want to hurt them. If the Americans are close, they can help me."

"If you're worried about another friend, I could take more than just you. I could help two or three of you escape."

"No, it's too dangerous for you and for us. I'll wait for the Americans."

"If you change your mind, I'll be here, waiting." He walked away with his hands buried deep in his overall pockets.

I suspected he might have been involved in the underground. If he could get false papers, he had to have connections. Still, I couldn't take the chance of the Germans shooting the others for my freedom. I prayed he was right about the end of the war being near.

Frieda and Eva worried I would open my big mouth at the wrong time or do something to get in trouble. While working in the underground, I developed a sixth sense about which people to approach and which ones to avoid. I planned to sneak over to the kitchen and find some bread.

"Are you a *meshuggeneh*, a crazy woman?" Frieda asked. "Do you want to get caught and beaten again?"

"What's she up to now?" Eva asked.

"I was thinking about going to the kitchen," I said. "I want to find some bread."

"You're going to get yourself killed one day, Sara," said Frieda. "You go too far."

I listened to her this time and didn't sneak out, but my stubborn nature didn't change.

Normally we slept during the day since we worked at night. One morning we were called outside to the *Appelplatz*. While we stood in our usual rows of five, wondering what was going on, two boys, one about sixteen and the other about seventeen, were paraded in front of the formation. Their hands were tied behind their backs with ropes, and they had been beaten.

I heard later that a transport came in and one of the boys had heard his mother was on the transport. The two boys, late last night, sneaked under the wires to go to another barrack to find the boy's mother. The guards caught them.

The Nazis were going to hang these teenagers for sneaking out of the barrack. They were put on a stool with a noose around their necks. I'll never forget the terror in their eyes.

We could not cry or look away; if we did, we would be beaten. We were forced to watch the whole thing as they pushed the stools from under the boys. Their bodies jerked with convulsions on the ropes. We wanted it to be over quickly, but it wasn't.

"If you do the same thing, this will happen to you," said one of the Nazis in charge of the hanging. "You will hang the same way."

After watching so much death and misery, I tried to find something that reminded me of home and normal things. While I worked on the tracks, I watched a gray bread wagon drawn by two brown horses. I can't explain my strange fascination with the horses, but I was drawn to stare at them whenever they passed. I couldn't make out the facial features of the driver who delivered bread with this wagon, but the horses were beautiful to watch.

People died at Kaufering, but usually from exhaustion or malnutrition. People there knew I had trained as a nurse and often sought my help when someone was injured. One time a young boy about sixteen or seventeen years old approached me while we were working.

"Why are you crying?" I asked him.

"Sophie told me to come to you and talk to you," he said.

Sophie was a girl who worked with me and stayed in the same barrack.

"What's the matter?"

"My arm's all blue," he said. "I'm afraid if the Germans see it, they'll kill me. I'll be shot. What should I do?"

The others in camp knew I had studied nursing before the war.

"Cut my arm off if you have to. Do what you have to do. I want you to help me."

I looked at the boy's infected arm, turning a bluish-black color. I knew I would have to amputate part of his thumb to allow the infection to drain. With a piece of wire, I severed about an inch of his thumb. He didn't feel it when I cut between the joints. Dark black blood and pus gushed out. He said he could feel his arm, but not the cut. I told him it would continue to drain and he would feel it soon enough. I clamped the flaps of skin together with the wire.

"Pee on the cut," I told him.

"Why?" he asked horrified. "I don't understand."

"Urine has acid in it. If you don't pee on it, you can get a worse infection and die."

When he came back, I tore off a piece of my dress and tied it around his hand. He went back to work as though nothing had happened. In a few days when it had completely drained, I sewed it up with stitches. I improvised with a piece of wire for a needle. He was moved to another barrack, and I didn't see him again for a long time.

During this time I shared a bunk with three teenage daughters of a Hungarian rabbi. Two of the girls sneaked to the kitchen, about ten to fifteen feet from our barrack, to get food. While they were in the kitchen, a Polish *Kapo* tried to rape one of the girls. Her sister ran back and told me what was happening.

When I got there, he had his shirt off and had her down on the ground. She struggled to fend him off. I wanted to kill him.Rushing him from the back, I pulled him by his hair off the girl. I punched him in the neck. Wanting to choke the life out of him, I hated everything he stood for. He was in his thirties and fat from working in the kitchen.

"How dare you do this to two children!" I yelled at him. "You try it again, and I'll kill you."

I didn't know how much anger I had bottled inside me nor how strong I had become working on the tracks. I truly believe I could have killed him with my bare hands.

Rubbing his neck and gasping for air, the *Kapo* didn't say anything. I think he knew better. Had he said anything to set me off again, I would have finished him.

"Let's go," I told the girl. I dread to think what would have happened to those teenage girls if I hadn't been there. The girl's sister was watching from the fence. When I got them back together, the one at the fence helped her trembling sister back to the barrack. I waited a few moments to make sure the *Kapo* wasn't going to follow us. Satisfied he wasn't, I returned to the barrack after the girls.

A few weeks later, I was going to warm myself up by huddling closer to my bunkmate, one of the Hungarian girls. She didn't move. I shook her, but again she didn't move. I feared the worst. She was dead, yet we hadn't realized it for two weeks. We worked different shifts and thought she was on another shift. We hadn't noticed the smell because we were living like animals. The stench was always with us.

Her body had begun to decompose. Even her sisters hadn't realized she was dead. When the *Kapos* came to oversee the removal of her body, the legs separated from the torso when we moved her. This ghoulish scene from a nightmare was everyday life in the camp, a Nazi hell on earth.

Here at Dachau more *Kapos* than guards carried out the Nazi commands. The *Kapos* were as cruel as the ones at Auschwitz, but the soldiers were not as sadistic. Maybe they sensed the end of the war was near, and they were losing. At the end of 1944 we saw the American bombers flying over. It filled us with hope to see them so near. We kept thinking the end couldn't be too far off.

More and more people kept arriving on transports. I suppose the Germans, who were losing ground to the Allied forces, were sending more prisoners to mainland German strongholds, such as Dachau. We heard about a transport of political prisoners arriving from Greece that had practiced cannibalism. They waited for people to die and ate pieces from the corpses to keep themselves alive. That was the first and only time we had heard about such a thing.

Sometime in the spring of 1945 we were taken out of the barrack when Allied airplanes flew over. The soldiers ordered us to wave handkerchiefs at the pilots. They wanted us to be human shields. Knowing the Allies wouldn't fire on people waving white flags, we would be bait to lure the aircraft closer before the Nazis opened fire. We refused, and the Nazis began to shoot people out in the field.

Just before my row was ordered to the front to wave the handkerchiefs or be shot, the German SS doctor from the infirmary called me out of the line. With trance like movements, I stepped toward him.

"Stay in this line," he told me. Turning to some soldiers of lesser rank, he said to them, "I need her. She's a nurse."

I remained in the forest while a thousand people were shot down with machine guns.

Row upon row fell on the bodies already on the ground. As quickly as the guns could be fired, people fell in waves, turning the green grass into a red sea. Not all died immediately. I heard their moans and saw them writhing on the ground, trying to crawl away. The SS Nazi machine gunners took special delight in picking off those who were still alive.

As the sound of the aircraft faded and all movement in the field stopped, we marched back to the barracks. Half did not return.

One of the men killed in the thousand had been a resistance fighter in Belgium. I had seen him at the courthouse in St. Gilles. A young, good-looking man, his life should not have ended in a field in Bavaria. All the time we were walking back, I kept thinking I should be dead right now. It should have been me.

I felt grateful to the doctor for saving my life, but I mourned the loss of the others. In return for his saving my life, I worked some in the infirmary in Landsberg, another subsidiary camp of Dachau. All I could give people who suffered terrible pain and were possibly dying was an aspirin. I didn't want to be in the infirmary, but I felt I owed it to the doctor.

After counting aspirins and putting the bottle in the cabinet, I talked to the doctor. I had heard some of the other Germans call him Heinrich, but I referred to him as *Herr Doktor.* I don't remember exactly how our conversation started, but I had the boldness to ask him some questions.

"Why did you save me?" I asked. "What difference does one Jewish life make?"

Moving a stack of papers from the corner of his desk, he sat down. "You're different, Sara. You have character. You're not afraid. You don't fight unless there's a reason, and you're not embarrassed to clean yourself in the snow."

"So what? Everyone has seen it before. I want to be clean. You Germans have taken away all my pride. I don't have any left. I do what I have to."

The words had come out before I could stop them and I waited with fear. Strangely enough, he allowed me to speak openly with him.

"Before the war I had never known a Jew. I believed all the propaganda in the newspapers and the newsreels. I believed all the stories about the Jews. You're the first Jewish person who's ever talked to me."

"If you know it's all lies, why do you continue to stay in the German army?" I moved a step closer.

"I have no choice now, but I won't stay much longer." He seemed to be lost in thought. "I'm not proud of what I've done," he said. "I was caught up in the spirit of nationalism for the Fatherland. I was young. I wanted to have the uniform and the boots. I wanted to belong. The uniform made a young man very attractive to the girls. Now I know better, but it's too late."

"Why?"

"You've seen the planes. It won't be long now. The Allies will find the records and know I was part of the SS. It doesn't matter what happens to me. I worry about what will happen to my wife and children."

"Where are they?"

"In Frankfurt. My son and daughter don't know I'm SS. I never told them."

That seemed strange to me because most SS soldiers wore their uniforms as badges of honor, but this man didn't want his children to know.

I didn't ask the doctor why he kept his activities in the SS secret from his children, and the subject never came up again.

True to his word, the German doctor didn't remain long in the camp. He left a few days after saving my life,

We heard tanks, but didn't know which side they were on. An older German soldier of the *Wehrmacht*, not SS, told us not to fight.

"The Americans are coming," he said. "Hold on."

Sometimes he would throw us some bread and would let us read the newspapers. He didn't like the SS officers and didn't want to be in the German army. Because he didn't want to fight, he was put in the camp as a guard. A lot of soldiers may have been in his same position. They didn't want to fight for Hitler, but they were afraid for their families if they refused. One day this older soldier just disappeared. We never learned what happened to him.

In April 1945 the SS guards came into the barrack and infirmary and told us not to come out. If we came out, we would be shot. For three or four days we kept hearing the tanks getting closer and closer. We were afraid to go out. On the fourth day, I could stand it no longer. When I looked out, I couldn't see soldiers anywhere. I was in the infirmary and said to a Jewish man who also worked there.

"Something's wrong here," I said to him. "I'm going out to see where the guards are."

"You're crazy. Don't go out. They'll shoot you."

"I'm dead anyway. I'm not going to stay in here any more and starve. I want to know what's going on."

"Let me go with you then."

"No, let me go first. I may have a better chance; they may not shoot a woman as quickly as they would you." When I looked out, I couldn't see anyone in the towers.

" No one is in the guard towers," I said.

"Let's go see."

The camp was empty except for us prisoners—no sounds and no guards anywhere. The SS headquarters was cleared out. They had taken everything. We went to the kitchen and saw food. Taking some bread, we went from barrack to barrack and told the others, "Come out. The Germans are gone."

We were afraid it might be some trap set for us by the Germans, so we didn't venture close to the fences and gates.

A day later the sound of the tanks grew louder. Some of the women nearly died of sheer fright from the sound. Thinking we were free, hundreds of people ran to the fences. These people didn't realize the electricity was still on. They were electrocuted, hands charred black by the voltage and their bodies clinging to the sparking wires. They had been so close to freedom.

A few heard the tanks and assumed they were German tanks returning. They died from heart failure, not realizing they were the American tanks coming to liberate us at long last.

Some Americans, wearing green uniforms, rode on the tanks and some walked along beside the tanks, holding their rifles ready to fire if necessary.

"We're Americans," the soldiers called to us, but we didn't know at the time what they were saying.

When we realized the Americans had arrived and the Germans were not returning, a great roar of triumph in a babble of languages soared to greet the soldiers. Standing inside the fences, we watched and waved in jubilation as the tanks stopped and the dust settled.

Then we saw the looks of horror on the faces of our liberators when they saw us. To them we were walking corpses fresh from the grave.

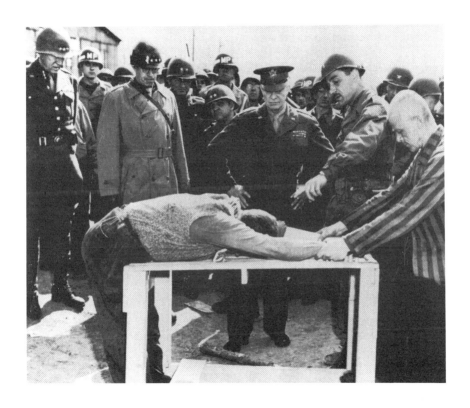

General Eisenhower watching demonstration of how Germans tortured prisoners at Ohrdruf Nord concentration camp. Sara was similarly punished for giving away her soup.
Courtesy of Eisenhower Presidential Library

CHAPTER 16—LIBERATION
APRIL, 1945

When our American liberators saw the prisoners electrocuted on the fences and people collapsing from heart attacks, they gaped in disbelief. Our miserable condition sickened them. These seasoned, battle-weary soldiers threw up when they saw what the Nazis had done to us. They held us and cried.

The soldiers got the electricity turned off and took the bodies down from the fences. They kept asking us questions, but none of us could speak English, and we didn't know what they were asking.

Feeling helpless, they began to hand us food—whatever they had with them. Some of them had chocolate bars and liquor. For many starving people, the rich food was too much because their stomachs were not used to it. People died because their systems could not process that much food so quickly. The GI's were trying to help, but their generosity overwhelmed those weakened by hunger. My fellow prisoners suffered from typhus, diarrhea, and an assortment of ailments too numerous to list.

The cruelest irony of the war manifested itself when hundreds of people died on liberation day. The Nazi legacy of death still reigned. For evil to have this much power was unimaginable.

One of the American officers must have told the GI's to bring us food and clothing. A couple of the GI's tried to let me know they were Jewish too. The words Jewish and *Jude* sounded similar. I understood what they were trying to tell me. Some soldiers showed me their Stars of David to let me know we were the same.

I was so excited and happy that I began to sing. Frieda and Eva joined me as we sang Jewish songs like *Hava Nagila*. The GI's clapped and cheered us on. Those of us who were able danced around and put on the American soldiers' caps. Then I sang the Belgian national anthem and other patriotic songs. A mixture of music filled the air as people from various countries began to sing their national anthems.

While the GI's continued to search the camp, looking for Nazis who might still be lingering in the vicinity, I told Frieda and Eva we should create American flags to wave. We took a white sheet from one of the Nazis' barracks and cut it up. We found red paint to use for the stripes and blue for the square with stars. Though crudely made, the flags served their purpose, and the GI's appreciated our efforts to thank them. The few able-bodied men hoisted the GI's on their shoulders and paraded them around.

The Nazis and the *Kapos* had disappeared before the Americans reached the gates. At least in our part of the camp, none were around. I don't know when they escaped, but they weren't there when I saw the Americans enter this subsidiary camp.

The soldiers found the supply of confiscated clothing, which the Nazis had taken from the prisoners. They showed us the clothing and pantomimed that we should take whatever we wanted. Having clothing that covered our bodies was a luxury. Simple items, such as underwear and socks, were *mitzvahs*, blessings.

Since Kaufering and Landsberg were so close to each other, they put the survivors who needed the most intensive medical attention together at Landsberg and set up an infirmary. Later this camp became a Displaced Persons camp or DP camp.

I don't know how much time elapsed between our liberation and the day General Eisenhower arrived. On that memorable day soldiers snapped to attention and checked their uniforms. An official-looking jeep drove up and parked in the middle of the camp. Eisenhower's chauffeur, a short, young woman wearing a uniform, tried to tell us something in English, but no one could understand her. Then she asked in French if anyone could speak the language.

"I can speak French," I answered.

Frieda and Eva pushed me forward to speak for all of us.

The young chauffeur told me the man next to her was General Eisenhower. She translated for the general. Even though she had a British accent, her French was beautiful.

General Eisenhower told her something in English. Smiling, this tall man came over and kissed my cheeks. "Oh, my God, I can speak to you," he said. The chauffeur translated his words for me. He was so happy. Then he asked me to attend a meeting and give them information concerning the camp.

On our way to a large meeting room, the general had his chauffeur translate for him.

"I'm glad I have someone to translate. We usually find someone who can speak English. We're sorry we couldn't get to you sooner," he said. The chauffeur added that the Russians had liberated Auschwitz.

Inside the office the officers wanted to know how long we had been in the camp, when I had last seen Germans in the camp, about the number of prisoners, the treatment by the Germans, and the condition of the people who had survived. The general said they would leave medical units to help us. He explained how vital my role would be as translator. Then he gave the chauffeur an MP armband, and she helped me put it on.

"You take care of them because you're the only one to speak the languages," she explained. "Don't let them out of the hospital. Will you wear this as an honor?"

"Yes, I'll do whatever I can."

"You're in good hands. The American doctors will take care of you."

As I was about to leave, General Eisenhower said to me through the chauffeur, "Come to the United States after the war. You would like it."

I never forgot his invitation. He planted a seed that day with those few words.

The Americans had other business to attend to, and I returned to my friends. Frieda and Eva examined my armband with admiration. They were proud of me for translating for such an important man. General Eisenhower left the same day, but as he had ordered, medical units were left behind to help us.

The doctors treated those who were the most ill with typhus first. People continued to die by the hundreds in spite of the medical help from the Americans. The entire compound was quarantined to protect those outside the camp from contracting typhus. In a way we were captives again, but we realized these doctors had a duty to protect the uninfected. They gave those of us without typhus inoculations against the disease. Frieda, Eva, and I received these shots. We were among the lucky few who were healthy enough to get around on our own. We fed those who were too weak to feed themselves.

The Americans served us feasts. I couldn't believe we had real loaves of soft, white bread. I could help myself to bread, butter, marmalade, honey, milk, and real coffee. My hands shook as I held that first cup of coffee. It had been so long since I had tasted real coffee that I began to cry and probably filled the cup with more tears than coffee. The American cooks prepared vegetable soup with pieces of meat in it, and we were given three meals a day. To me, it was manna from heaven.

For those too weak to help themselves, we gave them small amounts and nothing too rich, like butter. The American medical personnel would also hold people and feed them. If the sick people could hold down a few spoonfuls of soup, then later on we'd give them more. We had seen early on during the liberation what happened to those who ate too much at a time.

Even though the Americans brought medical supplies, hundreds of people still died daily. Intravenous medicines were available, but people still succumbed. Each day I reported the number of casualties to the commander's staff and helped in the infirmary. I also attended staff meetings with eight people whenever they needed me. Three doctors and two medics kept track of the hospital ward. The commanders in charge of the camp trusted me completely, and I was allowed to go any place in the camp that I wanted. Acting as an MP was a duty I was not going to take lightly.

One of the GI's told me a rumor about Stalin's son being held at Dachau. Certainly Dachau housed many political prisoners; however, this was news to me. More events that happened at the main camp were also news. What I witnessed at the liberation of our sub-camp was completely different than what happened at the main camp.

Within a short time the Americans caught thirteen SS women who had performed barbarous acts. One had used the skulls of inmates as grisly lamps with light bulbs in the eye sockets. Another had used the skin of Jewish people for wallpaper. These women treated the bodies of human beings like trophies to be displayed, and I was determined to see them hanged for their crimes.

On May 8, 1945, things changed for me. We heard the Nazis had surrendered officially to the Allies. Everyone reacted in different ways. Some cried with happiness, others drank too much, and some gave thanks that it was over. I just continued to perform my duties. There would be time for celebration later.

That same day in the hospital I saw two men who didn't need to be there.

"Why are those men in there?" I asked Frieda.

I had to account for whoever was in the infirmary, and these men had not checked with me. Furthermore, they were drunk. The American soldiers gave them liquor to celebrate the liberation, and one of these men was stinking drunk in the hospital. I was mad at the Jewish hospital guard for letting these men in and for giving them the bottle of alcohol. I started to shoo them out.

Then one of the men turned around. "Refka, what are you doing here? Where are the children?"

No one called me by my middle name. Only Nathan called me Refka. This drunken man with the broken nose couldn't be my Nathan. But when I stared at his face, his smile was unmistakable. It was Nathan.

The next thing I remember is smelling salts. I brushed them away from my nose. I realized I had fainted. The shock of seeing my husband, whom I thought was dead, must have overcome me. I was told later that he fainted too. Frantically, I sat up and realized Nathan was alive. I touched his arm to make sure he was real. "What are you doing here? I thought you went to the gas chamber."

"I did go to the gas chamber."

"How is it possible? Bolka told me you went to the gas chamber with your piece of bread."

"That's true. I didn't want to give him my piece of bread because he was a *Kapo*. I told him I was going to have a full stomach when I died. He didn't know what happened next because he left."

"So he told me the truth. But if you went to the gas chamber, how is it you're alive?"

"It's a long story. Let's sit on the cots."

Nathan was not as thin as some of the men, but he walked hunched over as though his shoulders ached.

After we sat down, he began his story. "I was working in the coal mines. When I came down with typhus, I was selected to go to the gas chamber. One of the SS soldiers heard my name being called at the door of the gas chamber. He yelled, 'Hauptman? Bring that Jewish *schwein* over here.' I was so weak I couldn't walk to him, but I was still holding my piece of bread in my hands. The other soldiers took me from the truck and dragged me to him. When the others left, he asked me, 'Is your father Moisha Hauptman?' I answered he was. Then this guard said, 'You're not going into the gas chamber. I knew your father. He was always good to me.' It turned out the soldier was the bellboy at the hotel where my father stayed when he was traveling or probably smuggling people out of the country. The soldier said, 'Mr. Hauptman always tipped me well. My whole family lived off those tips. I promised myself I would save the life of a Hauptman, whether he was related to Moisha or not. I could not help your father, but I can save the life of his son.' That's how I found out my father was dead." Nathan paused and wiped his eyes. He put his head in his hands.

"Nathan, I'm so sorry." I put my arm around his shoulder.

He sighed deeply and regained his composure. "That guard took me to an infirmary and told the *Kapos* to feed and clean me. He would be back for me the next morning. He kept me with him every day from then on. He wouldn't let me out of his sight for fear I would be sent to the gas chambers again. I worked as a tailor, and this soldier came every three days to give me food and keep me alive. Then he took me with him to clean up the Warsaw Ghetto. We removed the dead bodies from the buildings. When the soldier was ordered to go to the Russian front, he made sure I would be sent here to Dachau and given a job that had access to a lot of food. That soldier, who was the bellboy, is the only reason I'm alive today. I don't know what happened to him once he was sent to the Russian front. He was probably killed. That was in August of '44."

"What kind of work did you do?"

"When I came to Dachau, I delivered bread with a horse and buggy."

"Was it a gray wagon with two brown horses?"

"Yes. How did you know?"

"It was you. I saw that horse and wagon going by when I was working on the train tracks. I stared at it as though it had a magnetic hold on me. Now I know why I was drawn to it. You were in it."

"Yes." He smiled and asked me, "So where are the children?"

"The children are with Catherine. They're doing all right."

I was lightheaded from my euphoria. My husband, who had been dead to me, was alive again. It was the most joyous resurrection I had ever known, but I was still too shocked to even hug or kiss him. All I did was hold his hand. I noticed the number on his arm of 70442. His also had the Star of David tattooed by his number. I couldn't believe he had survived all these years.

"How did you make it so long in Auschwitz?" I asked him.

"People with this low a number were rare."

"If I had been sent back to the coal mines, I wouldn't be alive. When they realized I was good at making the uniforms, they kept me around. But when I fell asleep at the sewing machine, the Nazis would hit me in the back with their rifle butts to make me work. Since I was useful, they gave me a little food. When I came here, I thought I was in heaven with all the bread I could steal. I traded bread for better clothing, for cigarettes, for vegetables. The bread kept me alive."

I could only stare at him. It was a miracle. Then I remembered the other man who was with Nathan.

Nathan introduced me to his friend, Leon, who was from Germany. He and Nathan had become friends in the camp. They had been digging a tunnel under the barrack in case they needed a space to hide. They used it at the end when the SS came in to shoot the remaining people in the barracks at the sub-camp of Muhldorf. Before they came in, Leon, Nathan, and two other men got into the tunnel where they had also hidden some food and water. They remained in the underground tunnel for four days. When they heard no shots being fired, they thought it was safe to come out. Otherwise, the departing SS would have killed them as they had the other men. Nathan, Leon, and the other two were saved.

Nathan also told me about the dead SS he had seen in the courtyard of the main camp. The American liberators engaged the remaining SS soldiers in battle, killing many of them and taking the rest as prisoners. I was glad the SS members were shot. I hated them for how they enjoyed murdering us. I would have killed one if I had been able to. During my time in the camp, I had sworn if I ever found one of the townspeople who had laughed at me or one of my tormentors at the camp after liberation, I would kill that person. The rage within me overpowered my sense of morality.

While we were still in the infirmary, I introduced Nathan to the Catholic priest I had met on the work crew. Father John was performing last rites for those Catholic prisoners dying from typhus.

"How has she acted?" Nathan asked Father John.

His question stabbed me. *How could he question my behavior? What the hell was he implying?* I got up and stood by Father John.

Father John looked a little dumbfounded. "Sara's been good. She wasn't a *Kapo*, if that's what you want to know. She's a wonderful woman who helped everybody." Father John put his arm protectively around my shoulder.

"Yes, she's so wonderful she even wanted to make sure I had underwear," Father John told Nathan to ease the situation.

"That sounds like my wife." Somewhat embarrassed Nathan said, "She would do anything. One time back in Belgium she rang the doorbells for the entire apartment building just to watch everyone come down the stairs. I was so embarrassed I walked away from her. I didn't want to be blamed for her mischief."

Father John laughed. "Nathan, she was good in here."

"What's become of you in these camps?" Nathan asked. "You were just an innocent kid before. You don't act like the wife I knew in Belgium. How can you ask a priest about his underwear?"

I walked a few steps away from both of them. "I only asked him," I said in defense. "I didn't see anything."

Father John thought my comment was funny. He assured Nathan I had behaved above reproach during my captivity.

I never dreamed of asking others about Nathan's behavior before he spoke to the priest. It hurt me to know he was checking up on me, but I didn't have anything to hide.

I was glad Father John had spoken up for me the way he did. As Father John walked away, I didn't know that would be the last time I would see this kind priest.

Nathan continued his comments without any realization of how much he had hurt me. "Let's go home."

"No, you go home. I cannot go home yet. I want to see those thirteen SS women hanged."

"Sara, we're free. We don't need to stay."

"You go. I don't want to go yet. General Eisenhower made me an MP, and it's my duty to see them hanged."

"Is there someone else?" He pointed at the doctors in the infirmary. "Is that why you don't want to come with me?"

"Of course I don't have someone else."

Nathan's jealousy had not disappeared. I remembered how jealous he had been when I had gone to nursing school in Brussels.

"My gosh, what are you talking about?"

"Why don't you want to come home with me now?"

"I told you I have my duty here. I can't just leave." I was so hurt by his checking up on me that I wasn't sure I wanted to go with him. *How could he question my character like that? What kind of a man had he become?*

"Someone else can make sure those women are hanged."

"I'm not leaving." I looked away from him to hide the tears welling in my eyes. I made an excuse about having duties to perform and told him I'd talk to him tomorrow.

Again the next day Nathan asked me to leave.

"What do you expect me to do? Just walk out?I can't do that. People are counting on me."

Then he just smiled at me. That damn smile of his could make me forget where I was and what I was supposed to be doing. My anger subsided, and I returned his smile.

Nathan picked me up and carried me outside. Humming a Polish love song, he took the MP band from my arm and put me in the wagon. It turned out to be the same gray wagon with the two brown horses for delivering bread. The same magnetic hold on me took over as I stared at the beautiful horses.

He planned to leave right then. Nathan's friend, Leon, held the horses' reins. Frieda started crying. I asked her, "Why are you crying?"

"I'm happy for you," Frieda said.

Nathan had told her he was kidnapping me to take me back to Brussels. He knew I wouldn't leave without seeing the Nazi women hanged.

Nathan threw me in the buggy. As Leon yelled at the horses, off we went. When we passed through the gate, I couldn't breathe. I expected the Germans to appear and force us back inside. When I realized I was truly leaving, all I thought was, *Guy and Monique, I'll see you soon.*

CHAPTER 17—FROM THE JAWS OF DEATH

As Nathan, Leon, and I made our way through Augsburg and Stuttgart, Nathan was in such a hurry he wouldn't let the horses eat. We slept in parks, but each morning Nathan would get the horses ready to go again. I felt so sorry for those two horses. While we were near Stuttgart and Nathan was asleep, I took the horses and the wagon to a farm. I told the farmer to take care of them and feed them. "If I come back and see these horses are not fed, you'll be in trouble. You take care of them and feed them."

The farmer agreed, and I left the horses with him.

Then I went back to where Nathan was sleeping.

"Where are the horses and wagon?" Nathan asked when woke up.

"You weren't feeding them, and I'm not going to watch them die. I've watched enough suffering from starvation."

The veins in Nathan's neck grew larger and he gave me an exasperated look as though I had lost my mind. I didn't give him a chance to say what he was thinking.

"If you don't like it, I'll just go back. You weren't taking care of those horses."

He shook his head when he realized he wasn't going to change me. "Did you at least get some food—some sausages or salami—in exchange for the horses?"

"No, I was thinking about the horses, not our stomachs."

We began our walk back to our home, and Leon accompanied us. Even though he was twenty-two and well-educated, he didn't want to be on his own yet. He planned on traveling to Frankfurt to find out if anyone from his family had returned from the camps. If no one returned, he would join us in Brussels.

Along the way we found some American soldiers in Stuttgart and asked if they could arrange our transportation back to Brussels. They got us on board a train and supplied us with food. They gave me chocolate and gave Nathan vodka. I bristled when he took the bottle. Too recently I remembered his being drunk in the Landsberg infirmary. He saw the disapproval in my eyes and didn't drink the vodka.

On the train to Brussels, we saw a Belgian man who had been at Dachau with me.

"Sara, when we get home, a band and lots of people will be waiting for you," the man said.

"Why are people and a band waiting for you?" Nathan asked. "We're just Jews returning from the camps."

I hadn't told Nathan about my work in the resistance and was reluctant to tell him even now, but I had to. Nevertheless, I downplayed my part in the underground.

"I made false identity papers for people trying to escape."

"People don't usually meet a train for someone who was just a clerk," Nathan said, suspecting I had done more.

I shrugged.

He didn't pursue the topic. "We're getting off at the next stop." That was one stop ahead of our usual one. Nathan was a shy man who avoided recognition, and as his wife, I respected his wishes.

"You're right. I don't want any part of that."

We exited the train a station early to avoid a welcoming committee. After being in the camps, I felt like a wild animal. I had been sleeping outside, hadn't changed my clothes since I left the camp, and I hadn't brushed my hair in days. I couldn't face people, and I didn't feel like a heroine just for surviving.

With each landmark that we passed, my mind sped back to the war and my underground activities. Too many people had died. Fourteen underground workers were killed when a Belgian spy betrayed them. They had been tricked into going to the mountains and were killed there. One of the resistance women had been dating this Belgian spy and trusted him completely. Her love of the man blinded her to his true nature. That mistake cost fourteen people their lives.

That memory dredged up another disturbing one. An underground worker had been in Dachau with me. Nazi machine-gun fire killed him when the inmates would not wave the white flags. He and the others refused to become human shields. The memory of his death and the deaths of the others I had worked with were too vivid for me. I couldn't face a welcoming committee with a band and flowers.

Later I found out the resistance workers were disappointed with me for avoiding this reception, but I could not return this way. I was also scared that Nazi sympathizers were still around and would hurt my family for my part in the resistance. I wanted to see Jean Marie and Maurice Gilbert, but not if it meant someone might kill Nathan. It turned out I would never see Maurice again, and it would be a long time before I would meet Jean Marie.

In the weeks to come I learned that Nazis had arrested Jean Marie sometime after I was arrested. He was tortured, kept as a political prisoner, and shuttled from one prison to another. Luckily the Nazis never found the ledger book where Jean Marie had listed the names of the people who had false identities.

Near the end of the war a trainload of political prisoners was headed out of Brussels as the British forces approached. Jean Marie was on that train. The Nazis planned on using the prisoners in a hostage trade. When the train entered the Nazi-occupied area, the engineer somehow sabotaged one of the driving arms of the locomotive, and it would not move. Other engines were brought in to pull the train, but the Belgians who hooked up the other engines connected them at the western end of the train. The train went full-steam toward the Allies rather than toward the Nazis. The lives of hundreds of partisans were saved this way, including Jean Marie's.

Getting off a stop before our usual one meant we had to take a tram to our home. When we arrived close to our neighborhood, it was no longer there. Grief-stricken, we stared at our homes that had been bombed into rubble. The school was gutted, and no familiar buildings remained on our street.

Nathan and I were unsure where to turn. With our home destroyed, we wondered what other parts of the city had been affected and who was left. We decided to split up and go to our relatives' homes. Nathan would check with Mocha, and I would go to Jules's home. Maybe they had received news about Simon or Nathan's cousins.

When I rang the bell, Jules gasped. His face lost color, and his hands shook. Tears welled in his eyes as he reached out to me.

"You're alive. Oh, Surala, I thought you were dead."

"Don't cry, Jules." I hugged him and choked back my own tears. "I'm all right."

He touched my face. Then he held onto me as though he couldn't let go. We both cried, and tears streamed down our faces.

"They told me not to expect anyone to return. This is a miracle. Where's Nathan?" Jules asked and pulled me inside.

"Nathan went to see his cousin Mocha. He'll be here soon."

"Agnes, come see who's here." He motioned excitedly for her to come down the stairs. "Sara has returned!" All the while, he held my hand, reassuring himself that I was real.

"Sara!" Agnes exclaimed as she descended the stairs. "I can't believe it." She called the children to come see me.

They all hugged me. Tears covered everyone's face as we tried to choke out words of happiness. After the initial excitement, Jules had me sit on the sofa next to him. He asked me about *Maman*, Jean, and Albert. Since the children were present, I didn't give Jules any details of how they died.

I asked if they had heard anything about Simon, but they had not.

I was glad Jules had not been shipped out like the rest of my family when he was arrested and sent to Malines. Agnes was able to get him released by showing the children were not being raised in the Jewish faith, and she had no Jewish relatives in her ancestry for the last ten generations. Jules spent six weeks in the Malines ghetto before they released him. Why they freed him and kept others was a miracle. Agnes worked hard for weeks to get Jules released. She went to various churches tracing her religious lineage for the Nazis. Because of her hard work, my brother was saved.

While I stayed that afternoon with Jules and Agnes, Nathan found his cousin, Mocha. Unlike my joyous reunion with Jules, Mocha did not want to speak to Nathan. He had heard rumors about survivors and mistakenly thought if anyone had survived the camps, he must have cooperated with the Nazis in the role of a *Kapo*.

"I tried to explain to him," Nathan said, "that I wasn't a *Kapo*, but Mocha wouldn't listen. He slammed the door in my face."

I was furious with Mocha, but I knew Nathan had to deal with his family in his own way. If I interfered, it might only make things worse. I felt sorry that Nathan had survived so much, only to be treated like this by his own cousin. I was grateful Jules had not believed such a story about me.

I told Jules I had to see Guy and Monique. I was anxious to get to the little town where Catherine lived. Jules told us to come back as soon as we had the children, but Nathan and I couldn't stay with Jules and Agnes. They had seven children, and their apartment was too crowded.

After our reunion Nathan and I went to a Jewish aid organization that gave us 1500 francs to get us back on our feet. We needed the money for transportation to get our children, food, clothing and an apartment.

As soon as we had money, I headed to the little village where Catherine lived while Nathan looked for a place for us to stay.

I knocked on the door and was filled with joy to see my old nanny. She had aged while I was in the camps.

"Sara!" Catherine grabbed me and hugged me. "You're back. My baby's come back!"

Spending a few moments wrapped in her arms, it felt wonderful to be home where people loved me and cared about me. Anxious, I looked past her to see the children. If Guy had heard my voice, he would dash into the room to see me. However, there were no toys or signs of children in the house.

"Where are Monique and Guy? How are they?" I asked.

"Monique is at Susanna's house. I'll call her to bring Monique down." Catherine phoned her daughter. After a quick conversation, Catherine said, "She'll be here in a few moments." Catherine felt the side of the chair as she sat down.

"Where's Guy? Is he coming with Susanna too?"

"I had to put Guy in an orphanage," Catherine explained. "The Nazis became too suspicious. Being in an orphanage was safer than staying here. I took him to the closest orphanage, and he stayed there until some other boys noticed his circumcision. The priests told me they transferred him to Profondsart."

My heart sank as I heard this dire news. *Where was Guy now?* Before I could ask the question, Catherine continued.

"That's where Monique stayed too when I had the operation."

"What operation? What's wrong?" I kneeled in front of her.

"I have cancer in my eye. The doctors tried to stop the spread of it, but it's gone too far. I've lost the sight in my right eye." She pointed at her eye. "While I was in the hospital, Monique was in the orphanage with Guy. To protect the children, they were given different last names. Guy used the last name you gave him of Miodownik, and Monique went by the last name of Diamond."

"Oh, Catherine, I didn't know you had been through so much. How are you now?"

"During the operation the doctor removed as much cancer as he could, but I lost the sight in it."

"What can Nathan and I do for you?"

"Nothing. I'll be all right. Now that you're back, I can rest easy."

I pulled up a chair next to Catherine. While we chatted, I looked at the door, expecting Susanna any minute. *What was taking her so long?* I told Catherine only a little bit about the camps. I wanted to see Monique. She was now a little over two and a half years old. She must have changed a lot during that time. *Would she remember me? Would she react the way Guy had when I returned from the Paris prison?* Finally Susanna knocked briefly at the door and came in with Monique.

"Look who's here!" Catherine said to Monique. "It's your *Maman*, just like I told you."

"*Mon enfant*! My baby!" I said. "Come to *Maman*, Monique." I knelt down before her and opened my arms. Then I realized she didn't know me except for the pictures Catherine had shown her. I felt like I had been knocked down. I couldn't catch my breath. My child didn't want anything to do with me.

Twisting a strand of hair, Monique was reluctant to come to me. She said to Catherine, "No, *Bobonne*."

"She's your *Maman*." Catherine pushed her toward me a little. "Go to her." Catherine was able to get Monique to stand in front of me by coaxing her along.

I took her hand, and we hugged a little. She pulled away after a few seconds and ran back to Susanna. To her, Susanna was her mother and Catherine was her grandmother. I was simply a stranger, and she was being polite.

My heart was breaking, but I understood. Monique didn't know me. Catherine did what she could, but to Monique I was just some face in a picture.

I had survived for my children, and my own daughter didn't want to be with me. I knew I was expecting too much and that things would work out, but for the time being I ached inside. I bit my lip to keep from crying in front of Monique.

"My poor *cherie*," I said, still longing for Monique not to be standoffish. She was adorable with her dark brown, curly hair, but something was wrong with her eyes. They were crossed and she was wearing thick glasses.

"What's wrong with her eyes?" I asked Catherine.

"I've taken her to the doctor and he said when she's older he can do surgery to straighten them. He thinks she'll be able to see, but she'll have to wear glasses."

"Now that the war's over," Susanna said, "Mother will be able to see a specialist about her eyes too."

"It won't matter," Catherine said. "There's nothing more they can do."

"Mother, don't talk that way."

"You know it's true. I don't mind dying now that Sara's back, and you're grown and can take care of yourself. I wanted to live long enough to see the children back with Sara and you married. All my prayers have been answered."

"Susanna, are you married?" I asked.

"Not yet. We're not even officially engaged. We've been seeing each other, but we didn't want to get married during the war. Now that it's over, perhaps we will."

"Congratulations, I'm happy for you."

"Susanna will get married, and you're back," Catherine said, "so no one needs me any more. God will call me home soon."

"Catherine, we'll always need you." I hugged her and knelt by her chair. I couldn't bear the thought of losing another person who was so dear to me.

"I knew you would come back. I just knew it. After my operation I brought Monique home for a while. Guy could not return from the orphanage. I'm sorry, Sara. I did what I thought was best."

"It's all right, Catherine. Don't worry about it. You were protecting the children. Is Guy still at Profondsart?"

"Yes, he's there."

Profondsart wasn't far away, only about sixty miles, but this one small trip had exhausted me physically and mentally. I would have to get Guy another day. I told Catherine I would leave Monique with her for a while until Nathan and were settled. I could not rip Monique away from the only family she had known. Giving her some time to get used to me before taking her back to Brussels was the best choice. I could reason this out in my mind, but my heart didn't agree. I felt like my chest was caving in. I couldn't breathe except in short gasps as I walked away from her.

When I reunited with Nathan at Jules' apartment, I told him what had happened.

"You have to go with me to get Guy. I can't face another rejection like this on my own."

Nathan understood, and a few days later we went to Profondsart to get Guy. We told them who we were, but the Jewish aid organization required documentation to prove who we were. As we filled out the forms, they sent for Guy.

When he walked into the room, he ran to us and hugged us. At five and a half, Guy looked so much more like my father now. The first thing he asked was, "Are we going home?"

"Soon, *Cherie*. We're going to Nonnie's for a while first. We have a home, but we don't have a house to put it in." As we left, it felt so good to have the family back together. For all of us to survive was a miracle.

On the way I explained to Guy that he and Monique would stay with Catherine, their nonnie, until Nathan and I could find an apartment in Brussels. He wasn't happy with that, but I told him it would only be for a few nights until we could have a home again.

"Where's *Bobonne*, *Maman*?" Guy asked me. That question sliced through me, tearing at my insides. I had to tell him about his grandmother.

"*Cherie*, your *Bobonne* is not coming back. She and your Uncle Albert and Uncle Jean are dead. The Nazis killed them."

"Why, *Maman*? Did they do something wrong? Why did the Nazis kill them?"

"I don't know, *Cherie*. They were Jewish. The Nazis just killed them. Your *Bobonne* and your uncles were good people. They didn't do anything wrong. They never did anything bad in their lives."

To explain the insanity of a war to a child was impossible. I just hugged him and let him cry.

"They're never going to come back?" Guy asked.

"No, they will never come back." I sat there crying with Guy all the way to Catherine's house.

"*Maman*, are the Nazis still there?" Guy jerked his head from side to side as we neared the town.

"No, *Cherie*, they're gone. You're safe now."

"They were in church when I went with Nonnie. They scared me."

"They're not going to scare you any more, darling. Papa and I are back now and we'll take care of you. Don't worry."

I had to give the illusion of confidence in front of Guy, but I could only hope that the specter of Nazis torturing Jewish people was gone. How could they kill people and then go to church on Sundays? Such hypocrisy!

I also noticed how quiet and withdrawn Guy had become in the course of the war. At times he looked like a little, old man. He had been through far more than any person should ever experience in a lifetime. He told me once he and Monique had gone to the movies, and some Nazis came in. His little heart beat wildly. All he could do was hold Monique's hand and hope she wouldn't be as scared as he was. The Nazis didn't bother them, probably because Guy had blond hair and Monique had a reddish tint to her dark hair. Guy didn't mention other fears or nightmares, though I'm sure he had them. He internalized it all and didn't want to upset Nathan or me by talking about it any more. Guy would remain that way even into his adult life.

We went back to see Catherine before heading to Jules' home in Brussels. Catherine said she would keep the children for a few days until we could get settled. Before we left, she told us about Guy going to a fortuneteller. He had been given some money to go to a movie, but he used the money for the fortuneteller instead. Even the fortuneteller had given him hope his parents would be coming back.

The next morning Nathan and I left for Brussels again. We could not impose on Jules and Agnes and only stayed a few days with them while we looked for some place to stay. We would go back to see the children and then return to the city on a daily basis.

While we were looking for an apartment, Belgian policemen approached us asking for our papers. Anytime someone asked us for identity papers, it felt like the Nazis returning all over again.

"We've returned from the camps," Nathan said to them. "The Nazis destroyed our papers."

"What nationality are you?" asked one of the policemen.

"I'm Belgian," I said.

The policeman continued looking at Nathan. "And what about you?"

"I've lived in Belgium since I was thirteen," Nathan said.

"What about before you were thirteen?" The policeman was still suspicious. "Where were you from?"

"Poland."

"All people with Polish citizenship are to report to camps in Germany. They cannot stay here in Belgium."

My stomach tightened as visions of the German camps swirled through my mind.

"What do you mean he can't stay?" I asked horrified. "He's lived here twenty years, and now you want him to leave? This is ridiculous!"

"I'm not leaving my family," Nathan said. "My son and daughter were born here in Belgium. How can you expect us to split apart after we just returned from the camps? Who do I see about this?"

"Sir, you'll have to come with us to *Petite Chateau*. You can state your case there." He took Nathan by the arm as though he were some common criminal and started to lead him away.

Nathan turned around. "I'll talk to the person in charge. We'll get this straightened out shortly. I'll call you after I get there."

I couldn't believe it. We had returned home after years in the concentration camps only to be told Nathan could not stay in our home city and country. It was unbelievable.

When I got back, I told Jules and Agnes what had happened. They were just as outraged. How could our own Belgian people do this to us? I began to feel as though the anti-Semitism didn't leave with the Nazis.

Some officials in the Belgian government did not want the Jews to return to Belgium, nor did they want refugees being granted permission to stay in Belgium. I had heard rumors about King Leopold III's early capitulation to the Nazis, and now it made me suspect the rumors might be true. Even if he did not cooperate with the Nazis, he was not welcomed back in Belgium. His brother Charles was the regent while Leopold remained in exile. Leopold's second marriage was not popular among the people either. These official policies about refugees were anti-Semitic and did not gain any trust for the monarch among the Jewish population.

They took Nathan to *Petite Chateau* in Brussels, which was a place for detainees without papers, not a prison. Nathan was told he would have to stay there and could not move into an apartment since he was not a Belgian citizen.

I managed to get an apartment close to *Petite Chateau*, and I contacted a lawyer, a friend of Nathan's cousin, about trying to get Nathan released. Since this was a federal matter and not a local one, Jean Marie was not able to help us. While I was at the courthouse in St. Gilles, Jean Marie asked if I wanted to work there again, but I explained the situation with Nathan would take all my time. Jean Marie understood.

During this ordeal with Nathan's citizenship, my dear nanny and friend, Catherine, passed away. It had been only a few months since our return to Belgium. She had survived long enough to see us reunited with the children. Even though I knew she had been sick, the news of her death left me devastated. *Would I ever stop losing those I loved?* Catherine had been more than just a nanny to my children and me. She had saved my children. My debt to her and her daughter Susanna could never be repaid. Susanna had treated Monique and Guy like her younger brother and sister. I felt so lost and numb without Catherine. In the past I had depended on her to be there for the children and me. Now she was gone.

Susanna got married after the war, but the young man whom she married was not as comfortable about having Jewish friends as she was. I think he may have been jealous of the attention both of the women gave my family. It's probably lucky Susanna did not marry this man while my children were hiding with her and her mother. He might have turned them in.

Thankfully, others were able to help my family and me. The Displaced Persons organization, run by sympathetic Jewish people, helped returning refugees. They gave me some money for the apartment and food, tried to help me with Nathan's situation, began looking for my brothers and sisters, and kept us refugees informed about new arrivals from the camps.

Daily I searched for Simon's name on the list, and one day when I found it, I was ecstatic. Jules and I were waiting for the transport when it arrived, but Simon did not appear. Then we were told he was supposed to have taken a flight. That seemed strange because none of the refugees were flown back to their home countries.

On that transport we did meet our former bookkeeper, Lezke, who had worked in my father's store. We went to the kitchen set up for the refugees, and he told us Simon had survived in Auschwitz until near the end. He had been given the job of feeding the pigs, a humiliating job for a Jewish person. Lezke had worked as a bookkeeper in Auschwitz and saw Simon, but did not know what had happened to him near the end of the war. He did know that Abram Bolka, the *Kapo* who got me to Dachau, hanged himself at Auschwitz when the Russian troops advanced. Most *Kapos* knew they would receive retribution for their actions once the prisoners were free, and many ran or committed suicide.

We checked with officials and asked why Simon's name was on the list along with one of Nathan's cousins. Neither one of them ever showed up on the transport. The Americans assured us no plane had been dispatched to bring refugees back to Belgium. We never learned what happened to Simon and Nathan's cousin, but they never returned to Belgium. The only thing we could determine was Simon probably died at Auschwitz from typhus.

We had to assume they both died, and someone had used their names on the transport list. Someone such as a *Kapo* who wanted to return to Belgium may have used their names to obtain entry and then dropped the name as soon as they were safely back within Belgium's borders. We'll never know for sure.

Two people who did return from the camps in late July or early August were Frieda and Eva. I saw their names on a transport list and went to meet them at the train station. They were some of the few whose house was not damaged in the war, but their belongings were gone. Since they both held Belgian citizenship, they faced no legal issues concerning deportation. We visited often and talked about our experiences together, like getting Frieda's shoes back for her.

Eva's brother also returned from Dachau and told her the thirteen SS women who were arrested near the camp were, indeed, hanged for their crimes. Frieda and Eva had lost many family members also, but at least they had each other. Eva was in bad health from her experiences in the camps and did not live very long after her return. Shortly afterward Frieda decided to immigrate to Israel. She married, but her sterilization at Auschwitz meant she couldn't have children. I was glad I had had my children before the war, but I knew Frieda was scarred the rest of her life. She would always want children and would never be able to have any. The Nazi legacy of cruelty continued to torment us.

Sara and Frieda, 1947

My health was wrecked from my years in the camps. When Nathan and I crossed the border to Belgium, health officials examined us to make sure we were not carriers of a contagious disease. Even though we could enter the country, our health issues were severe. I was having problems breathing. My lungs had filled with fluid and I had to go to the hospital to have them drained. During the week I was there, the doctor told me about some of the damage caused by my time in the camps. The exposure to the elements in the camps, the dehydration, the starvation, and the sterilization had taken their toll. My stomach had shrunk to a quarter of its normal size. The doctors wanted to insert a colostomy bag, but I didn't want it. I wouldn't let them operate even though my digestive system was full of tumors, bleeding ulcers, and hernias. My feet were swollen, my circulatory system was affected, my heart was bad, my gums were abscessed, my eyebrows never grew back, and my teeth were loose. I had severe headaches and arthritis. I was weak nearly all the time. Two years passed before I had a menstrual cycle again. After the camps my health was never the same. One doctor listed me as 100% disabled.

Even fifty years later I still suffer from the abuse I endured in the camps. For several years I had to have my stomach pumped every three months or so, and this made my esophagus bleed. I have arthritis so bad I cannot sleep through most of the night, and I have to use oxygen almost daily. I've suffered two heart attacks, had tumors and fourteen inches of my colon removed, and been hospitalized much of my life. At night I cannot sleep with the door closed; I'm afraid I'm being put into a gas chamber when the door closes. Survival costs even years later.

Nathan's health also suffered from being in the camps. With a bad heart and kidney stones, he wound up having six bi-passes and an operation to remove the stones. When he worked in a coal mine near Auschwitz, Nathan had a piece of coal lodge under his left eye. It impaired his vision and almost blinded him. Years later he had it removed. He had mild lung problems, a smaller stomach, digestive problems, and scars on his feet from the coal mines and going barefoot in the winter. His feet would swell easily. Also he had scars on his buttocks and back from being struck with bayonets in the camps. If he fell asleep at the sewing machine at Auschwitz, the guards would come along and hit him in his back with the butt of the rifle to wake him up. Those scars he carried with him forever. After having his head shaved, the top of his hair did not grow back. He was bald on top with hair growing only on the sides of his head. Many of his health problems would continue to plague him later in life also.

In 1946 Leonard, the circus ringmaster, found me at our first floor apartment in Brussels. He had been looking for me in all the camps in Europe for two years. When the circus had traveled to Nuremberg and Frankfurt, he tried to locate me in the camps, but was not allowed entry. He wanted me to return to my job as a lion tamer at the *Cirque Royal*. Leonard had no idea I had been sent to Auschwitz and Dachau.

I introduced Leonard to Nathan. On occasions, I could smuggle Nathan out of the camps. Leonard and Nathan sat down to discuss the job offer.

"She's a fine woman," Leonard said, "and she was a fine girl when we met. She worked so hard and she risked her life for everybody. Please let me have her back to work for the circus. You can travel with us. You don't have to work for the circus. Just let her work with us."

I wanted to return to work. I enjoyed the act and I was good at it. I liked showing off, but Nathan wouldn't hear of it. In the old European fashion, he didn't want his wife to work.

"I love my wife and she doesn't have to work," Nathan said to him. "She doesn't have to make a living for me."

I was disappointed, but Nathan was the head of the family. We could have traveled all over Europe with the circus, but Nathan didn't want it. I suppose having his wife work was too much of a blow to his ego. He didn't want me showing off in public. I could be Nathan's star, but not a public figure.

We did go see the circus at *Cirque Royal* and we visited with Leonard several times, but my career in the circus was not to be. I was already thinking about immigrating to America. On our last visit to the circus Leonard said to me, "Out of the 120 people working for the circus, I will miss you most of all. My whole family respected you and loved you. We would have gone to hell for you." Then he turned to Nathan and said, "Take care of Sara." I never saw Leonard again.

I was able to smuggle Nathan out of the camp, but never on a permanent basis. It was almost like a game of cat and mouse. On another one of these occasions, Nathan and I heard about a refugee gathering in Paris. We decided we would go and try to find out more about what may have happened to other people we had known. Word of mouth was the only way we had to find out the fate of relatives. When the Allied forces entered the camps, they found the Nazis had burned many of the records. Therefore, we relied on other people who had been in the camps to let us know what had happened to friends and family members.

While we were in Paris at a get-together, the most unexpected event happened. While I was talking to some people, a young man ran and hugged me. He was a clean-cut young man around eighteen or nineteen years old with dark hair. I didn't recognize him until he said, "Papa, come here. This is the lady who saved my life. This is the lady who cut off my thumb."

I recognized him as the young man from Dachau who had blood poisoning. I was so pleased he had survived the camp and was doing well.

His husky father came over and thanked me repeatedly. The father was a butcher and wanted to supply me with meat, but his son's survival was enough for me. Though we didn't hear news about our relatives, this reunion with the young man from Dachau made the trip worthwhile.

When we returned to Brussels, Nathan was again taken to *Petite Chateau*. After all efforts to get him permanently released were in vain, Nathan was sent to another camp, this one near the Holland border. I told the children he was sick; I could not tell them the true reason their father was being detained. They were too young to understand. I took the children to see Nathan in the camp. All they could do was wave at him through a window. One of the guards tried to explain to Guy that Nathan had done nothing wrong, but Nathan spent another six months in this camp.

During this time Monique had an operation to correct her cross-eyed condition. She was in the hospital a couple of days, and the surgery went well. She wore glasses, but could see normally. The operation did not cost me anything because Belgium had socialized medicine and all citizens were given free medical care.

After the Nazis arrested my mother, my other brothers and sisters were placed in different orphanages around Brussels. During the war they had stayed with Catholic nuns and priests and farm families. Later they were put in orphanages. They were not kept together for fear if the Nazis discovered one, the entire family would be taken. It took a while for me to discover the whereabouts of all of them. For most of the war Esther and Henri were together at Castle La Bas. Henri saw Mariette occasionally, but none of the others saw each other. Before they had been separated, Henri taught Mariette how to throw a knife and jump off trains or streetcars or buildings. He knew she would need these skills to survive.

After the war when Esther was in an orphanage, a girl told her about someone who sounded like Mariette. The girl had a younger sister in another orphanage and told Esther the child she had seen looked exactly like Esther. Esther knew it must be Mariette. Since Esther was a minor, she could not get Mariette from that home to stay with her, but one of the older sisters, who was eighteen, went with her. When Esther found Mariette, she was dirty, full of lice and ticks, and had not been taken care of properly. And worst of all, Mariette ran away when she saw Esther. Esther found out later that Jean had instructed Mariette not to speak to family members if she saw them because it might endanger their lives if she did. It took Esther and the other girl a long time to convince Mariette she could be seen with a family member. The older sister and Esther had to wash Mariette with lye soap and a floor brush because Mariette had a skin disease called "La Gall" or impetigo, which was contagious. Her skin reddened and became itchy. Then small blisters formed. When they broke, they left a tan crust, which could be removed with gentle washing. Sulfur, a new and expensive treatment, was also used to get the infection out. Even though Mariette was sick and had to be hospitalized, Esther was happy to be reunited with her.

After the war, the girls were usually put in one home and the boys in another. The Jewish organization, UNRA, took care of the houses. The older girls took care of the younger ones, like big sisters. The name of the home, *Maison des Hirondelles*, translates as the "home of the swallows." Jacques stayed with Esther there for a while.

When I found Esther after I returned to Belgium, she came to live with me for about three months and helped take care of Guy and Monique. She was around fourteen at the time. With Nathan being detained at Petite Chateau, I could not really establish a home. Having Esther take care of Guy and Monique while I constantly visited lawyers and the Jewish aid organization was fortunate, but I could not bring all of my brothers and sisters to live with me. Not enough room, food, or money was available to take care of them. They were at least all placed at the same orphanage after the war. I would have them over on weekends and take them places, but during the week, they stayed at the orphanage. They were able to leave the orphanage to visit me, but I could not keep all of them in our small apartment.

Nathan and I became like parents to my brothers and sisters. The younger ones could not remember *Maman* and Papa. To them, we were *Maman* and Papa. Any time I had to discipline Esther or one of the children, they would run to Nathan and tell on me, as if I were in the wrong, but Mariette never had to be disciplined. She was a child of silence and never rocked the boat.

The war had taken its toll on Mariette's childhood. She could never be a child again and look at the world with the eyes of innocence. No one hugged or kissed Mariette during her years in hiding. She was hidden in dark, underground places in barns, fields, or hay boxes. Sometimes the places were on farms, in churches, or in convents. In one forest, dead people hung from tree branches. A little child should not witness these scenes of death, yet Mariette did. She learned to count to ten after a bomb because she knew the bomb would explode and shrapnel would fall from the sky, showering metal death on those below it. People were cut to ribbons by the shrapnel. All these images scarred Mariette's younger years.

Wild after being on his own for so long during the war, Henri gave us a lot of trouble. No one looked after him. Throughout the years of Nazi occupation, he had to fend for himself. He didn't consider it stealing when he took something he wanted. He had noticed where Nathan kept some gold coins in the headboard of the bed. After Nathan put them there, Henri took them.

Nathan caught him and called him "little *gonif*," thief, but that didn't phase Henri. When Nathan asked him about the coins, he denied he had taken them. If he'd see us on the tram, he'd jump off, afraid we were looking for him for some theft. At sixteen years old, Henri would sneak into nightclubs and go to prostitutes.

Nathan wanted him to live with us and learn to be a tailor, but Henri refused. He wanted to work with some friends of ours in a jewelry business. While he was there, he stole some pieces and tried to tell me he had made the little spoon he had given to me. When we discovered what he had done, he took a bicycle and ran away. He was afraid of what we were going to do. As a sixteen-year-old, he was making bad choices.

We couldn't understand at the time why he was doing this to us, but he was acting out his anger at the world, not just at us. It wasn't our fault that we were taken to the camps, but Henri couldn't understand he was hurting us. He couldn't understand what was going on in his life either. The pain was horrible in all of us. Even though people didn't think the children in hiding were suffering like the others, they still felt the terror and the loss the adults felt. We were all hurting and showing it in different ways.

With my physical limitations, I knew I could not take care of my own children and my brothers and sisters properly. With Nathan being deported to the border whenever the Belgian authorities caught him, we were all in constant turmoil. I had to put my brothers and sisters back in the orphanages.

In 1946 my oldest brother Charles returned from Switzerland to find out what had happened to the family. All of us had trouble forgiving my oldest brother who had abandoned *Maman* during the war. His refusal to take *Maman* and the younger children was burned into their memories. I could not forgive him either.

Charles, his wife, and their family returned to Belgium after the war. When Charles asked about *Maman*, Jean, Simon, and Albert, he didn't believe they were dead. "*Maman*'s dead," I told him. The Nazis killed her."

"How can you talk like that about our mother?" Charles asked. He was angry at me for talking so bluntly.

I was livid. I didn't care how I talked to him any more. After all, if he had found room to take *Maman* and the children with him when he fled Brussels, I believe she would have lived.

"She died in the camp," I told him. "She was taken to the oven."

"You shouldn't talk like that about *Maman*."

"You killed *Maman*!" I screamed at him. "She would still be here if you had taken her. You made your choice of family. You took your wife's family. We're not your family any more. You'll have this on your conscience."

"Don't talk like that." He slapped me.

I wasn't going to shut up. What he did to me didn't matter. A slap in the face paled in comparison to what I had endured. I railed back at him. "You had the trucks. You didn't have room for one person? Your mother? Your little sister? How dare you even come back and ask about them! None of us can forget what you did."

"I have a right to know what happened to them."

"You have no rights. You weren't in the camps. You don't know what it was like. I only lived for the sake of my children. Six million people died. I feel guilty enough for surviving. I don't need you to make me feel worse. You're not my brother any more. Go away. We don't need you."

Out of guilt, Charles and Renee, his wife, agreed to house my youngest sister Mariette, but Renee treated her like a servant, not a sister-in-law. Though Charles and Renee's oldest daughter was only nineteen months younger than Mariette, Mariette was Charles's sister and should have been treated better. Renee would push Mariette out of the house to sit on the stairs after her work was done. When Mariette refused to do any more cleaning or washing, Renee wouldn't allow her inside. The tension between them was great. Mariette was better off in the orphanage.

When Charles and his family were preparing to immigrate to Rio de Janeiro, Brazil, he came by to see the remnant of the family before he left. I asked if he were going to take Mariette too, but he said no. I said, "She's better off without you." That was the last time I talked to him until 1966. For twenty years my brother was dead to me.

The Jewish Congress of Canada asked my brothers and sisters if they wanted to immigrate there. Bernard, a teenager of about seventeen or eighteen at the time, did not want to go to Canada. Instead he chose to immigrate to Israel. At first Jacques was scheduled to go with a group of children, the *Shamer Atzayer*, to Palestine, but he cried and didn't want to leave the others. The officials allowed him to join my brothers and sisters, thus giving Bernard the opportunity to go to Palestine. He had always wanted to become a rabbi and he felt this was where he wanted to be. Esther, Henri, Jacques, and Mariette went to Canada to start new lives. Canadian Jewish foster families were willing to take refugee children. I could do little for my brothers and sisters in my current situation, and they decided Canada would be the place for them.

Being a Zionist, Bernard went to Israel and lived in a kibbutz. Later he became part of the Israeli army and fought to liberate Israel. When he finally retired, he went to Vancouver to be around my other brothers and sisters. Mariette sponsored him and his family to live in Vancouver and be reunited with the family.

Nathan and I were thinking about immigrating to Palestine. I had secured passage on a boat and had our luggage ready to go. When we were preparing to go, a Jewish man from Germany who was working in the passport office talked us out of it because no employment was available for a tailor in Palestine at the time. We changed our minds, got our belongings off the boat, and looked for another place to go. Staying in Brussels was too hard. Furthermore, the Belgian government wouldn't allow Nathan to stay legally.

Finally in 1947 I was told the only way to be with Nathan was to relinquish my Belgian citizenship, re-marry him in a civil ceremony, and accompany him to a displaced persons camp in Frankfurt am Main, Germany. I couldn't believe it, but I had no choice.

When I agreed to give up my citizenship and re-marry Nathan, the Belgian officials had to make sure Nathan had never been married to anyone else before. For six weeks they advertised in public bulletins asking if anyone would claim a marriage to Naftali Hauptman. The officiousness was ridiculous. The fact that Nathan and I had been married in a Jewish ceremony before the war wasn't enough for them. So I gave up my citizenship, remarried Nathan in a civil ceremony complete with the officials wearing white Colonial wigs and costumes and having a red carpet rolled out for us, and prepared to leave Brussels for Frankfurt.

I did not want to take Guy and Monique with us to Frankfurt at first because we had no place to stay. I put them into a Jewish orphanage until Nathan and I could return or send for them. Over and over again, I was forced to split my family. Poor Guy was always afraid we would be separated permanently.

When my brothers and sisters immigrated to Canada in November 1947, I was preparing to leave for Frankfurt. I couldn't even see them off at the ship. All I knew was they were headed to Canada. I wouldn't find out where they had gone until years later when Mariette would contact me by letter.

Upon our departure for Frankfurt, Jules agreed to do any paperwork to try and get reparations for our belongings, but I knew we would probably never see any of them again. How can mere money replace all the memories of a lifetime? I had very few material possessions, but at least I had my children and my husband. Agnes held onto a picture Leonard had taken of me with the lion cub. She also had some photographs of my brothers and sisters and mother and father. We were lucky because most people didn't have these few items left. Many people wish they could have had just one photograph, but they had nothing at all except their lives. And those of us who survived felt guilty just for having that, our lives. The nightmare begun by the Nazis years ago would haunt us day and night for the rest of our lives.

Also before we left, Mocha, Nathan's cousin, came to see Nathan and apologized for how he had treated him. Apparently, he had found out Nathan had told him the truth about the camps. Nathan could not have been a *Kapo*. *Kapos* were killed at liberation or they hanged themselves. He wanted Nathan to come to his house. I was glad they had reconciled before we left for Frankfurt.

Also Mocha had seen me working at the courthouse in St. Gilles, and I think he told Nathan what he suspected about my work in the underground. However, I never told Nathan more than my work with the false papers. All of us workers had given our word never to reveal what all we had done. This soon after the war was still too risky.

In 1947 Nathan and I started another new life in Germany. All the time we were in the refugee neighborhood, I knew I wanted to immigrate to the United States. Nothing was left for me in Europe. Besides General Eisenhower had invited me himself. He had convinced many refugees that becoming an American is what we should pursue. So I did. People in the United States were funding the Jewish organization, but we weren't going to live like this forever. We had to make plans for our future. I wanted to immigrate to the United States. Nathan didn't want to, but I told him I could not stay in Europe.

"What are we going to do in the United States?" he asked me. "We don't know the language. The children won't know anybody."

"I don't want my children to go through what I did. I want them to grow up where Jews are not hated just for being Jews. I want a new life for my children. For myself, it's not important, but for them it is."

"You go first then and I'll come later."

"Nathan, I'm going. I want you to come with us, but if you won't, I'll go by myself with the children. I'm going. Too many memories surround me here. *Maman* didn't come back. Albert didn't come back. Simon didn't come back. Why do you want to stay here?"

He cried and finally agreed we would go. Nathan had searched many Displaced Persons camps throughout Germany for relatives who may have survived, but he never found anyone on his side of the family. Now we were being forced out of Belgium, the only country we had ever loved and had thought was our home.

CHAPTER 18—BEARDING THE LION IN ITS DEN

In Frankfurt we were able to find an efficiency apartment of three rooms—a tiny kitchen, bathroom, and a main room that doubled as bedroom and living room—all we could afford while we applied for immigration to the United States. In 1951 after I had convinced Nathan nothing was left for us in Europe, except bitter memories, we decided to immigrate to the United States.

We had heard King Leopold III had returned to Belgium in March of 1950 and would abdicate his throne to his son, Baudouin, soon, but we had no desire to return to Belgium. Because Nathan still had Polish citizenship, it took longer for us to be granted permission to immigrate. We were scared to start all over, but I felt we needed this fresh beginning in a new country.

I didn't want the children to see how we had to live now. The neighborhood was not a place for children. They were better off in the orphanage in Belgium. My health had deteriorated more. I wasn't sure I could care for the children without help. Nathan had taken the only job he could find, smuggling cigarettes. It was not a life.

I went back to visit the children in the orphanage and explained our situation. I told them I was trying to get our immigration to the United States approved. Every two weeks I told them I would come back to visit them. Guy was doing well on his soccer team, and Monique was progressing in her studies. Her former eye problem was not a factor any more. In addition, the children were learning piano. These were "luxuries" they would not have where we were in Frankfurt. I made the decision to leave them in the orphanage until a few weeks before we were approved for immigration.

Other people in this little Jewish "neighborhood" were worse off than Nathan and I. One man described his return to Poland after the concentration camps to search for his relatives. When he knocked on the door of his former home, the person now inhabiting his home arrogantly asked him, "What are you doing here?" The Jewish man did not understand. All he wanted was to find someone in his family still alive.

"What do you mean what I'm doing here?" the Jewish man asked. "This is my home. I want to see if any of my family has returned."

"Go away. They're all gone," the Polish man said.

"What do you mean they're all gone? Can't I even come into my own home and see if something is left?"

"No!" The Polish man blocked the doorway.

"Where are my parents?"

"They're all dead." Then the Pole pointed to a cemetery plot next to the house and said, "They're buried there."

When the Jewish man went next to the house, he saw the graves of his entire family, even the tiny baby. The Polish man threatened to kill him if he tried to get back his belongings or land. "The same will happen to you as happened to them."

The Polish authorities wouldn't help him. When he went to a Jewish organization seeking help, they told him the Polish man inhabiting the house had killed his parents and family. The Polish authorities weren't going to help him because they hated Jews as much after the war as before it. The Jewish man had no choice but to immigrate to another country.

Some of the refugees had lost every member of their family. They were totally alone in the world and just wanted to die. They were empty shells. I remember one conversation with a man who had lost his whole family. He didn't want to start over, and he didn't care if he bathed or not. I told him he smelled, but he didn't care. He had lost all hope and all desire to live. He had no strength to start over and said to me, "I only lived until liberation. Once I was free I didn't care if I died or not. I have no will to live any more."

"Don't do this to yourself," I said. "If Hitler could not kill you, why do you have to kill yourself?"

"You're a smart woman, but what do I have in life? I'm alone."

"You're young. You can make a life. You can have another family."

"What I lost I can never have again."

"You can ease the pain when you have another family. Live. Don't let the Nazis rob you of more life. Live in spite of what they did."

I was good at putting up a positive front for others. Inside, I was not the same as before the war. Then I was full of life, and now I felt empty. None of us smiled as much, went out with friends as much, or talked about the past. When I lay awake at night, I would think, *A year ago I was lying on some straw with lice covering me.* The adjustment back to a "normal" life was difficult. I could understand why some people tried to drown their sorrows in a bottle.

Alcoholism was widespread after the war. Many people drank to forget their pain. Many of us tried to help them, but they didn't want our help. They were too far gone. Some men would even get drunk and then purposely pick fights with the local Germans. They were full of rage and would look for any reason to hit a German.

I understood their anger and experienced it myself. I hit a German woman who was dating Moisha, a friend of Nathan's. On one occasion Moisha told a German girl, Johanna, he didn't come to see her because he was playing cards with Nathan. This was a lie to cover up his liaison with a prostitute. When Johanna came into the restaurant and starting yelling at Nathan, I lost all restraint. She insulted him without reason.

"Why are you covering up for Moisha?" Johanna yelled. "He told me he was playing cards with you."

"I don't know what you're talking about," Nathan said. "I wasn't playing cards with Moisha."

"You *schweinhund*! Moisha told me when you got through playing cards you went to the hotel."

When she called him a pig dog, the nastiest insult in the German language, she was implying Nathan would lie for Moisha and also go to a prostitute himself. That was it for me. I was afraid Nathan would have a heart attack.

"Don't you dare talk to my husband like that." I stood up. "My husband has nothing to do with you. If you insult my husband, you have to deal with me."

I grabbed her by the hair and threw her against the wall. After I had thrown her and she lay there unconscious, I realized her hair was still in my hands. I had torn a huge chunk of hair from her bleeding scalp. Right away an ambulance came and picked her up, and she was taken to the hospital.

"Sara, why did you do this?" Nathan said to me afterward. "Why are you so savage, so wild? You've changed."

"After all those years in the camps, I'm not taking insults from a German. You were with me in the house. How dare Moisha involve you in one of his lies! How dare she talk that way to you!"

"I don't care what she says. Her opinion doesn't matter to me."

"It matters to me. As long as I'm alive, no German is going to insult you or me."

The next day we were sitting in the large eating area where many of the refugees gathered. About two hundred people were in the area, listening to accordion music, when I saw three men approaching us with two German shepherds. Someone said to me, "Uh oh, Sara, I think they're coming for you."

I suspected they might be Johanna's father and two brothers. They were asking around for me. Nathan begged me not to say anything. He didn't want me to fight with them too. After a waiter identified me to them, they came over to our table.

"Are you Sara Hauptman?" the father asked me.

"Yes."

"Do you know who I am?" He adjusted the dog's leash in his hand, allowing the dog to get a little nearer to me.

"No. What do you want with me?" I faced him without any fear of the dog.

"I'm Johanna's father. These are my sons," he said as he motioned to the other two men.

"What do you want?"

"I wanted to see who hurt my daughter."

"I did it." I sat back a little in my chair. "Did she tell you why?"

"No."

"She insulted my husband. Her boyfriend implicated Nathan in his scheme and tried to use Nathan's good name to cover up his own actions. If she wanted to yell at someone, she should have yelled at Moisha, not Nathan. She called him a *schweinhund* in public. I don't have to take that from her."

"My daughter doesn't yell," her father defended. "She said you screamed at her."

"I'm sorry," I said with restraint, "but yes she did yell. Am I screaming at you right now? Well, I didn't scream at her either. My husband became pale when she railed at him in front of all our friends. I wasn't going to sit there and let her cause him to have a heart attack. Ask anyone who was there and they can tell you the same thing." I motioned around the room.

People around me were nodding their heads in agreement. I guess I must have convinced him.

"Thank you," he said. "I apologize. I had to find out what happened." He and his sons left with the dogs. I'm not sure why they brought the dogs along unless they thought they could intimidate me with their presence. Lions and tigers didn't scare me, so I wasn't afraid of two dogs.

Later on when I saw Moisha, I was still mad. "Moisha, how dare you include my husband in one of your stories! Why are you dating a German girl anyway?"

"I'm just using her. I don't plan on marrying her." He lit a cigarette and slid into a chair, propping up his feet on the table.

"It's not right, Moisha. Don't include Nathan's name in one of your cover-ups ever again."

A few weeks later Moisha brought Johanna over to our table at a restaurant. "Sara, Johanna wants to say something to you," Moisha said.

"I don't want to see you or her," I said. I turned my back to them.

"Sara, don't be so hard on them," Nathan interceded. "Moisha is still one of ours."

"Nathan, I don't want people to think you're worse than they are. I won't take an insult from any German."

"I'm sorry I yelled at you and Nathan," Johanna said. She put her hand on my shoulder. "I was just so upset."

I brushed off her hand. "Then why didn't you come to me and ask what had happened. Nathan doesn't go out like that. If he goes out somewhere, I go with him."

Johanna cried. "I'm sorry. I made a mistake. If you want me to apologize publicly, I'll put it in the paper."

When I didn't answer her, she pointed to her bald spot and said, "Look what you did to my hair. How can you be so hard on me now?"

"You did it to yourself. Be glad I didn't kill you. After being in the camps, I could kill."

"Sara, I don't believe you could kill someone."

Standing up and looking her in the eye, I said icily, "I could. Stay away from me."

Moisha led Johanna away, but I still seethed inside. Nathan knew better than to try and say anything else. I didn't care if her father had supposedly helped in the underground.

Sara after the war with a friend

Sara, Johanna, and Johanna's mother in Frankfurt, Germany

After the camps I was wild with rage, and uncontrolled anger would surge through me. About a week later I was having coffee with my German landlady. She had another friend of hers for coffee with us too. In the middle of the conversation she said, "If Hitler were still alive, I would vote for him all over again."

I couldn't believe she could say such a thing to me. After all I had endured at the concentration camps and having lost my mother and three brothers to the Nazi death machine, I couldn't restrain myself.

I jumped up on the table, grabbed her hair with both hands, pulled her to the floor, and pounded her with my fists. All the rage and grief erupted inside me.

"You dirty Hitler!" I yelled. "How can you have Jewish people in your house and still talk about Hitler?"

Even though she was quite a large woman, nearly six feet tall, I had her down on the floor crying. The other woman was screaming, "You're killing her!"

I hit this Nazi sympathizer with all my might. The other woman tried to pull me off the landlady, but she could not. Then she must have called the police when she realized she couldn't get me to stop hitting the German landlady.

The landlady was bleeding all over. I had knocked out her two front teeth. Her eyes were swollen and bruised. I didn't care. She deserved what she got. When the police came, they could not believe I had beaten her so. They looked at how big she was and how short I was. They took the landlady to the hospital, where she stayed for a week, and they took me to the police station.

At the police station, the policemen asked me why I had attacked her, and I told them everything that had happened.

"How dare that woman! She eats my bread and has the audacity to say that to me. How can she do that? Even if she felt that way, she shouldn't say that to me after I was in the camps. I couldn't just sit there and let her say that."

The policemen let me go after he filled out the report. Nathan had come down to the station when he heard what I had done.

"If you can beat up a woman twice your size, you're a good fighter," one of the policemen said. "Just go home."

Nathan even joked with them at the end by saying, "I'm afraid to go home. She might beat me up too. I've been married to her all these years, and she couldn't even kill a fly. Now she does this. I'm not going home."

The policemen just laughed and sent me home. By their light-hearted reaction, I knew they weren't Nazi sympathizers. Otherwise, I might have spent a long time in jail. A lot of Germans opposed Hitler, but too often people stereotype all Germans as being Nazis, which was not necessarily true.

From then on, the Nazi-loving landlady never opened her mouth to me again. She avoided me entirely. But when word got out in the refugee neighborhood that I had beaten up a Nazi-loving woman, people would come over just to see who I was and congratulate me. I had never planned to be infamous for hitting someone, but this was the result.

A few months before we were to leave Frankfurt for the United States, we arranged to take Guy and Monique out of the orphanage in March 1951. Unfortunately we couldn't cross the Belgian border to get the children back with us, so we sent a friend of ours in a black car to pick up the children and bring them across the border where we were waiting in Germany.

In a forested area we saw the children again. Little Guy carried a stamp collection book and dropped it when he saw Nathan. He ran to him and hugged his Papa. In the excitement Guy's stamps blew all over the place. We collected as many as we could, and he hung onto that little blue-checkered book as though it were his most precious possession. I remember his words, "Is this the last time? Can we be together now?"

"Yes, *Cherie*," I assured him. "We'll be together always."

Guy remembered this last orphanage quite well. He learned the address at 128 Rue van Rusenbek with the telephone number 489802. Also he became a talented soccer player and was invited to join a junior traveling soccer team, but we planned to leave Europe before he had a chance to play on the team.

In May 1951 the children and I stayed a few days at a hotel near the harbor where the ship, the *Captain Blackford*, would leave for America. I had argued with Nathan about coming, and I thought he had changed his mind and was going to stay in Germany. I knew I couldn't because staying was too painful. Two days before we were to leave, we went through a series of health screenings, such as blood tests and chest x-rays. Nathan showed up after all, but he had lost all of our money, all two hundred dollars, in a gambling game.

Just before we were to depart, an official told Nathan he could not board because he was sick and was put in quarantine. I was furious with him. The first thought that came to my mind was he had been with some other woman and contracted a disease from her. I accused him of awful things, but Nathan swore to me he had not been with someone else.

Finally one of our friends asked if we had tipped the health examiner $50. We had no idea we had to do this. I dug out the $50 from my money and paid the man. I said to the health examiner, "How dare you do this to a family with two children! You knew he was healthy. You made me think my husband was not faithful to me. Why didn't you just tell me I had to give you the $50? Why would you want to break a family apart?"

I was so mad I was ready to kill him. The German health examiner didn't say a word. He took the money and wrote out a clean bill of health for Nathan.

I wanted to escape from Europe and all the violence. No matter where we turned, we suffered injustices. I wanted to be in a place where we wouldn't be singled out, and we could feel some control over our lives again. America was that place, and we were on our way.

Sara immigrating to the United States aboard the Captain Blackford

CHAPTER 19—ESTABLISHING A NEW LIFE
1951

On board the ship, the *Captain Blackford*, we were separated into different areas for men and women. Though we were below the deck, Monique and I slept on a higher level than Nathan and Guy. This ship was an old military transport that had been de-commissioned and bought by private individuals. Immigrants coming out of Europe were often transported on such ships. We had cots and pallets, and many people spent most of the voyage in their beds because they were so seasick. The pitching and rolling of the boat in the large ocean waves affected Guy and Nathan, but Monique and I were fine. Embarrassment of throwing up in front of other kept Nathan below. It didn't affect me, and I could eat in the dining room, work in the kitchen, take food to those who were too sick to get up, and walk around the boat without any problems. Two to three other women were also unaffected by the rolling of the boat in the pounding waves, and we helped take care of others.

I had never experienced such a voyage before and was unaware of the effects of the salt air, billowing waves, and humid conditions. My lungs reacted to the humidity, but my stomach remained balanced.

The captain of the ship could speak French, and many of the crew spoke different languages, including German, but most of the immigrants were from Eastern Europe and could not communicate with the crew or captain. All of the immigrants on board were Jewish refugees seeking a better life in the United States.

When I was talking to the captain, he asked me if I had considered changing my last name. I wasn't quite sure what he meant at first, and he explained about the Lindbergh baby kidnapping case. A man named Bruno Hauptmann was found guilty in the kidnapping. The captain was concerned people would associate me with this man. I asked how the man in the Lindbergh case spelled his last name. When the captain told me that he spelled it with two "n's," I said I wasn't worried because my last name only had one "n." People should not associate him with me. The captain said I was smart to think of that difference. Naturally, I had no desire to change my name.

To keep up the spirits of people who could manage to get around, the captain planned a dance. I felt like going even though Nathan didn't. Dancing with the captain and chatting with the others about our new life in the United States, I enjoyed myself.

The boat trip took us thirteen days between the end of May and the beginning of June. We arrived without incident in New York. Guy was eleven years old at the time, and Monique was eight. When we arrived at Ellis Island, the American immigration officials asked people their names, but none of them could speak English. The officials often didn't wait to find someone who could speak the other language. Names were written in English phonetically and misspelled, especially the Hungarian and Czech names. In one incident after the official asked for the name, the immigrant asked in German, "*Was?*" *Was* in German means "what," and the German "w" is pronounced as a "v." The official, mistakenly, wrote "Vas" as the person's last name. Also some names were shortened. One person's last name was Wasserman, but during the process, an official shortened it to Wasser. At least I could understand when they wanted the name, and I spelled mine, Hauptman, proudly with one "n."

In the large hall with a lot of benches people from the Hebrew International Aid Society, HIAS, were calling out names to link the refugees with sponsors. I was in terrible shape because the humidity and heat brought on a bout of asthma. I couldn't breathe well, my lips and tips of my fingers were turning blue, and I wasn't sure I was going to make it. The Jewish officials decided I should not stay in New York. The climate was bad for my health, and too many tailors were in New York for Nathan to establish a business anyway. The officials told us we would be going to a place with a hot, dry climate, which turned out to be El Paso, Texas. We were given train tickets to this strange, new place that we had only heard about in the movies. Guy imagined all sorts of Wild West adventures, complete with cowboys and Indians.

On the train he even asked, "When do I get a horse?"

All we had in the world was $3.50. We tried to explain to the waiter on the train that we wanted some eggs to eat. He only spoke English, and we didn't know English. Even though I could speak six languages, none of them helped me here. Guy resorted to crowing like a rooster to get across what we wanted to eat.

The new American cuisine was difficult to get used to. We considered jelly on bread with our eggs foreign. In Europe we didn't mix our sweets with eggs. Guy could also remember stopping in St. Louis where he got a chocolate ice cream, the biggest one in the world. He hadn't tasted many sweets during the war in Europe, and this was a memorable event for him.

Upon our arrival in El Paso, the barrenness of the land inflicted a sense of depression. Living in a near desert climate was quite a change from the lush vegetation of Brussels. I wanted to cry, but I knew I couldn't show my disappointment to the children. Our sponsors from the small Jewish organization of El Paso met us and took us to a two-bedroom basement apartment to live. Monique and Guy were not used to sharing a room with each other, but I hoped they would adjust as all of us would. This three-room apartment located at 1505 Stanton Street was only a block away from the synagogue and close to the downtown area. Nathan was able to get work as a tailor at $35 a week. Our new lives as Americans had begun.

Within one year we earned enough to pay back the Jewish organization who sponsored us, HIAS. They did not ask for repayment, but we didn't want charity. The organization in El Paso had sponsored over 200 families from Europe. We were one of the last families to arrive. When other refugees found out we repaid HIAS, they thought we were trying to be "big shots." They didn't understand that we did not want to feel obligated to anyone. We wanted to "pull our own weight." We even refused charity for our food. If we went a little hungry at times, we could bear it. We had suffered far worse than this in the concentration camps. The kids would cry, but we would manage. We had a little money after we sold my silver fox fur coat, which Jules had kept for me during the war. To make ends meet, Nathan also sold some family jewelry Mocha had hidden for him during the war.

After a few months in our basement apartment we were able to find a better place to live. We found a duplex at 108 W. Nevada Street, which was just around the block from our old apartment on Stanton.

We were so poor all we had to eat in the house was bread, butter, and some cottage cheese. Guy didn't want to eat the cottage cheese, but I insisted he eat it. I didn't want him to go hungry. This was the first time Guy had ever acted so stubbornly. I was tempted to bring up the fact I had nearly starved in the camps and he should be grateful for this food, but I resisted that urge because he had suffered too. Losing patience, I finally got tired of his protests and whines and whipped him. He ate the cottage cheese, but threw it up. I sat down and cried. I couldn't believe I had sunk so low as to spank my child over some cottage cheese. Homesick, I was tired of trying to make a living in this new place. America wasn't the land of milk and honey we had imagined.

A lady from our temple brought some hand-me-down clothes for Guy and Monique. Nathan told her we could not accept her charity. The kids needed the clothes, but our pride wouldn't allow us to accept the clothes. She didn't understand the blow to our self-esteem and thought we didn't want the clothes. Our inability to speak English caused a rift between her and us. How could we explain to someone that we were trying to maintain a shred of self-respect by not accepting charity? They did not understand.

Poor Guy and Monique could only speak French. The language barrier created difficulty in school. The administrators put Guy back in second grade because he could not speak English, though he had been in the seventh grade in Belgium. He was in the same grade as Monique. What a blow to a young boy's self-esteem to be put back so far just because he could not speak the language! English as a second language was not even considered as a class in the 1950's in American schools. He cried and begged me to take him back to Europe. I told him we could not go back.

He picked up English from children in the neighborhood and in school. As he would do his homework at night, I would watch what he was doing and try to help. One time he told me I would have an *A* in English if I were taking the course with him. That was quite a compliment coming from my son.

In the meantime the gentile kids at school called Guy "Frenchie." The kids didn't know the French pronunciation of Guy's name was GEE. They would call him the American version and he would always have to correct them. Monique decided to change her name to a more American-sounding one, Monica. We still called her Monique at home. Both children learned English and Spanish quickly. Living so close to the border made Spanish a must for inhabitants. Even though school was hard for Guy and Monique, they managed to graduate at the same age as the American students their ages by attending summer school and working twice as hard as their peers.

In the meantime I tried to find a job to make ends meet. Nathan did not want me working. In Europe wives did not work. A husband's success was measured by allowing his wife to stay home. Nathan would have been irate if he found out that I was looking for employment. I heard from some friends about a Jewish man who worked at the Levi clothing factory who could speak Yiddish. The bookkeeper's wife was French, and he could speak the language, so I applied at the factory, located close enough for me to walk to work.

The manager gave me a job working on the assembly line putting size labels on the jeans. There I met many Spanish-speaking workers who tried to teach me some Spanish and some English. Spanish was similar to French and I picked it up readily. However, one jokester in the factory, Juanito, decided to teach me the wrong meaning of some words. He taught me some cuss words, but told me they meant, "Watch out." That led to an embarrassing moment.

When the boss's son would enter the assembly line area, he was so tall he bumped his head. When he did that, I told him in Spanish what I thought was "Watch out." He looked at me askance and continued on his way. It got to be a regular thing with him. Every time he would come down, I would say "Watch out." He must have lost his tolerance for my remarks because one day I was called into the boss's office.

The boss addressed me in Yiddish. "Sara, do you speak Spanish?"

"No. You know I don't speak Spanish."

"Every time my son goes down, he said you insult him in Spanish."

"What?" I asked with surprise. "I just tell him to watch where he's going. He hits his head a lot because he's so tall."

"What is it you say to him?" After I told him the Spanish words, he smiled at me and shook his head. "Sara, that doesn't mean 'Watch out.'"

When he told me what it did mean, I turned beet red and could have crawled under a rock. I apologized to the boss and explained the error. He wanted to know which employee had misinformed me, but I didn't want to get him in trouble. It was my fault because I didn't ask someone else what the phrase meant. I'd tell that guy off, but I didn't want him to lose his job over this incident. The boss let me go and gave an explanation to his son.

As soon as I got back to the factory area, I looked for the jokester who had set me up, but Juanito was nowhere to be found. Everyone must have warned him to stay away from me because I was mad. I got over it in a few weeks, but learned never to use a translation without verifying it first.

I was able to work and not let Nathan know because our work hours were so different. He left for work at 6:30 AM and returned around 9 PM. He worked so long and hard to support us. I left for work at 8 AM and returned by 3 PM. Therefore, Nathan was not aware of my employment. He never questioned how I was able to buy better food until I made a mistake one day at the grocery store. I usually cashed my check separately from his. I don't know what I was thinking, but I handed the cashier both checks. He noticed it right away.

"Sara, where did you get that check from Levi's?"

I knew "the cat was out of the bag," a new American idiom I had learned.

"I've been working there. We need the money."

"How is it possible? You're home when I come home, you have the house cleaned, the meals cooked, and the kids are OK."

"I leave after you do and return before you come back. The kids play at the house and don't leave when I go to work. I do all the housework when I get home. I can manage. I've been working there for eight weeks now."

Nathan's face reddened and the veins in his neck bulged. He was too proud to have his wife work, but he certainly wasn't going to discuss it in public.

He pulled at his collar and smiled at the cashier as he paid for the groceries. His nice recovery only masked momentarily how upset he was with my working. I'd hear about it at home.

When we returned to the apartment, I put the groceries away. Nathan sat at the kitchen table, waiting for me to finish.

"Why didn't you tell me? We should have discussed your getting a job."

"You would've said no. I can manage, and we need the money." I twisted a napkin around my fingers. "If I work, maybe we can find a better place to live."

"My wife shouldn't have to work."

"Nathan, you didn't tell me to get a job. I made that choice. It's different here in America. Lots of women have jobs. We're Americans now."

Nathan shook his head and shrugged in resignation. He knew thirty-five dollars a week didn't adequately feed or support four people. He smiled at me, kissed me on the forehead, and went to the bedroom.

I knew I could keep working, and we never discussed it again.

After about four months we could afford to move out of the basement apartment. We found a small house to rent from one of the Jewish men in the temple. The living conditions were better, but money was still tight. I would not use money to wash clothes in a Laundromat. A woman from the temple offered the refugees a place to wash clothes, but again I would not take charity. I washed our clothes and linens in our bathtub.

Around 1952 or 1953, Nathan complained about abdominal pain. At first the doctors had diagnosed a stomach problem. Luckily, a French-speaking doctor came by the hospital room and heard us. For two years Nathan was told his stomach was causing the pain, but after this doctor examined Nathan, he realized Nathan had kidney stones. He went into surgery and recovered very well.

During Nathan's hospitalization, a rabbi came into the room to visit with us. "What are *you* doing here?" I asked.

"I heard you were refugees," the rabbi answered. "I wanted to check on you."

"I'm sorry; I don't need you." After the war, I was so bitter against God I didn't want anything to do with a rabbi or religion. Nathan grimaced and motioned me aside.

"Sara, don't do this," Nathan said in French. "He's a rabbi."

"I don't care. I don't want him in here."

The rabbi couldn't understand us when we spoke French. We talked to him in Yiddish. I was cordial to the rabbi while he was in Nathan's room, but I didn't want anything to do with him, religion, or God. If the rabbi stayed in the room, I was going to leave. I told Nathan this and walked out. Even though Nathan and I were conversing in French, I guess the rabbi got the message and left shortly after I exited Nathan's room.

Later on the next week, the same Rabbi Roth came to check on Nathan again. "What are you doing here? We don't need you here," I said to him,

"I came to see your husband and talk with him."

"I don't care. We don't want anything to do with you."

After he left, Nathan was livid with me, but I didn't care. *How could there be a God if He let so many people perish in the concentration camps?* We were both mad at God. After what we had seen and experienced, believing in a loving God was almost impossible. *What had we done to deserve such a fate? Where was God when people were going to the gas chambers? Why did God let my mother and brothers die? Why did Nathan have to lose everyone in his family?*

I didn't want to hear what the rabbi said. Nothing he could say would matter to me. His words would fall on deaf ears, deafened by the cries of the millions who went to the gas chambers when God would not listen to them.

A short while after Nathan was dismissed from the hospital, Rabbi Roth again visited Nathan, only this time we were at our house. We could not turn him away from our home. Our customary hospitality would not permit us to treat him poorly. Rabbi Roth asked for a cup of tea, and I said I would get him one. Right away I made up a table of tea and cookies. He sat down, and Nathan smiled.

"How's Nathan doing?" the rabbi asked me.

"Thank God, he's doing OK."

"That's all I wanted to hear," Rabbi Roth said. "Nathan, I'll see you in the synagogue." He got up and left, satisfied when I said "Thank God," that I did believe in God and would return to our religion.

After he left, I thought a lot about what I had said. I did believe, no matter what had happened during the war. That was the beginning of the return of my faith. I discussed how I felt with Nathan. He recognized the need to take the kids to *shul*, especially when Guy would turn thirteen soon and go through his *bar mitzvah*. Rabbi Roth had patiently waited for our icy hearts to melt, and that little chipping away at the iceberg inside us made it possible for us to return to our religion.

Later on I talked to the rabbi. "I'm not against God. I'm mad at Him. I cannot forgive Him for what happened to the little children in the concentration camps. I could defend myself, but little children could not. They didn't do anything wrong. Little children who couldn't even walk were taken to the gas chambers. Is it right?"

"Sara, I'm sorry," Rabbi Roth said with tears in his eyes. "I cannot tell you. There are no words for what you went through. I cannot talk for God. I can only talk for myself." He did not try to explain God's ways.

"I cannot forgive Him and I cannot forget. It's very hard. Every time I see a synagogue, I ask why He allowed this to happen. For six months after the war in Belgium, I was not myself. I was crazy and acted wild at times. My brother Jules tried to talk to me after the war about God, but he had not been in the camps. He had not witnessed what I had."

Even though Nathan and I wondered how God could allow such horrors to happen, we didn't want our children to grow up bitter. When Guy went through his bar mitzvah, Nathan went back to the temple for the first time to pray since we were in the camps. This was an important rite of passage for a Jewish boy, and we wanted to be there for Guy. For the bar mitzvah, Nathan made Guy a beautiful suit. Having a tailor in the family certainly had its advantages. Guy was the best-dressed young man.

After Guy's *bar mitzvah*, Nathan went to the temple only once a year for the high holidays to pray for his parents. Once I even heard him say to God in *shul*, "I'm not going for You. You took my parents away from me. I'm only going for their sakes."

When Monique was old enough, she went through a bat mitzvah, a ceremony similar to a boy's bar mitzvah, but for girls. In Europe we didn't have this, but here in the United States, girls were trained in Hebrew as the boys were. We were very proud of both of our children for learning Hebrew and reading from the Torah.

Nathan returned to the Jewish services because of the children, but a part of me was still hardened against God. I desired to change what I felt in my heart. After all, Nathan had lost more of his family in the Holocaust than I had. He lost 175 relatives in the concentration camps and ghettos. His seven brothers and four sisters all died. He had always been the optimist, but now he had little to believe in. Over time my heart became less hard, but I still wonder why the senseless killing had to take place. I suppose I will never have that answer until I die.

Guy, age 11, and Monique, age 8, in El Paso

CHAPTER 20--THE LION'S SHARE

In 1952 I received a letter from Mariette, which included her address, phone number, a rose and two Canadian dollars. This was the first contact I had had with my sister in five years. Mariette was seventeen years old now. I immediately called the number.

"Mariette, come over," I said when she answered the phone.

She didn't know who I was at first. After the initial excitement, she asked me where I was, thinking I was somewhere in Vancouver.

"I'm in El Paso, Texas. Come now. I want to see you."

She had to explain to me that Vancouver was a long distance away from El Paso. When she realized I was in the United States and not Canada, she cried. She couldn't leave Canada and come all the way to Texas to visit me. I had no concept of distances between the United States and Canada. Then we both cried. After a while I gave her my address, and we discussed our corresponding until she was old enough to leave Canada or I had saved enough money to travel to Canada.

She explained that the Jewish Congress and the Red Cross had helped her locate me in El Paso. Though thrilled to hear from her, I was still saddened we couldn't be together sooner.

I asked her about the $2.00 and the rose that she had sent me.

"It was all I had from a baby-sitting job that was my own money," she said. "I thought you might need it. The rose is from our garden."

This really touched my heart. My baby sister was worried about me. I told her we were doing all right, and she should keep her money for herself. Of course that wasn't entirely true, but I didn't want her to know.

She also gave me an update on Esther, Henri, and Jacques over the years. After the Jewish Congress officials came to the orphanage in Brussels, the children were given a choice of going to Australia, the United States, or Israel, and 1,000 could go to Canada. In November of 1947 when they decided to immigrate to Canada, Esther was fifteen years old, Henri was sixteen years old, Jacques was fourteen, and Mariette was twelve. As part of a group of fifty children who left Belgium, they traveled by bus, train, and boat to England, crossing the English Channel en route to Canada. Mariette got seasick during this voyage.

In England the children were housed temporarily in a castle, where no one spoke French, and the children were unable to communicate with their English guardians. When Mariette asked for paper to write a letter to me to tell me where they were and where they were headed, no one could translate her request.

They sailed for Canada aboard the *Aquitania*. Along the way Esther was mad at Mariette for getting seasick. She was afraid they couldn't disembark in Canada with Mariette being sick. Esther tried to scare Mariette into getting well by threatening to throw her overboard if they couldn't land in Canada. Esther had learned to be tough as nails during the war, even with her family. Compassion was a luxury the war didn't allow.

It took a week to cross, a week to get to Winnipeg, and another month in Winnipeg before foster families were arranged. Esther, Henri, Jacques, Mariette, and another boy named David were sent to Vancouver. They were the first refugees to arrive; others came later.

Arriving in Halifax, Canada, on November 17, 1947, the children were taken to an austere building that looked a prison. After all they had endured during the war Mariette thought, *I came out of the war to come to a free country and they are putting us in prison.* After entering a large room, medical personnel roughly examined the children for any illness. The physicians examined the children's eyes, noses, and teeth. Every inch, it seemed, was poked and prodded. Then the children were given shots to prevent diseases. Mariette didn't want anyone to touch her.

During this exam the children were told to give their jewelry to an official. When Mariette's ring that Nathan gave her was returned, the diamond was gone. All the money the children had was also confiscated. None of the children spoke up because they had no idea this was illegal. They were too scared they would be sent back to war-ravaged Europe.

From Halifax the children boarded a train to Montreal and then Winnipeg. In Winnipeg they stayed with a family called Smith, famous for their corned beef. They stayed there about two or three weeks. Mariette followed Esther like a shadow, much to Esther's chagrin, especially since Esther wanted to talk to Larry, another refugee teenager. Winnipeg's plethora of snow piled up higher than the windows of most houses and freezing weather scared Mariette. She asked the Jewish Congress if they could leave. Esther and Jacques were content to stay in Winnipeg, but Mariette and Henri wanted to leave for a warmer climate.

"There is only one more place to go," said the woman accompanying the children across Canada. "That place is Vancouver."

According to Mariette, they arrived in 1947 in Vancouver. The beautiful city with its mild climate, lush greenery and no snow was a welcomed sight. The children were taken to foster homes of different families in the same town. They were separated once again although this time they could have contact with each other. Even though the families that took them in wanted to adopt them, my sisters and one brother decided to keep their own last name of Rozen. Jacques took the last name of his adopted family, Brown, until he married. Then he resumed the use of Rozen once again.

Esther suffered greatly in the transition. She had learned to be totally independent during the war years and didn't want her new foster family to help her. They were middle-aged foster parents who didn't know how to help a teenage refugee adjust. When this situation didn't work out after three months, Esther became an *au pair* to a widow with three children. Unfortunately, the lady treated her like a servant, even to the point of having her eat a lettuce sandwich and canned beans in the kitchen when the rest of the family ate roast beef. Life for her was not easy, but she was determined to finish high school.

She did finish her education, and while she was in school she continued to see Larry. He, too, had been a refugee and had come to Canada on the same boat as my brothers and sisters. Originally from Czechoslovakia, Larry went into the concentration camps at age fourteen to come out at age fifteen. He survived Auschwitz and Bergen Belsen. During his time in Auschwitz, he had worked in the same coal mines as Nathan, but they never knew each other then. After the war Larry spent a year and a half in England. From there he was sent to Vancouver. Esther became engaged to Larry at age seventeen. He had to get a court approval to marry her because she was under the age of nineteen, and in Canada that was considered a minor. At age eighteen, Esther married Larry on June 17, 1951. I didn't even know she was married until I talked to Mariette. My first thought was she's too young to be married, but then I remembered how young I was when I eloped with Nathan.

Henri had a foster family at first, but he didn't get along very well. Having learned to be independent, Henri's relying on a family was too strange now. It became a defensive mechanism with Henri not to get too close to people because as soon as he did, he knew from past experience that he'd have to move again. When he was seventeen, he moved to Vancouver Island and took a job in construction. He and Esther were close, but he would always be a loner.

Jacques loved his foster mother dearly. He was close to his foster sister too, but never to his foster father. After his foster mother died, Jacques was kicked out and terribly hurt. Losing two families was too much for him. He remained close to his foster sister and her husband, but the idea of having a home would always be foreign to him.

Bottom left-- Jacques and Henri in Vancouver with friends

Mariette's situation was the best of all. Her foster family was wonderful and treated her like their very own daughter and only child. Though in the best situation, Mariette still had difficulty adjusting. During her first year, she ran away twelve times and was afraid of all men, thinking they were Nazi soldiers.

Each time she ran away, her foster father would bring her back and reassure her by saying, "You're mine. I will always bring you back and you will learn to live with us."

It took her three months to learn to say a sentence without thinking first in French. Everything in English seemed backward to French language structure.

Mariette's foster family sent packages to my brother Bernard in Israel, allowed her to see her brothers and sisters, provided her with a good education, and saw to it that she lacked for nothing. Mariette and Jacques went to different schools, but kept in touch with each other.

No English as second language classes existed at the time, so the Jewish Congress arranged for the refugee children to be in the Peretz school, a Jewish language school. After a week in this school Mariette drew a picture of a school, showed it to her foster parents, and they were able to communicate. They understood she wanted to go to school, which she had never experienced. At twelve years of age Mariette was able to attend school for the first time. In Belgium she was not allowed to go to school because she was in hiding. She only learned a little underneath someone's table. It was remarkable she learned as much as she did. She could speak Yiddish, French, Flemish, and a little Dutch and Polish. Unfortunately since Mariette could not speak English, she was put in first grade. Though she was much older than the other children, she had to start somewhere, just as Guy had.

In 1949 Jules contacted the Red Cross and the Jewish Congress to locate our brothers and sisters. A social worker in Vancouver contacted Esther and told her someone in Belgium was looking for her. Jules wrote letters and kept in touch with her and the others. Even though my brother had been in contact with them, I did not hear anything about them until Mariette sent me the letter in 1952.

After Jacques, who now called himself Jack, found out we were in El Paso, he let us know his foster sister's husband was coming to Fort Bliss for a visit. He wanted his foster brother-in-law to meet us. I wanted to meet him too, but I was afraid we would not make a very good impression. Even with my working, we still lived in virtual poverty. We used two orange crates for end tables. I was almost in tears, but Nathan told me he would take care of it. He sold his watch to his friend Paul Berstein for $10. That was enough to prepare a grand meal for Jack's brother-in-law. Paul didn't want to take the watch and told Nathan he would hold it for him. Nathan wouldn't take the $10 unless Paul took the watch. Eventually Nathan paid him back. We were lucky to have such good friends who understood us. At least we were not embarrassed to have Jack's brother-in-law visit us. He gave Jack a glowing report of us, even though we had pretended to have more than we actually did.

Trying to make a decent living wasn't easy for refugees. Learning a new language and adapting to a new culture were difficult, and in addition, we had to take jobs that paid very little. After working for Levi's a year, I worked in a piece-goods store and then some clothing stores.

In 1954 while I worked for Aaronson's, I thought I was pregnant. For years Nathan and I had tried to have more children. In Europe we had gone to specialists in Vienna and other places to find out if I could become pregnant. The doctors told me I could never conceive again. The Nazis had not sterilized Nathan, but I had been sterilized. I hoped the doctors were wrong since I had not had a hysterectomy, and I visited one doctor in El Paso who gave me some encouragement about having another child.

I was so excited and hopeful. While I was at work, I had terrible cramps and went to the hospital. Nathan was concerned I had worked too much, but that wasn't the case. Instead of my being pregnant, I had a four-and-a-half pound tumor in my womb probably caused by the sterilization drug Mengele had given me. In doing research years later, I read that this drug was most likely a mixture of silver nitrate or citobarium called F12. The violent inflammation I had experienced after the insertion closed the oviducts, leading to permanent sterility.

The depth of my depression seemed endless. My hopes of having more children were dashed completely, and I was horrified to know the drug Mengele gave me could create a tumor like this. I would never have another child. The Nazis had robbed my future.

I wanted to adopt more children and Nathan was willing, but sixteen-year-old Guy disagreed. He tried to console me by saying he would give us grandchildren someday.

Guy was much easier to raise than Monique. I suppose a lot of teenage girls give their mothers grief during those formative years, and Monique was no exception. She was probably too much like me in temperament. I remember I was angry when *Maman* would not let me go to dances.

Sometimes I wondered if Monique had problems when she was a teenager because I hadn't been around when she was young. *Was there something she experienced with Catherine or in the orphanages afterward that made her rebellious?* I'll never know. Irrationally, she was angry with me because she looked like her father with his large ears and nose. I couldn't help that, but she would use it as an excuse for her behavior.

While we were living in El Paso, Mariette came to visit us on her honeymoon. We had not seen her since she was a child in Belgium. During the time she grew up in Vancouver, Canada, we had been unable to afford a trip to see her and my other siblings.

Mariette and Nathan had a special friendship that was difficult to explain. He would tell her secrets, take her places, and treat her more like a daughter than a sister-in-law. Nathan and I could trust Mariette with anything. She had learned to survive during her time in hiding and depend on herself. When we talked about the war, she would often ask us questions, trying to remember things even though it was painful. She once said, "I have to find out if I dreamed my life or lived it." For survivors, only a thin veil separates our nightmares and our reality. Finally Mariette was happy with my new brother-in-law, Sid.

In 1956 Nathan and I were ready to take our citizenship tests. We had been in the United States five years and knew we wanted to become citizens. Other refugees said the test was hard and that we probably couldn't pass it on the first try. I obtained the study booklet from the courthouse and read it. It didn't seem that difficult. A friend of ours, Paul, a former Russian officer who had immigrated to the United States, tried to convince me if he couldn't pass the test the first time, I wouldn't either. I was determined to prove him wrong. Nathan encouraged me and told Paul, "You'll be surprised. She'll pass."

We needed two witnesses to vouch for us. Nathan's boss, Fred, and his brother came to the courthouse with us. After they testified that we would be good citizens, we were given a written test. They gave me some sentences to write in English, such as "I go to school" or "I came from work." They weren't difficult for me. After I passed, I spoke to the judge about Nathan. I explained that he had not received as much education as I had, but he would make a good citizen. While the judge talked to me, he asked how many languages I could speak. I told him English was my eighth language after learning French, Flemish,

German, Yiddish, some Polish and some Hungarian, and Spanish. I asked the judge, "Why don't Americans have to learn all this history and pass a test to become citizens?"

"They're born Americans," he answered. It seemed a strange answer, but true.

Monique and Guy took their citizenship tests on the same day and also passed. When Guy was asked if a war were to break out between Belgium and the United States, for which country he would fight, he said, "The United States." That was good enough for the examiner.

While I was taking my test, Nathan had been talking to a Spanish-speaking lady in the waiting room. She told him he could take the test in another language, and Nathan had the false impression he could take the test in Polish. When he went to take the test and wrote the answers in Polish, he failed. He didn't understand why he had failed. Later on, we found out Spanish was an acceptable language to use on the answers, but Polish wasn't. He had to take the exam again three weeks later. The second time he wrote in English and passed.

At the ceremony we said the Pledge of Allegiance and sang the national anthem, one of the proudest moments of our lives. As I sang those words, I recalled Eisenhower's face and how much pride had shown in his face when he talked about his country. I could sense that same intense love for America as I had felt for Belgium. Now we were Americans.

CHAPTER 21—COLORADO SPRINGS

After high school Guy served in the Marines. When he finished his years in the service, he wanted to go to college on the GI bill and was interested in the University of Colorado at Boulder. He and Nathan went to see the campus and talk with school officials. On the way back Nathan stopped to visit a friend, Behrman Pena. Behrman was a fellow tailor we had known in El Paso who had moved to Colorado Springs. He told Nathan he was the only tailor in town with plenty of business.

Nathan went to the largest department store in town at the time, Waymire's, and inquired if they needed a tailor. When the owner saw Nathan take a thimble out and put it on his finger, he said Nathan had the job. He didn't have to prove more than that. Nathan was offered $125 a week for thirty-six hours of work. He could do alterations at home too. Nathan called me to tell me about the offer. I was ready to move from El Paso, and the opportunity to move to Colorado sounded wonderful. I told him to take the job.

In the meantime, I hired a moving company to pack up our belongings. By the time Nathan and Guy returned that Sunday, the household items and furniture were packed. We had to sleep on the floor that night, but I was ready to move.

Although the move was a *mitzvah*, a blessing, the trip to Colorado wasn't so wonderful. In those days seatbelts were unheard of. Close to Pueblo we were involved in a car wreck. When the other car hit us, I was afraid Nathan would be propelled through the windshield. I put my legs across his waist to hold him in place. He probably would have been killed if I had not held him. He was all right, but I was hurt in the accident. Glass imbedded in my back and head. Guy, who was following in a car behind us, ran up to see what had happened. He and Nathan cried, thinking I was dead. Nathan prayed to God, and I remember thinking to myself, *If you don't believe in God, Nathan, how can you pray?*

Our car looked like an accordion after the accident. I was surprised we had all survived. To sew up my scalp, the doctor had to use sixty to seventy stitches in the back of my head. He also did a skin graft to cover where the stitches had been. I still have scars on my back from that accident. Added to the scars from my beating in Dachau, my back looks like a macabre mosaic.

Life in Colorado Springs was beautiful for us. Nathan enjoyed working at Waymire's, and I took a job at Fashion Bar, a women's clothing store. Guy moved back to El Paso, and Monique had finished school. We bought our own house, and it seemed everything was finally going our way.

Over the years we managed to save enough money for a trip to Canada to see my family. Mariette wanted us to stay with her and also spend some time with Esther. Unfortunately, my brother Charles would be there. I was surprised Mariette would even have him in her home, but it was the only house big enough for all of us. After Charles and I parted with angry words when he left for Rio de Janeiro, I hadn't talked to him. I didn't know how I would act when I saw him, but I was willing to be civil. This time I could only hope he would be different.

At that family reunion in 1966 at Mariette's house in Vancouver, Esther was still angry with Charles, and she would not say anything to him. His leaving our mother stranded was too deeply ingrained in the memories of both Esther and Mariette. When Charles tried to absolve himself from all blame for *Maman*'s death, Mariette gave him a piece of her mind.

"Keep your damn mouth shut," Mariette told him. "I don't want to hear anything from you. Do you think because I was only five years old I forgot when you told *Maman* and me there was no room? I remember. *Maman* pleaded with you to take me because I was a little child. You refused. Until the day you die, I will not forgive you."

I talked to him because I didn't want to stay angry the rest of my life, but my sisters did not feel the same way. We tried to get along even though great tension mounted. We tried telling jokes, but they were all in different languages. Sidney, Mariette's husband, said, "We are the foreigners here," as he left the room with the other spouses who could not understand the different languages we were using.

We tried to construct the facade of a family reuniting, but too many bitter memories blocked the way. We were a family of strangers.

On returning to Colorado Springs, we were constantly reminded of how important family was. Nathan worked with Joe, an eleven-year-old boy who was a part-time presser because he and his family needed the money. Nathan always called him Little Joe. Because Joe's home life was so dysfunctional, Nathan felt sorry for him. Joe was the fifth child of twelve and had a lot of younger brothers and sisters to take care of because his father was an alcoholic. Nathan would bring Joe home with him and tell him he could always consider our home his home. Even though Joe was a teenager, Nathan and I considered him another one of our kids for over five years.

One time when Joe was in Pueblo, he had a flat tire. The man at the garage refused to wait on him because Joe was African-American. When Joe called Nathan and told him the situation, Nathan was furious. We drove to Pueblo to the garage that had refused Joe service, only this time Nathan went in. The man offered to fix the flat for Nathan. This is one of the rare times I had ever seen Nathan angry. He asked the mechanic, "Why did you refuse to change the flat for my son?"

"I didn't refuse your son service," the garageman said, looking shocked.

Then Nathan brought Joe in. "This is my son. You refused to change his flat tire. What's the problem?"

The mechanic only stammered, but Nathan made sure Joe got his tire fixed and got home safely.

I never knew until this moment that Americans could be racists. In Belgium we had grown up with people of all colors and beliefs. Tolerance was something we had ingrained in us. Our neighbors were from the Belgian Congo. We never thought of them as different just because they were black. In addition, my family had been tolerant of other religions. My father supported the Catholic nuns whenever they would go door to door asking for charity for their projects. The fact we were Jewish and they were Catholic never crossed my father's mind. He gave because he saw the need, not because he only helped one religion or color of people. We grew up color-blind and tolerant of all religions.

The situation of hate and racism in America made our stomachs turn. We were not aware how some Americans treated others until we moved here. Under the Nazi regime, we had seen what racism and hate could do and we certainly didn't want that to happen to Little Joe. Nathan and I wanted to protect him from people like the garage mechanic, but he would have to face bigots everywhere.

When we first moved to Colorado Springs, the buses were segregated. I hated this situation and would sit in the back of the bus with the Blacks. Racism was rampant in the United States, and we could only offer Little Joe our love and support in the face of hate.

However some good news also arrived. Guy was getting married to a girl from Juarez named Margie who had converted to Judaism. After they were married, they were blessed with a son whom they named Simeon. He was named after my brother Simon who died in Auschwitz. Later on they were blessed with two other children, Esther and Jacob. Esther Anne, born on August 24, 1974, was named after Nathan's mother. Jacob, who was born on November 20, 1979, was named in honor of my brother Jean. The rabbi had told us if the name had the same first letter, that it would honor Jean. Guy had always promised me he would give me grandchildren, and he certainly gave me three wonderful ones. They are all very talented, smart, and good-looking. Naturally as their grandmother, I say that objectively.

With new additions to my family, I suddenly had a desire to see my relatives again and return to my native Belgium. I hadn't been back to Belgium in over twenty years, and it would be good to see everyone.

After I flew there in 1971, I tried to find my father's grave. During the war the cemetery had been bombed, and the graves were in total disarray. Bodies were buried in various places, and the markers were put back up, but we could never be sure my father's body was placed in the correct grave, a tragic circumstance of war.

I enjoyed seeing Jules, Agnes, and their family. While we were visiting them, Nathan asked Agnes for the picture of me with the lion cub. For some reason, she felt compelled to keep it. I don't know why since the picture belonged to me. I was content to let it go, but Nathan managed to sneak the picture into our suitcase when we left. Though I would never return to the ring as a lion tamer, I had greater "beasts" to face.

CHAPTER 22--BEASTS AND FEARS TO FACE

In 1983 I had a heart attack. While working for Fashion Bar at a moonlight sale, I collapsed. I felt a wrenching pain in my chest and fainted. When I woke up, I was at the hospital. I stayed two months before they allowed me to go home, and I weighed only eighty-seven pounds. I nearly died. During this time I had a dream of a garden-like place where people were dancing and golfing. I wanted to join them, but Nathan wouldn't let me go. I had gotten out of bed and crawled toward the door when Nathan found me. Somehow I knew if I stayed in bed I would go the other way to the beautiful garden. Had Nathan not been there that moment, I suppose I might have crossed the chasm between life and death.

Nathan and Monique had been in my room just minutes before I had this dream, and they told me I appeared to be sleeping soundly. No one wanted to wake me, not even the nurses who checked on me. They had no idea what I was dreaming about or what may have been happening. Nathan and Monique had left the room while I slept. When I got out of bed, I knew I had to find Nathan. I fought to get to the door. After I woke up and saw Nathan, I told him about my dream. I remember telling him, "No wonder no one wants to return after death; it's so beautiful there."

Later I asked the doctor if my work at the store had triggered the attack. He said my heart condition was probably a result of what I had suffered in the camps. After that I had to quit working. I helped Nathan in his shop at home, but I could never return to work full-time. I take nitroglycerin tablets whenever I have chest pains. Also I had an operation on my esophagus that required 119 stitches. My health took a plunge, but it didn't matter any more because not long after this, a tragedy occurred that altered my life forever.

While Monique was driving on Interstate 25, a truck hit her car. She was put on life-support. Monique could only communicate by nodding her head a bit. The doctor told me if they took her off the machines, she might not live, and she would be on the machines indefinitely. I told her what the doctor had said and when I asked her if she wanted me to take the machines away, she nodded "Yes." I knew she didn't want to live this way, hooked up to machines to breathe for her and not able to communicate or live normally. I couldn't sleep and tossed and turned each time I tried to make that final decision. After all, Monique was only forty-one years old.

Again Nathan and I talked to the doctor to make sure there was nothing more he could do for Monique. For days I prayed for some miracle, but nothing changed. Monique was slipping away from us. I couldn't bear to look at her with the tubes and wires covering her. Nathan and I finally made the decision to take her off life-support. On February 28, 1983, the doctor removed the breathing apparatus. Within a few minutes, my beautiful daughter was gone.

One of the reasons I lived through the camps was to see my children. All that time I had lived for them. Now I felt like I had nothing to live for. Monique was gone. Her life was ended far too soon. She was so full of life and had so much love to offer.

I felt empty. At times I didn't want to wake up because Monique wouldn't be there. I knew I still had Nathan and Guy, but my soul ached over the loss of my daughter. Part of me died with her.

A short time after Monique's death Nathan' heart condition worsened, and he couldn't work any more. By 1985 he was in a wheel chair. At one point he was on so much medication, he didn't recognize me. He thought I was some impostor who had taken the place of his wife. He saw me as an old woman, and he was thinking of me as his young wife in Belgium years ago. His mind could not reconcile the passage of the years. When my sister Mariette came to visit him, he told her, "Marietteka, this strange woman killed Sara and took her place."

That hurt me more than anything I could ever imagine, more than any pain I had endured during the war. My own husband didn't recognize me. I talked to Mariette the rest of the night in Nathan's room.

The next day when Mariette came into the room, he snapped out of it. He recognized her right away. "I have to talk to you," he said to her. "Look what happened to Sara."

"What happened to Sara?" Mariette asked him.

"She's all gray."

"She became gray because you're so sick."

"Look how old she's become."

"Did you see how old you are? Look at yourself in the mirror. Look at me. I'm not young either."

In his mind I had aged, but he had not.

"Nathan, who am I?" Mariette continued.

"You're my little girl. You're my little darling, my little Shirley Temple."

When he said that, we knew that he was thinking clearly again.

"And who is Sara to me?" Mariette asked.

"She's your sister. Do you think I'm crazy or something? She's your sister."

I never mentioned what he had said ever again. It may have been caused by his medication, but whatever it was, it passed and Nathan never forgot who I was again.

That was the last time Mariette saw Nathan. He was too sick for them to enjoy the old times together when they used to play cards, eat smoked eels, *shmaltz* herring with onions, rye bread, and drink vodka. They were so close to each other.

Even back in Brussels after the war when he was avoiding the police because he had no papers, he used to meet Mariette at a bar and let her have black beer. He would give her money in a hanky and put a knot in it to keep the money safe. After his by-pass surgery years later in the United States, Nathan gave Mariette a special pin made of diamonds and a large sapphire and his lucky pinky ring made of red rubies. She always wore them because he gave them to her. They both knew this was their last visit.

For three months from August to October, he was in the hospital. I didn't spend a night at home that whole time. Nathan told me he would always take care of me. He would guide me, and I would be all right. He urged me to stay in our house after he was gone and not move in with Guy or anyone else.

He began to talk about people he had known who were now dead. This scared me because once people do this, their time on earth is short. I told him not to scold our daughter Monique. He laughed so hard at this statement that tears came from his eyes. I told him,

"Promise me you'll leave her alone."

"I promise." The tears ran down his cheeks, and I knew he was ready to go. Nathan had told Dr. David Greenberg, a close friend of the family, that he was ready to go, but I wouldn't let him go. He told Dr. Greenberg I had awakened him three times before when he was ready to go. On one of those occasions, he described his own beautiful garden scene where he had been. I knew that garden well from my own close brush with death.

Dr. Greenberg came out when I was in the hall outside of Nathan's room and said, "Sara, let him go. His heart cannot take it any more. He wants to go. He's ready. Let him go."

"I didn't do anything."

"Don't tell me you didn't do anything. He told me you woke him up last night."

"Yes, because I heard him snoring." That's when I realized he wasn't snoring. He was dying, and I didn't want to let go.

When the orderlies took Nathan downstairs for x-rays, I heard him moan once. I knew right away that it was the end. I held his hand, and I wouldn't let anyone touch him. I told the nurse to call Dr. Smith and tell him Nathan's gone. The orderlies took Nathan's body back to the room.

Nathan died October 6, 1989, on Monique's birthday and at the exact time she was born, 3:30 in the afternoon. I cannot believe it was a coincidence that it was a Friday, the same day of the week on which she was born. Somehow I felt Monique needed him, and he died on her birthday.

I came home alone and looked at the portrait of Nathan and talked to him. I knew he was gone, but I felt close to him when I looked at his portrait. Even little Toby, our white poodle, sat in front of the portrait and pricked his ears as though he were listening to Nathan.

Nathan had been my strength and the love of my life. No one could ever replace him. I went to the hall closet, got out his sweater, and put it on. It smelled like Nathan, and it felt as though he was putting his arms around me when I wore the sweater. I picked up Toby, sat in front of the portrait and sobbed into Toby's hair.

Before Nathan died, he said to me, "I will guide you. Don't be scared. Don't be afraid." I always feel that Nathan is still watching over me.

CHAPTER 23--THE HEART OF A LION

After Nathan died, I needed to keep myself busy. I helped in Temple Shalom whenever they needed me, and I also became involved in our community outreach programs for the hungry and elderly in Colorado Springs. Even before Nathan died, I had given food to the needy. The bakery closest to my house, Continental Bakery, gave away the day-old bread products. I picked these up and also purchased some sweets to take to families who needed food. Another program involved Temple Shalom and the Presbyterian Church collecting food for the homeless and hungry. I've also volunteered my time with the Marion House Soup Kitchen, the Senior Center, Golden Circle Advisory Council and the Housing Authority of Colorado Springs, an organization that collects food for needy elderly people. After nearly starving to death, I did not want anyone else to suffer that way.

I felt compelled to tell my story and bear witness to the truth of the Holocaust by speaking in schools. We had been asked to speak about our experiences before Nathan died, but he didn't want me to do it. Nathan only spoke about his experiences to me, Guy, his brother-in-law Larry, and two rabbis in El Paso and in Colorado Springs. He asked me to wait until he was gone before I spoke to schools about the concentration camps. I think he knew how hard it would be on me, and he wanted to protect me from all those past experiences rushing back in full force. It was bad enough when Nathan and I talked about it. We would cry, and often nightmares of being back in the camps woke us in the middle of the night.

In 1989 when a teacher called the temple about Holocaust speakers, I was ready to tell my story. The rabbi told her about David Bram,

Sidney Gritz, and me. David is a survivor of Auschwitz and Ebensee. Sidney is a retired brigadier general from the United States Army who liberated Buchenwald.

I was scared to death to speak publicly. Sid Gritz is a natural speaker. After all, he was a general and was used to speaking to large groups of people. I had never addressed a large group of people before. Speaking in public is the number one fear in adults, and definitely my public speaking anxiety was high. I managed to overcome my fear and tell the children my story. I had to learn to slow down when I spoke. Whenever I'm nervous, I speak faster. Also I have to speak slowly because the children have a hard time listening to me with my Belgian accent.

Usually I don't tell them about my time as a lion tamer, my work with the underground, or about the harsh adjustments after the war. I tell them about Auschwitz and Dachau; that's enough. I also temper my remarks based on the age of the audience. With high school and college students, I tell them bluntly what the concentration camps were like. With the younger children, I spare them some of the harsher descriptions. I won't speak to children younger than fifth grade. The youngest children aren't mature enough to understand what happened.

Sometimes I spoke by myself. At other times David or Sidney spoke with me. I also traveled to Denver and Canon City to tell audiences everywhere about the Holocaust, but revisionists are now trying to say the Holocaust never happened.

Once I did confront a young man who denied the Holocaust. I spoke at Colorado College, and an exchange student from Nuremberg, Germany, was in the audience. While I was speaking, he raised his hand and told me the Holocaust never happened the way I was describing it. I was so angry and shocked all I could say was, "How dare you! I was there. You weren't even born when the Holocaust happened. How can you deny what you weren't a witness to? I was there. I know what happened. The German people mocked us every day as we went by them. Of course they want to hide what they did. They don't want people to remember how heartless and cruel they were. I know the truth. If you want to go on believing lies, then just get the hell out."

This made me as angry as the time the German woman said she would vote for Hitler again.

The professor told the young man to leave, and I continued to speak to the rest of the audience. I could tell I wasn't the only one shocked and angered by his remark. The rest of the audience was ready to tell him off too. During the time I was talking, the professor must have spoken to him because after my speech, the young man apologized. Although he was apologetic, I didn't want to accept it. I was still too angry. I told him, "I don't have to accept your apology. What are you? A KKK member or an SS? Are you from Germany?"

"Yes. I'm an exchange student."

"How can you deny it? Some of the camps still remain in Germany. The older German people sat on their front porches and watched us go by daily. Your grandparents may have been the ones who laughed at us. How dare you tell me it never happened! Many German people are still living in our Jewish homes, eating from Jewish plates, and sleeping in Jewish beds. They live in beautiful homes that were once ours. And you tell me it never happened." After that, I left.

My lawyer, who was with me, wanted to intervene, but I told him, "Leave it alone. I can defend myself." Since then I have never encountered another person in the audience who denied the Holocaust, but I'm not through speaking. It may happen again.

As the older witnesses to the Holocaust pass away, it's easier for the revisionists to plant their lies in the minds of young people. That's why I continue to speak even though I become physically ill and drained every time I speak. After telling my story so many times I should be used to it and not be as affected, but it doesn't happen that way. I relive the entire experience each time I tell it—the smells from the ovens, the cries of the helpless going to slaughter, the taste of the horrible soup, the feel of the whip on my backside. The sights of walking corpses return in my memory, fresh and alive once more, and I'm imprisoned in the camps all over again.

I still feel guilty I came back when so many died. Why me? It's difficult to explain to someone who was not there how all the images can resurrect themselves so vividly. Men who have had flashbacks of war can understand. The nightmare is never-ending.

I still speak though. It doesn't matter how large or how small the audience is. I've spoken to as few as one class of children to gymnasiums filled to capacity of 1,900 or more. I know if one child hears my story, sees the tattoo on my arm, and absorbs the truth, that child will bear witness to future generations. If a fifth grader can tell his or her children about me, then it will be more difficult for the revisionists to carry out their insidious plan of denial. These children to whom I speak will be witnesses because they heard it from me, and I was there.

As I look back on my life, I wish I could have changed many parts. I would never want anyone to experience what I did during the Holocaust. When I watch world events unfold, I worry another Hitler will rise up and sweep people into a nationalistic frenzy. It bothers me when so much racism exists in our country or any country. Anti-Semites in the United States still undermine the very work of tracking down Nazis who live here with impunity

Not a day goes by that I don't think about my mother and my brothers being murdered by the Nazis. Every breath I draw is labored as a result of the extreme conditions I was forced to endure. Daily I see the tattoo on my arm and wonder why it had to happen.

Even though I cannot forgive what the Nazis did, I cannot hold the children responsible for what their parents or grandparents did. The youth of Germany can overcome their past. My hope is that the whole world will become a more humane place. People must treat each other better, and education and learning to love are the answer. Only when we realize that "those other people" are just like us will we have a chance of stopping racism. People must not be judged by the color of their skin or by their religion. Unfortunately, too many wars have been fought over religion. If we worship the same benevolent God, how can we wage war on those who also love God? I suppose there are some answers I will never have in my lifetime.

Many events in my life I can't explain. I don't know why Nathan and I found each other again after the war. We didn't try to change each other, and we danced when the music played. At the end of the war we were so glad to have found each other that we never wanted to lose sight of each other again. That made us treat each other more carefully. He loved me above all others and made me feel like I was the most special person in the world. When we walked, he would always reach for my hand to hold. He never complained about anything, and he had the same love for me in old age as he did when I was a teenager. I was his darling. We had a beautiful life together.

Having lost a daughter, I have learned to appreciate life and hold onto it dearly. At times I just want to share some news with her, and I have to remind myself she's not here. Then the pain is as fresh as the day she died. At other times it feels like she's been gone forever.

I'm so grateful I have Guy and his family. He called me every weekend to check on me when I was in Colorado Springs. He wanted me to move closer to him, and I moved back to El Paso in 1997 when my lungs couldn't take the altitude any more.

One great surprise I had in life was meeting Amy, the little granddaughter of Maurice Gilbert, again. Fifty years after being involved in the resistance, I met a lady in Colorado Springs who told me about a French-speaking woman with whom she was acquainted. Amy Hughes came over to my house, but I didn't recognize her until she made a remark about the picture of me as a blond during my time with the underground. "I know her," she said. "That's Agnes De Vos. She kicked me out of my grandfather's house when I was little."

When she said that, my knees went weak. I didn't know who she was or how she could have recognized me. "No, that's me," I said. "Agnes De Vos was my sister-in-law's name. I used that during the war. Who was your grandfather?"

"Maurice Gilbert. Agnes came to his house and told me to leave when I was twelve years old during the war."

"That was me. Oh my gosh, you're little Amy. I didn't recognize you with your married name." After that short conversation, we had a much longer one about what we each remembered during the war. I couldn't believe I had met little Amy again.

It seems as though my entire life has been sprinkled with narrow escapes and miracles. Just being alive in my present state of health is a miracle in itself. In December of 1996 I had a severe bout with the flu and had to be hospitalized. The scary part was I was fine just before this. It came on suddenly, and I couldn't get out of bed for several days. Either I couldn't hear the doorbell or the telephone when they rang or no one came by in three days. As I lay in bed, I had no idea of the passage of time. I threw up so much I became dehydrated. Luckily my tutor who was helping me with my English, Curt Stauffer, came by to check on me. When I couldn't answer the door and he saw my dog Toby through the window, he knew I was in trouble. With the help of the next door neighbor, Frank, Curt got the back door open, found me, and took me to the hospital. Had he not come when he did, I might have died.

While I was hospitalized, I became delirious and thought I was in the camps again. I fought the nurses and the orderlies, thinking they were Nazi soldiers putting me in a gas chamber. Never had I experienced such delirium before. I had had dreams of the camp, but never had I been in such a state that I couldn't distinguish the past from the present. It frightened me enough to realize I needed to be closer to Guy and his family.

Moving from my home of thirty years was one of the most difficult things I've ever had to do. I had so many close friends, like Vivian Dietzen and Flora Holmes, that I didn't want to leave them. Also I didn't want to be a burden on anyone, and I didn't want my family feeling like they had to take care of me; however I had to move back to El Paso to be near my son and his family.

After settling into my apartment in El Paso, I made new friends, began volunteer work at a PBS station, and enjoyed being around my family. At eighty-seven years of age I still enjoy baking, visiting my family in Vancouver, listening to the rabbi, and sitting on the back porch gossiping with my friends at night. These simple pleasures of life I have learned to cherish.

It is for my son, my grandchildren, my great-granddaughters, great-grandson, and future great grandchildren that I have written this book. They must know what happened and never forget.

It is also written for all the survivors who could not talk about their experiences. I hope more survivors will tell their stories and let their families know the truth, but I know many have been too traumatized to talk about it at all. Hopefully, my story can speak for them too.

We must speak. We must not remain silent. Too many were silenced over sixty years ago, and they must not be forgotten. For our children's sakes, the truth must be told in every language. That may be why God kept me alive. I am a witness. I fought back, and I survived.

Sara and Guy
Hauptman

Madison, Simeon, Linda,
and Lauren Hauptman

Elise, Esther, Buck,
and Avery Zengerle

Jacob, Katelyn, and Pamela
Hauptman

Jacques, Esther, Mariette and Sara in Vancouver

Sara's sister, Mariette

Index

Photographic and Art Credits

Campbell, Leonora. Glamour Shots. 9515 Gateway Blvd. W #C. El Paso, Tx. 79925.

Esmiol, Kathleen. Photographs of Auschwitz-Birkenau.

Kelly, Rebecca. Logo design. www.beccakelly.com.

Thompson, Linda. Photographs of Auschwitz-Birkenau.

United States Holocaust Memorial Museum. Map of Subcamps of Dachau. p. 102